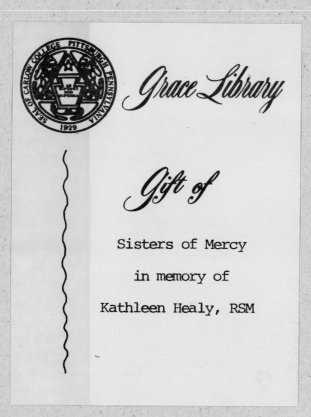

*Southern Literary Studies*
Fred Hobson, Editor

Eudora Welty and Politics

# EUDORA WELTY AND POLITICS
## *Did the Writer Crusade?*

Edited by *Harriet Pollack* and *Suzanne Marrs*

Louisiana State University Press

Baton Rouge

Copyright © 2001 by Louisiana State University Press
All rights reserved
Manufactured in the United States of America
First printing
10  09  08  07  06  05  04  03  02  01
5  4  3  2  1

Designer: Laura Roubique Gleason
Typeface: Trump Mediaeval
Typesetter: Coghill Composition Co., Inc.
Printer and binder: Thomson-Shore, Inc.

Library of Congress Cataloging-in-Publication Data:

Eudora Welty and politics : did the writer crusade? / edited by Harriet Pollack and
Suzanne Marrs.
     p.  cm. (Southern literary studies)
Includes bibliographical references and index.
  ISBN 0-8071-2618-7 (alk. paper)
  1.  Welty, Eudora, 1909—Political and social views.   2.  Politics and
literature—United States—History—20th century.   3.  Political fiction,
American—History and criticism.   I.  Pollack, Harriet.   II.  Marrs,
Suzanne.   III.  Title.
  PS3545.E6 E84   2000
  813'.52—dc21

00-009837

# Contents

*Harriet Pollack*
Eudora Welty and Politics
*Did the Writer Crusade?*                                              1

*Peggy Prenshaw*
Welty's Transformations of the Public, the Private, and
the Political                                                        19

*Noel Polk*
Engaging the Political
*In Our Texts, in Our Classrooms*                                     47

*Suzanne Marrs*
"The Huge Fateful Stage of the Outside World"
*Eudora Welty's Life in Politics*                                     69

*Suzan Harrison*
"Racial Content Espied"
*Modernist Politics, Textuality, and Race in Eudora Welty's
"The Demonstrators"*                                                  89

*Ann Romines*
A Voice from a Jackson Interior
*Eudora Welty and the Politics of Filial Piety*                      109

*Rebecca Mark*
A "Cross-mark Ploughed into the Center"
*Civil Rights and Eudora Welty's* Losing Battles                     123

*Barbara Ladd*
"Writing against Death"
*Totalitarianism and the Nonfiction of Eudora Welty
at Midcentury*                                              155

*Sharon Deykin Baris*
Judgments of *The Ponder Heart*
*Welty's Trials of the 1950s*                               179

*Danièle Pitavy-Souques*
Private and Political Thought in *One Writer's Beginnings*   203

*Harriet Pollack and Suzanne Marrs*
Seeing Welty's Political Vision in Her Photographs          223


Contributors                                               253

Index                                                      257

# Eudora Welty and Politics

*Harriet Pollack*

# Eudora Welty and Politics

## Did the Writer Crusade?

The most political of my closest literary friends came to me one day in 1995 with an uncharacteristically guarded hesitation in her face, wanting to tell me she had just had her first encounter with Eudora Welty, in the form of the author's essay "Must the Novelist Crusade?" The doubtful and deeply uncertain look on her face was shock. Did I love the fiction of a woman who had answered the question "Is writing a novel something we can do about [racism in the South]?"[1] by explaining why "fiction has, and must keep, a private address" ("Crusade," 153)? "Must the Novelist Crusade?" is not an essay that communicates effortlessly today, however boldly it was written in the early 1960s in response to calls presumably placed by an assortment of activist interviewers, critics, friends, and editors. The era in which art was comfortably understood as politically detached—and better for it—has vanished. I measure the distance between the moment in which Welty wrote her essay and the one in which my friend read it by recalling another woman's essay, composed in 1977, midway between the other two events. In "On the Politics of Literature," the introductory essay in *The Resisting Reader*, Judith Fetterly in an inaugural feminist analysis undercuts Keats's objection to "poetry that has a palpable design on us." Mounting a lateral attack on the New Critical establishment's insistence on the separateness of art and politics, Fetterly rejects pronouncements that art should be and is aesthetic rather than political: "Literature is political. It is painful to have to insist on

---

1. Eudora Welty, "Must the Novelist Crusade?" in *The Eye of the Story: Selected Essays and Reviews* (New York: Random House, 1978), 148. Hereafter cited parenthetically as "Crusade."

this fact, but the necessity of such insistence indicates the dimensions of the problem."[2] The "problem," of course, was a general unawareness of how narrative is *always* political, forcefully bringing readers to interpretative acts that are as ideological as aesthetic.

Welty's professional readers who have published beyond the New Critical moment and into the 1990s have met her work with interpretations increasingly centered on the politics of literature. As a consequence, their interest in "Must the Novelist Crusade?" first dwindled and now has grown elaborate. In the first of the essays collected here, Peggy Prenshaw sets these later readings in motion. Prenshaw views Welty's repudiation of the political in the cultural/historical context of the 1960s contempt for the corrupt "political," rather than the New Critical context in which Welty has usually been understood as asserting aesthetics over politics. Prenshaw demonstrates that the Welty of the 1960s associates political space with rigidity, silencing, and self-limiting closures. The writer's dislike of crusading fiction—a combination she fears "distort[s] a work of passion for the sake of a cause" ("Crusade," 157)—is an aversion to a definition of "political" that reflects Welty's time and place, twentieth-century Mississippi leading up to the 1960s. This essay and the others collected here, some of which were first presented in two sessions on "Welty and Politics" at the Eudora Welty Society conference "Home Ties," held in Jackson, Mississippi, in April 1997, rethink Welty's relationship to politics. The various pieces look closely at how surprisingly often Welty's fiction and criticism may have responded to such public political issues as political corruption, racial apartheid in Mississippi, McCarthyism and the Rosenberg trials, the violent resistance to the civil rights movement in the 1960s, and the integration debate in education as well as to southern reverence and filial piety for the identities of the cultural past, including and yet reaching beyond the issues of gender and family politics.

The collection, then, illustrates a shift that is taking place in how Welty is read. I measure this transformation in part by a memory from graduate school in the late '70s—a conversation I had with a cultural

2. Judith Fetterly, *The Resisting Reader* (Bloomington: Indiana University Press, 1978), xi.

historian who wondered, out loud and right away when we had just met, about my decision to work on Eudora Welty. Sympathetically, he questioned my special regard for a writer who was, as he put it, neither historically representative nor political, whose short fictions made her a "regionalist" rather than a southern writer. It was a pronouncement that I hadn't heard in so many words or with such in-my-face bluntness, although at the same time I recognized it as familiar. I remember that while my head was clearing I flashed on the Welty stories that were strictly and even officially "historical"—"First Love," "A Still Moment, " "The Burning"—and immediately sensed, with a woman's instinct for hopeless discussions, that only "The Burning" would qualify as "historical" in the developing conversation. I was already wondering to myself if this conversation were really—albeit indirectly—about women, and women writers, being outside of history, or if it were about Welty's approaching the public and historical through the private. Or were those two possibilities actually the same for Welty characters such as Phoenix Jackson, Joel Mayes, and Virgie Rainey? Academic theory at that minute was coming to acknowledge that for the marginalized historical subject, history was not the chronicle of great deeds and battles, borders, territories, legislation, or ratification, but consisted rather of accounts of lives on the periphery of official history and culture—of lives silent in history because they stood outside official power and event.

When this unforgettable conversation occurred, I had of course already been to the library to read Diana Trilling's 1943 review in the *Nation* in which she had explored her "distaste" for what she said she could no longer separate—Welty's style and her cultural attitude. Her accusation that Welty's fiction was, at best, apolitical and insensitive to important historical and social concerns came from a similar but slightly different angle. Welty was not just female, but also southern. Consider Trilling's reactions to *Delta Wedding*:

> Doll's houses, birds, moonlight, snow, the minutiae of vulnerable young life and the sudden revelations of nature may have their distressingly persistent way of agitating the modern female literary psyche, but only on a Southern plantation would the chance remark of a gardener to the effect that he wished there "wouldn't be a rose in the

world" set the lady of the house to trembling . . . as at some impudence. . . .

In the best of Welty's stories, and they were the earliest ones, Welty gave us what was really a new view of the South, indeed a new kind of realism about the South; and for this she used, not a dance prose, but a prose that walked on its feet in the world of reality. But increasingly Miss Welty has turned away from the lower-middle-class milieu of, say, "Petrified Man," to . . . narcissistic Southern fantasy and for this her prose has risen more and more on tiptoe. As a result, one of our most promising young writers gives signs of becoming, instead of the trenchant and objective commentator we hoped she would be, just another if more ingenious dreamer on the Southern past.

Clearly, my historian and Trilling might have had a sympathetic conversation about Welty's work, agreeing about her apolitical "female literary psyche" even while one labeled her "not southern" and the other "too southern." It was nearly a year later when, to this group of comments, I added Richard King's pronouncement in *A Southern Renaissance* that Welty and other southern women writers were ahistorical and apolitical—not primarily "concerned . . . with the larger cultural, racial, and political themes" of his focus, "for whatever reasons" and regardless of the "merits of their work."[3] By now the cluster was provoking me.

How quickly did my response sort itself out? I thought of Welty as someone who understood story itself as obviously political—in spite of the contradictory pronouncements in "Must the Novelist Crusade?" That is, she understood that story was not at all an innocent form, and constructed literature that seemed to me to be—more often than not—suspicious of, and *about* her suspicion of, old story patterns. "We start from scratch, and words don't, which is the thing that matters—matters over and over again," she knowingly wrote in another essay.[4] Her play with and obstruction of all kinds of old stories and story expectations resisted and altered their meanings. Albert Devlin

---

3. Diana Trilling, "Fiction in Review," *Nation*, 11 May 1946, 578; Richard H. King, *A Southern Renaissance: The Cultural Awakening of the American South, 1940–1955* (New York: Oxford University Press, 1980), 9.

4. Eudora Welty, "Words into Fiction," in *Eye of the Story*, 134.

and Prenshaw and then Peter Schmidt, Rebecca Mark, Ruth Weston, Susan Donaldson, and Suzan Harrison all knew this too, although their vocabulary of knowing may not have always identified these narrative strategies as "political."

I note a shift toward the political in our vocabulary for addressing these not-at-all-new issues from and following Barbara Ladd's 1995 article "Too Positive a Shape Not to Be Hurt: *Go Down Moses*, History, and the Woman Artist in *The Golden Apples*." Ladd wrote that despite scholars' having shown Welty's work as grounded in the historical, there persists a tendency to treat it as focused on the private single consciousness and so to call it ahistorical. Ladd attempted to correct this tendency by examining Welty intertextually with Faulkner—particularly in the pairing of *Go Down Moses* and *The Golden Apples*—and exploring Welty's displacement of Faulkner's plots. Ladd termed this a gender-based strategy for bringing attention to Welty's characters' indifference to, forgetfulness of, and obstruction of official cultural histories, echoed in the woman writer's own displacement of official southern history.[5] This sort of displacement—in its reinvention and recentering of the story to tell— is clearly political in nature.

The ten papers in this collection move forward from that disclosure to develop vocabulary for an increasingly significant discussion of Welty and the political and variously open the topic that was once presumed to be closed tight. Prenshaw initiates the process in "Welty's Transformations of the Public, the Private, and the Political." She argues that "the space in which Welty places what one might call acts of political behavior—listening, talking, debating, evaluating argument"—is rarely found in town halls, although the fiction nonetheless "displays a persistent regard for political negotiations" displaced to "the private sphere, private, perhaps, because these sites are so often the domain of women." For example, when *A Curtain of Green* opens with "Lily

---

5. Barbara Ladd, " 'Too Positive a Shape Not to Be Hurt': *Go Down Moses*, History, and the Woman Artist in Eudora Welty's *The Golden Apples*," in *Having Our Way: Women Rewriting Tradition in Twentieth-Century America (Bucknell Review* 39), ed. Harriet Pollack (Lewisburg, Pa.: Bucknell University Press, 1996), 79–103.

Daw and the Three Ladies," the comic story is humorously centered on "the question of what constitutes the good life for Lily Daw, a young woman who is effectively the ward of the town. Is her welfare best served by the protections offered by the state in the form of the Ellisville Institute for the Feeble-Minded of Mississippi? Or should she be mainstreamed into marriage with a traveling xylophone player and thus into a society of bourgeois individualism?"

Prenshaw uses Hannah Arendt's description of the Greek polis as "a site for contesting speech and action . . . the sphere of freedom" in her argument that *Losing Battles* is Welty's culminating portrait of positive and free political negotiation, of a polis-in-action where "a parliament of vigorous voices, freely speaking, [debate] the issues of authority and legitimacy, and the boundaries between the self, the nuclear family, and the larger group"—debate, that is, "the nature of justice and the knowledge most worth knowing." Various members of the Beecham-Renfro clan, vigorously and freely and with not a thought to being silenced by ordinance, dispute the standing of Judge Moody and the "accumulated power" of Julia Mortimer's authority in "an almost idealized political occasion when the stump speakers have knowledge of the subjects debated and full standing in the forum of exchange." Prenshaw finds that over a lifetime Welty's fiction has moved to this vision of community political debate from the earlier vision of *A Curtain of Green* in which endurance and self-silencing are more typical than the give-and-take of debate. To explain the continuity and the contrast between the Welty of "Death of a Traveling Salesman" and the Welty of *Losing Battles,* Prenshaw probes Mississippi politics as well as the alternative public sphere of evangelical Protestant reform with its emphasis on personal "redress of civil grievance." She reads "Keela, the Outcast Indian Maiden," *Delta Wedding, Losing Battles, The Optimist's Daughter,* "The Demonstrators," and "Must the Novelist Crusade?"—as well as Welty's own political photographs—to disclose the writer's perception of public venues as empty and inconsequential in comparison with "the private and local sphere, which is also . . . the habitation of fiction . . . the place where informed and persuasive deliberation occurs, where speech legitimated by authority of experience and identity can be spoken and heard."

"Engaging the Political: In Our Texts, in Our Classrooms" moves from issues of political debate to those of pedagogical debate. In this essay, Noel Polk muses over a trilogy of Hollywood films—*The Chamber, Ghosts of Mississippi,* and *A Time to Kill*—and their cultural representations of racial crimes in Mississippi, examining particularly the mitigation of guilt by a cultural argument about racial traditions. Polk uses the films to raise questions about the relationship between politics, art, and the university—that is, "between history, politics, and literature, and what teachers do, and in *how* and in *what forms* our history gets transmitted through the very institutions, our classrooms, that are the designated purveyors of that history." Cultural studies turns to memoir as Polk recollects his own first encounters with narratives about the South, handed to him as an unsuspecting undergraduate: "a modern canon filled with the ungodliest of racial problematics . . . depictions of the racial tensions in my home state . . . that were erupting in violence not more than seven or eight miles from where, in the sixties, I sat being instructed," but viewed through a critical tradition that separated art and politics and "would never demand of me that I go to sit-ins or perhaps to jail." Being "moved to tears . . . was enough." The aesthetic, Polk drolly observes, was confused with political *"an*esthetic." From the vantage point of his knowledge that "literature can become merely a part of those larger fictions out of which we constitute ourselves in the present moment, by constructing ourselves a coherent and meaningful past—a past by which, in the name of which, we hope to control the future," he hopes that "students will not just be deeply moved by what they read but will take their deep feelings . . . to the next step . . . to [change] the way they live." And from this vantage point Polk ponders Welty's response to the question "Eudora Welty, what are you going to do about it?" ("Crusade," 147).

As if in response to Polk's question, Suzanne Marrs in "'The Huge Fateful Stage of the Outside World': Eudora Welty's Life in Politics" documents Welty's unproclaimed lifetime of political reaction and action and focuses on the political views that Welty has expressed, and not always in private. A letter to the editor of the *Jackson Clarion-Ledger* written in 1945 in protest of "the spirit that would eventually be called McCarthyism. . . . prefigured Welty's active participation in the presidential election of 1952," in which she supported a candidate who represented intelligence, communication, learning, and imagination. Marrs argues that "for Welty, Stevenson's greatness lay in his recognition that political situations were too complex for simple answers. . . . [His] discussion of the multifaceted and perhaps impenetrable nature of reality held vital appeal" for the writer, who had declared that "all the opposites on earth were close together." "If public and private [were opposites that] thus converged for Welty in the campaign of 1952, if the fiction writer found her most interior values being championed 'on the huge fateful stage of the outside world,' she herself championed those values on [the] Mississippi stage in the 1960s" at Millsaps and Tougaloo Colleges. In a rich history of how civil rights conflicts were played out from the late fifties to mid-sixties on these two campuses, white and black, in and near Welty's Jackson, Marrs tells how on April 18, 1963, officials at Millsaps, fearing racial conflict in an integrated audience, suggested that its Southern Literary Festival be restricted to whites. Welty responded with the request that her lecture—later published as "Words into Fiction"—not be segregated.

In the presentation, after discussing the difference between reader and writer in their relationship to a work being "'neither so strange nor so important as the vital fact that a connection has been made between them,'[6] Welty read 'Powerhouse' to her interracial audience." This bold risk-taking built on her earlier readings and attendance at Tougaloo College's Social Sciences Forum, which had been "designed . . . to provide a 'model of an integrated society.'" And it led to another occasion a year later when, in a continuingly tense racial environment, she as Millsaps's writer-in-residence read a lecture entitled "The Southern Writer Today: An Interior Affair," which is the essay now known as "Must the Novelist Crusade?" Readers' understanding of the piece is considerably altered and powerfully clarified by the simple fact of that inaugural context. The paper's vocabulary, when heard at a far remove from its original time, place, and stage, is almost inevitably oversimplified. In its historical moment, it was a subtle and complex speech act. And Welty combined this act with another risky choice: a reading of "Keela, the Outcast Indian Maiden." "Keela," Marrs notes, "examines the complexities of human relationships":

6. Welty, "Words into Fiction," 144.

with Leroy's nostalgia for his importance in the drama of his victimization, with Steve's "inability . . . to overcome the separation of race," and finally, with a white "bystander's courting of detachment from both the horror and guilt Keela represents." Marrs proposes that by presenting the two pieces together, Welty made clear that fiction that did not overtly crusade could nevertheless be complexly political, even while accepting and even championing her judgment that "there is absolutely everything in great fiction but a clear answer" ("Crusade," 149).

As we close in on the secret of Welty and politics, a substitute secret appears: Welty and race. Welty's risk in self-presentation, apparent in the 1960 Mississippi settings Marrs documents, provides a point of departure for Suzan Harrison's "'Racial Content Espied': Modernist Politics, Textuality, and Race in Eudora Welty's 'The Demonstrators.'" Harrison argues that this story, "marked by various racial constructions," is "about reading and writing race and about resisting and obstructing racial readings." She recalls Toni Morrison's words regarding "the characteristics and associations traditionally projected onto the black Other by white culture: 'the power of illicit sexuality, chaos, madness, impropriety, anarchy, strangeness, and helpless, hapless desire.'" From this perspective, Harrison looks closely at Dr. Strickland's experience in Ruby's mother's house, an experience of "radical otherness, charged with sexuality, violence, and exotic chaos. . . . The story positions Ruby as a text that Strickland cannot interpret because the expectations and strategies he brings to the act of interpretation—racially inflected strategies—interfere with his ability to see what is in front of him." The doctor is authority ready to read authoritatively. He is delayed and affected by the associations he projects onto Ruby's body and community, his catalog of white projections onto black. "A maid?" he wonders, before he reads Ruby as "the breast" and then "the wound below the breast"—that is, sexuality and violence. The doctor does not recognize Ruby Gaddy, the woman who works in the building where he has his office—and in the dim room he labors to recognize the other members of Ruby's community who are surrounding him, impressed by what he does not make out. "'Don't you know her?'" they ask, "as if he was never going to hit on the right question." Adding to the story of Ruby's textuality, Harrison considers the Strickland narrative—in which "the doctor's barren life associates him with the general misery of the land"—as a transformation of Eliot's *Waste Land*, one that critiques modernist nostalgia and longings to hold old myths in place, a reading that enables Harrison to unfold the image of the fugitive Dove, golden, pollen-coated, and dying.

In the next essay, "A Voice from a Jackson Interior: Eudora Welty and the Politics of Filial Piety," Ann Romines reapproaches the relationship between the political, the private, and the past. Romines finds "the circumstances of the 'private woman' Eudora Welty . . . deeply and importantly implicated in her short fiction of the 1960s" in ways that extend the obviously political. Romines pursues the double meaning of filial—referring to both the "relation of a child to a parent, and the 'sequence of generations'"—a sequence in which inheritances are personal, cultural, and sometimes costly. The period of these stories coincides with a time when Welty experienced "trouble in the house"—the long illnesses and deaths of her mother and two brothers—a situation to which, Romines argues, she responded with years of filial devotion. The "constraints of 'illness in the house'" dominate these years when she, a devoted daughter attending a failing mother, is more housebound than at any previous time in her life. Romines considers a reason for Welty's feeling "oddly in touch" with her character Miss Eckhart.[7] Beyond their mutual love of art, they both came to be "single, childless, passionate middle-aged daughters, living in close filial relations with their disabled mothers."

Romines concurrently calls on the phrase "trouble in the house" in its other meaning to refer to the large dramas of U.S. political life, which were simultaneously being "acted out closer and closer to Welty's home, culminating in Medgar Evers's 1963 murder in Jackson." In her 1960s stories, Welty draws on "another close personal relationship, vaguely filial/familial itself: [her] close ties to her home state." Her response to the Evers murder—"Where Is the Voice Coming From?"—is written "extraordinarily, in the murderer's first-person voice. Welty described writing this political story in terms of near familial intimacy: 'I wrote from the interior . . . that world of hate that I

7. Eudora Welty, *One Writer's Beginnings* (Cambridge: Harvard University Press, 1984), 100.

felt I had grown up with and I felt I could speak as someone who knew it." A manuscript of the story titled "A Voice from a Jackson Interior" suggests that in Welty's mind, "politics was 'in here'"—and "might be closely linked with private spaces—in her case a domestic Jackson interior." Romines argues that Welty's two stories from the 1960s—her most overtly political—are about the filial piety of two "pious white" sons. The narrator of "A Voice," "whatever else he may be, is a dutiful son" who denies all authority with one patriarchal and determining exception. Dr. Strickland is another who has "'inherited' paternal legacies"—his occupation, his position in the town, his assumption of authority—but we meet him in the midst of a "power failure more disabling than the temporary electrical emergency" in progress at Ruby Gaddy's mother's house, and catch him as the filial links between generations have been severed by the deaths of his parents and his daughter. Romines's argument is about the political ramifications of filial piety for the past, and it complements Harrison's discussion of modernist nostalgic longing to hold old myths in place.

Rebecca Mark's "'A Cross-mark Ploughed into the Center': Civil Rights and Eudora Welty's *Losing Battles*" takes an unexpected turn in the critical reception of the 1970 novel. Sharing Prenshaw's view that *Losing Battles* is Welty's culminating portrait of the political, Mark examines the choices made in the creation of this novel by considering—as Sharon Baris will in her provocative second glance at *The Ponder Heart*—the political backdrop that dominated the news while Welty was writing. As Mark points out, these were the years when Emmett Till was lynched (1955), when James Meredith fought to integrate the University of Mississippi (1962), when the Jackson lunch counter sit-ins occurred, and when the debate over desegregation of the schools—accompanied by fury over school busing—raged. This fifteen-year period of composition corresponds exactly to the time frame between the *Brown* v. *Board of Education* ruling, which called segregated facilities unconstitutional, and the Swann ruling, which called for enforced integration. From this angle, Mark asks why Welty chose to place this novel about a schoolteacher and a community's educational philosophies in Tishomingo County, which had one of the smallest black populations in Mississippi, and then proposes a number of unexpected answers. Recalling Charles Bunting's question to Welty about "the rather conspicuous absence of Negroes in *Losing Battles*," Mark speculates on the meaning of the author's response: "There is, all the same, a very telling and essential incident . . . that involves a Negro as such. Perhaps you remember?"[8] Although Bunting seemingly did not, Mark does. The incident is the lynching of a black man for a white man's crime—that is, for the murder of Herman Dearman perpetrated by Nathan Beecham. In light of Welty's oblique response, Mark speculates about the political significance of Gloria's mysterious parentage, Julia's letters, Nathan's motives for murder, the novel's attitude toward mob mentalities, and crimes far worse than Jack's that Judge Moody has never brought to trial. She speculates further about the implications that Dearman's murder and the anonymous man's lynching would seem to have for Julia Mortimer, for public education, for constitutional law, and for Welty's mystery plot. Mark argues that viewed alongside *Losing Battles*, "Must the Novelist Crusade?" is a "description of exactly how the novelist *can* contribute to social change" by creating a plot that is, to use Welty's words, "a thousand times more unsettling than an argument, which may be answered." In *Losing Battles*, lynching and the school bus are two threads in a plot weaving unsettling political commentary as well as comic satire.

In "'Writing against Death': Totalitarianism and the Nonfiction of Eudora Welty at Midcentury," Barbara Ladd places Welty's nonfiction of 1935 to 1961—her photographs, her appreciation of "A Pageant of Birds" (1943), her responses to the fiction of Hemingway (1949) and Henry Green (1961)—into the political context of the mid–twentieth century, and focuses on the power of Welty's appeal to the private life during the years in which fascist and totalitarian regimes threatened from abroad. At the time, the rhetoric of individualism evoked "the human factor as potential" in the face of increasing State repression; this rhetoric provided an alternate vocabulary for political and personal freedom, increasingly "defined by contrast to 'totalitarianism' as represented by Mussolini, Hitler, and Stalin." Ladd depicts a young Welty in her relationship with agent Diarmuid Russell as the two

8. Charles Bunting, "'The Interior World': An Interview with Eudora Welty" in Peggy Prenshaw, *Conversations with Eudora Welty* (Jackson: University Press of Mississippi, 1984), 48.

shared suspicion of the growing power of the State and its preference for the reportorial and the material. She suggests a link to Russell's famous father, the Irish visionary writer AE, and the subject of his *Candle of Vision:* the threat represented by the State and its materialism to the individual's spiritual sensibility "with its admission of incalculable mystery," to borrow the phrase from the visionary's *Imaginations and Reveries.* AE's incalculable mystery perhaps suggested a vocabulary of resistance at a time when "Welty's subject also was becoming human mystery." Ladd suggests too that Welty's early stories are not so much about the plight of "the simple, the obscure, the feebleminded, the impoverished, and the alienated" in a "materialistic and progressive world as [they are about] the plight of the progressive and materialistic sensibility when confronted with these characters." Ladd goes on to place Welty's photographs in the context of the writer's objections to the reportorial, which violates the individual, and shows her interest in Maude Thompson's "A Pageant of Birds" at Farish Street Baptist Church to be an interest in the Jackson African American community's imaginative and political play with "symbols . . . chiefly patriotic and commercial"—"images of flags, dollars, and easy chairs"—conjoined in creative play that alludes to "both military and economic might." The refrain among the birds is a desire; they each sing:

> And I want TWO wings
> To veil my face,
> And the world can't do me no harm.

Ladd presents "A Pageant of Birds" in terms that suggest to me a signifying ceremony—a jiving parallel to the mule funeral of Zora Neale Hurston's *Their Eyes Were Watching God,* a pre-rap performance piece in which the eagle is central but kindred to the blackbird as well as the dove. Ladd calls this an "allegory [that] draws a good deal of its significance from the religious and political traditions of the African American church, linking political and commercial symbols subversively with religious discourse and community (rather than State) activism."

Finally, Ladd notes that Welty's responsive writing about Henry Green's work reflects the context of the cold war. Writing in the nuclear age following the bombing of Hiroshima, Welty repeatedly called on a critical vocabulary emphasizing personal commitment, using such words as "love, vulnerability, and daring" as well as the celebratory word "radiance," provocative in the postnuclear context. These words articulate a profoundly political "resistance to the impact of State power upon private life." And, tellingly, when Welty wrote of Green's fiction (1961), she demonstrated her attraction to a work that "announces on every page . . . the vulnerability of its characters to the threat of State power." Her reasons for admiring Green reflect her political concern; she characterized him as "writing against death"and as "reflect[ing] on the fate of individual man set down very much alive in a dying society."

In a different way, this sense of Welty's dismay with State power and her desire to uphold freedom is the subject of Sharon Baris's contiguous essay, which considers the trial of *The Ponder Heart* against the backdrop of the notorious trials of the 1950s, the Rosenberg trials and the McCarthy hearings. In "Judgments of *The Ponder Heart:* Welty's Trials of the 1950s," Baris recalls one particular response of Welty's to those many requests to crusade that came to her in the 1960s. In a 1972 interview Welty had chafed, recollecting that she had "felt like saying [she] didn't need their pointers to know that there was injustice among human beings"; she had been "writing about that *steadily right along*" (*Conversations*, 182). With this assertion in mind, Baris looks back to *The Ponder Heart*, completed in 1953. Sidestepping the tale's usual reception as light in heart and perhaps in weight as well, Baris considers it against the political backdrop that dominated the news while Welty was writing; she views the comic trial against the climate of the national trials of the 1950s, which connects exhibits into monolithic proofs "as if joining 'link after link' in a 'chain,'" a chain that for Baris expresses an idea of America that evokes the scriptural Daniel's prophecies—predictions that were the basis for the whole world's Manifest Destiny with America at the End. Examining the "fraily held together" trial of Uncle Daniel, she finds a possible parody of dark events, a lampoon that would draw a thoughtful if waggish line between Americanist presumptions and Welty's own. But even as Baris discovers surprising coincidences between the Rosenberg trial and Daniel's, she gently undercuts her own linkages, refusing to collaborate with the "menace of neatness" in evidence ("Crusade," 149) that Welty too had refused. She sees Welty writing as if to undo the idea of linkages in evidence "demanded as proof of American (or un-American) activities"; the comic trial works to undercut legalistic courtroom assumptions about truths of history and proof which in the actual and infamous American trials of the 1950s were used to decide matters of life and death. Baris sees the history of Welty's writing of this novella—her difficulty bringing it to conclusion as the Rosenberg trial actually came to conclusion—as reflecting Welty's uneasiness with both the actual trial and her fiction's relationship to it; once Ethel Rosenberg was sentenced to electrocution, there was no longer room for even the relief of despairing comic farce.

In "Private and Political Thought in *One Writer's Beginnings*," Danièle Pitavy-Souques considers Welty's self-portrait—first drafted for the William E. Massey lecture series on American civilization at Harvard in April 1983—as political in the tradition of southern women writing "from a region where the violence of History doubled their responsibilities as writers and artists." She argues that, like Zora Neale Hurston in *Dust Tracks on a Road*, Welty uses the genre of self-portrait (distinct from autobiography) "to rewrite a history of the development of the American imagination, with all its cultural components, and that these two works address the issue of the political at its highest level." Ultimately resisting critical response to Welty as a "regionalist," Pitavy-Souques strives to uncover "Welty's Americanness . . . within the canon of American literature." Calling up Benjamin Franklin as a literary ancestor, she argues that "language becomes theme when it serves Welty's purpose to present a general picture of America rather than the private picture of her own life" and that she "achieves a balance between the specificity of the self and the representative depiction of a life." Pitavy-Souques elaborates:

> Since Welty builds her narrative upon an accumulation of small details, she multiplies information about her home life and family background, schools and libraries in Jackson, summer travels through the country, and life in the early days of the pioneers, always insisting on mirror effects through endless echoes and multiple repetitions that work like so many small touches of paint on a canvas, or like Mondri-

an's grid, to convey the intellectual perception of what life was like in America at a certain time. At the end of our reading, we feel the simultaneity of hundreds of perceptions and thoughts, rather than the sequentially organized sensory experience of impressionism. The background has become exactly coincident with the foreground.

Pitavy-Souques argues that, using the possibilities offered by this technique, Welty expresses herself on the topic of racism by showing that "black voices and black talents for storytelling were part of her education as a fiction writer. . . . She shows how Jackson taught her the sounds of life, and . . . how early she became aware of the creative power of . . . storytellers, . . . [placing] Fannie, the African American seamstress, . . . side by side with her mother's white friends in the acknowledgment of her debt as a writer." And this is also the technique in Welty's treatment of her family's political background as she "uses short genealogical sketches to draw a political map of the United States, establishing, for instance, West Virginia as a place where slavery was refused." She creates in "the figures of her mother and father the paradoxical quality of . . . American myths. . . . With her mother's ancestors—preachers and lawyers, schoolteachers and scholars—she establishes the link with the drafters of the American Constitution and . . . with New Beginnings. . . . She identifies West Virginia, her mother's country, as both Eden and Promised Land—an Eden for her mother, but the wild promised land where she will have to fight ceaselessly to ensure her independence. . . . Ohio, on the other hand, her father's country, becomes the place where, for her, the myths of American pragmatism and simplicity and efficiency begin." Pitavy-Souques notes that Welty depicts her father as an American pragmatist and as pioneer experimenter with new technologies, and "further presents him as filled with the pioneer's love of change and movement . . . eager to reenact, with the same spirit of adventure, the exploration of the width and depth of the North American continent. Welty's insistence on the role played upon her creative imagination by railroad journeys with her father defines, it seems, wandering as the quintessential American dream and shows how deeply ingrained the wanderer is in the heart of a writer . . . [and] in the nation's imagination."

The final essay of the collection is photographic. In "Seeing Welty's

Political Vision in Her Photographs," Suzanne Marrs and I have annotated thirteen of Welty's images from the 1930s, published here with
the permission of the Eudora Welty Collection, Mississippi Department of Archives and History, to bring the writer-photographer's framing and exposing political vision into focus. These images are texts
that complement and clarify the representatives of race, class, gender,
power, and politics visible in Welty's fiction. We hope that, viewed in
this context, the pictures—most of which have been familiar since
1971 when Welty first published *One Time, One Place*—may develop
freshly.

Here, then, are ten complementary essays, based on various notions of
the political, the private, and the complex, that raise questions about
how we have interpreted Welty's importance, both private and political. Together they shed light on the deceptive opposition of "private"
and "political" as terms that, like "all the opposites on earth, [are]
close together," illustrating the writer's pronouncement in *The
Golden Apples*.[9] The time for understanding this paradox in its particular historical and cultural context has come.

   The 1998 Library of America Edition of Welty has summoned many
retrospectives of her work and speculations on its significance, including Claudia Roth Pierpont's "A Perfect Lady" in the *New Yorker*. Pierpont's analysis focuses precisely on the issue of the political and—in
light of the stories after *A Curtain of Green* and with the one exception of "Where Is the Voice Coming From?"—charges Welty with having averted her eyes from the political issues of her time and place. Unlike Baris, who connects *The Ponder Heart* to the Rosenberg and
McCarthy hearings, Pierpont views that novella as proof of Welty's determined avoidance of social significance during the years of racial up-
heaval in her home state and envisions her becoming "Mississippi's favorite daughter," and winning prizes for the oversight. Unlike Rebecca
Mark, who understands *Losing Battles* as a complex response to the
attitudes that allowed the lynching of Emmett Till and to ideas about
public education circulating after *Brown* v. *Board of Education* termed
segregated facilities unconstitutional, Pierpont reads *Losing Battles* as

9. Eudora Welty, *The Golden Apples* (New York: Random House, 1947), 265.

giving "no weight" to the revelation that "Uncle Nathan . . . murdered a man and 'let 'em hang a sawmill nigger for it.'" Stepping out from Malcolm Cowley's remark that Welty's "writing is . . . fastidious, scrupulous, marked by delicate discrimination," Pierpont does her worst:

> And this is the image of Welty that has prevailed, firmly shutting out the old, indelicate discriminations . . . the world of hate she split wide open [in a few stories] and exposed with expert hands. But, clearly this change has been her choice. A born outsider in a stifling, hypocritical, yet tantalizingly charming society, Welty discovered that she could write her way into acceptance; year by year, book by book, she came to be wholly embraced. Who would not find such acceptance irresistible? Who would not be glad and grateful? In terms of her art, however, it was a hard bargain. These new volumes make it all too clear how an intrepid explorer turned into a perfect lady—a nearly Petrified Woman—with eyes averted and mouth set in a smile, who from time to time let out a bloodcurdling cry, as though she, too, could not forget what had been lost.[10]

This riskily ventured, entirely unjust, and damaging as well as insulting view is not shared by the critics writing here. Yet in its misguided condescension, it makes startlingly, even achingly, clear the need for this collection, and for clarification on the controversial subject of Welty and the political. The essays that follow attempt to meet that need.

10. Claudia Roth Pierpont, "A Perfect Lady," *New Yorker*, 5 October 1998, 94–104.

*Peggy Whitman Prenshaw*

# Welty's Transformations of the Public, the Private, and the Political

For some years I have been interested to read Eudora Welty for the many ways she suggests in her fiction, essays, and interviews that the personal *is* political, though to use this familiar feminist phrase is not Welty's way. The outpouring of enlightening critical studies of Welty over the past two decades has not only enriched my understanding of the essential feminism informing Welty's work but has corroborated my long-held view that she gives us a fictional world that profoundly challenges the roles men and women have been given to play in Western culture—that is, that questions conventional systems of sexual politics.[1]

What I wish to do here, however, is not so much to revisit topics well explored by recent critics who have written knowledgeably and expansively of Welty's feminism. Instead, I intend to employ a conventional definition of "politics" as the means by which a society governs itself, or to discuss what one might call simply "public affairs," in an exploration of Welty's views of the public, the private, and the political spheres of human activity. In particular, I want to inquire into Welty's practice of relocating, or displacing, the public and the political spheres to private and moral ones—and to ask why she so deeply distrusts "politics" in fiction and in life.

Providing a point of departure is a recollection of an interview with Eudora Welty that Albert Devlin and I undertook in 1986 in her home

1. An early reading of gender roles in Welty's fiction was my "Woman's World, Man's Place: The Fiction of Eudora Welty," in *Eudora Welty: A Form of Thanks*, ed. Louis Dollarhide and Ann J. Abadie (Jackson: University Press of Mississippi, 1979), 46–77. The present essay is a revised and extended version of a paper appearing in *Mississippi Quarterly* 50 (1997): 617–30.

in Jackson, Mississippi. For several hours we engaged in a lively but relaxed conversation, mostly concerning other writers, but toward the end of the visit the discussion became quite intense. The change in tone occurred as Welty replied to a question about her political assessment of the nation and the times, the mid-1980s. Her response is notable in several respects, most especially in revealing the negative connotations she associates with the word *politics*, linked as it was in her mind with demagogic leaders and racism.

As recorded in the published interview, Devlin begins the sequence of questions by noting that he became interested in politics in the early 1960s, inspired by President Kennedy and civil rights legislation, which he said had given him "a sense of unity . . . and also a national purpose." By contrast, he had come two decades later to have "no idea where we are, either nationally or individually." Then he asks, "You've seen this over a longer period of time, do you have a sense of perplexity too?"

"I do, I feel that the perplexity is all over the nation," Welty answered. "And I also loved John F. Kennedy; I thought something wonderful was going to happen in the world when he was elected. And that really vanished with his assassination."

Turning from the national scene to consider her own local experience of "politics," she voiced not so much grief as deep frustration. "When I was growing up here, politics was everywhere, but there was not any kind of glorification of politics in my family on either of my parents' sides." Distancing herself from immoderate politics by claiming a familial disposition for reasonable moderation, she remembers Mississippians "like Bilbo and Vardaman who were almost unbelievable. And that is the kind of thinking that a lot of Jackson who were on the wrong side of Civil Rights hark back to: 'What we need is somebody like . . . !' So that's where their ideals led them, an idiotic return to something that was not any good in the first place."

Welty sharply dismissed such politics, registering her exasperation, and then made in quick succession a series of assertions that summarize the main points I want to pursue in this analysis of her "political" thought. Of the ideals of those who canonize Bilbo and Vardaman, she said, "Well, that's not anything to place too much confidence in. I can't talk. Such a tremendous—I do feel that private relationships between blacks and white have always been the steadying thing. I believe in private human relations anyway, for understanding. And I've always had faith that they would resolve problems."[2]

Here we find Welty silencing herself as she attempts to speak about "politics," a silencing that she accomplishes, one notices, with passion and resignation. Her hope for a better society lies not with "political ideals," compromised as they are for her by group conformity and racism, but rather in the individual heart, which is most effectively reached through private relations or art, not politics. The distinction between the domains of art and of politics (which she refers to variously as crusading, propagandizing, exhorting, etc.) is one Welty returns to again and again in essays and interviews. Steadfastly skeptical of politics, she does not pin hopes for individual rights or social justice upon a linking of the personal and the political. Instead, she makes a case for the superior efficacy of the separate, personal sphere as the venue where understanding of the Other takes place, where self-knowledge occurs, and where one's political beliefs may therefore take humane shape. "I don't think literature—I'm talking about fiction now—I don't think it can exhort. Or it loses every bit of its reality and value. I think it speaks to what is more deeply within, that is, the personal, and conveys its meaning that way. And then one hopes that a person made alert or aroused to be more sensitive to other human beings would go on to look at things on a larger scale by himself. I wouldn't like to read a work of fiction that I thought had an ulterior motive, to persuade me politically. I automatically react the other way." A little later she concluded her rather lengthy commentary on politics and fiction with a reassertion of her separateness from group affiliations, even literary ones, such as Bloomsbury. "I'm just interested in people as individuals . . . caring for individuals so much."[3]

Welty's frequently stated aversion to the politicizing of fiction and her fictional practice of steering well clear of overtly political topics, except in a few exceptional cases,[4] have made it commonplace

2. Albert J. Devlin and Peggy Whitman Prenshaw, "A Conversation with Eudora Welty," in *More Conversations with Eudora Welty,* ed. Peggy Whitman Prenshaw (Jackson: University Press of Mississippi, 1996), 114.

3. Ibid., 118–9.

4. The two final stories in *The Collected Stories of Eudora Welty* (New York: Harcourt Brace, 1980), "Where Is the Voice Coming From?"(1963) and "The Demonstrators" (1966), portray contrasting responses of white southerners to

throughout the nearly sixty years of her literary career for reviewers and critics to think and write of her fiction as nonpolitical. Diana Trilling's reviews of *The Wide Net* and *Delta Wedding* spoke of a fictional vision that was like a ballet—stylized, elegant, too often precious, and lacking in a realistic engagement with the South as it actually existed in a social, political manifestation. "Cloud Cuckoo Land" was the label given by a *Time* magazine reviewer to Welty's portrait of the 1923 Mississippi Delta, the nod to Aristophanes serving to indict what the reviewer regarded as the novel's political naïveté. A generation later, in his 1980 study of the Southern Renaissance, Richard King made the problematical assertion, often rebutted in the intervening years, that Welty, along with other southern women writers (excepting Lillian Smith), was "not concerned with the larger cultural, racial, and political themes" that he was focusing upon. According to King, Welty and the others "did not place the region at the center of their imaginative visions."[5]

For many years there have also been rumors of repeated Nobel Prize nominations that have met resistance because of judges' perception of a lack of social-political consciousness in Welty. And Welty herself

---

events that resulted from the civil rights movement of the 1960s. In a 1978 interview with Tom Royals and John Little, Welty spoke of "The Demonstrators" as "a reflection of society at the time" and not primarily a civil rights story. She also mentioned in the interview her intention to publish a collection of stories that "reflect the way we were deeply troubled in that society and within ourselves at what was going on in the sixties." To date no such book has been published. See Royals and Little, "A Conversation with Eudora Welty," in *Conversations with Eudora Welty*, ed. Peggy Whitman Prenshaw (Jackson: University Press of Mississippi, 1984), 259.

5. "Fiction in Review," *Nation*, 2 October 1943, 386–7, and 11 May 1946, 578; "Cloud-Cuckoo Symphony," *Time*, 22 April 1946, 104 ff.; Richard H. King, *A Southern Renaissance: The Cultural Awakening of the American South, 1930–1955* (New York: Oxford University Press, 1980), 9. Representative of the many well-argued rebuttals to King's assertion are those of Susan V. Donaldson, "Gender and the Profession of Letters in the South," in *Rewriting the South: History and Fiction*, ed. Lothar Honnighausen and Valeria Gennaro Lerda (Tubingen: Francke, 1993), 35–46, and Carol S. Manning, *With Ears Opening Like Morning Glories: Eudora Welty and the Love of Storytelling* (Westport, Conn.: Greenwood Press, 1985), 70 ff.

has, of course, somewhat exacerbated her reputation for apoliticality by such pieces as "Must the Novelist Crusade?" Published in the *Atlantic* in October 1965, the essay pointedly differentiates the arena of the novelist from that of the social or political crusader. "The writing of a novel is taking life as it already exists," Welty writes, "not to report it but to make an object, toward the end that the finished work might contain this life inside it, and offer it to the reader. . . . What distinguishes it above all from the raw material, and what distinguishes it from journalism, is that inherent in the novel is the possibility of a shared act of the imagination between its writer and its reader." For Welty, a crusading novelist is damned from the start by the deadening effects for fiction of totalizing generalities. These generalities, the pronouncements the crusader is trying to drive home, "make too much noise," as Welty personifies them, "for us to hear what people might be trying to say." By contrast, she says, "there is absolutely everything in great fiction but a clear answer."[6]

In interviews she has frequently spoken dismissively of efforts by social activists to engage her in causes. Jonathan Yardley reported in 1973 that, "as a Southerner and a woman," Welty was "constantly pressed for her opinions on race and Women's Liberation." She told Yardley, "I've never had any prejudice shown to me, so I have no bone to pick. I do think women should be paid as much as men, which I don't suppose anyone would disagree with. I don't see why, just because I write stories, that should give me the authority about, say, what should happen about abortion. Maybe I'm shirking responsibility, but I don't think so. Everything I feel is in my stories."[7]

Without engaging here the question of Welty's construction of "prejudice," I should like to inquire into her assumptions about what constitutes public space and political action, as distinguished from the private domain, and how these assumptions are related to the South in which she grew up and began seriously to write about in the 1930s.

The space in which Welty places what one might call acts of politi-

6. Eudora Welty, "Must the Novelist Crusade?" in *The Eye of the Story: Selected Essays and Reviews* (New York: Random House, 1978), 147–9.
7. "A Quiet Lady in the Limelight," in *More Conversations with Eudora Welty*, ed. Prenshaw, 11.

cal behavior—listening, talking, debating, evaluating argument, coming to evaluative positions regarding competing arguments about the society's good—that is, a free political arena—is only infrequently located in town halls, state capitols, political campaign sites, or union halls. Nonetheless, I would argue that the fiction displays a persistent regard for political negotiations but displaces such negotiations from political sites to what she regards as—and indeed, what has traditionally been regarded as—the private sphere, private, perhaps, because these sites are so often the domain of women. Welty's first collection of short stories, *A Curtain of Green* (1941), later included in *The Collected Stories of Eudora Welty*, opens with "Lily Daw and the Three Ladies," a story centered upon the question of what constitutes the good life for Lily Daw, a young woman who is effectively the ward of the town. Is her welfare best served by the protection offered by the state in the form of the Ellisville Institute for the Feeble-Minded of Mississippi? Or should she be mainstreamed into marriage with a traveling xylophone player and thus into the society of bourgeois individualism? The debate, held by three main female personages of Victory, Mississippi, is intense, impersonal, and conducted in the civic space of the post office, the street, the foot of the water tank, Lily's house, and the train station. But the political import of the story is oblique, camouflaged from most readers by Welty's humor, her genial but subversive mockery of the three ladies' exaggerated self importance, and a general readiness to read female outcomes as private, domestic matters rather than political ones.

When Welty depicts a condition or site where debate freely occurs, which engages persons of equal standing in speech and action—and which leads to a consequence of persuasion, rather than despotic enforcement of will—she is usually describing what is conventionally regarded as a private, rather than public, realm. She presents, however, a display of political negotiation, one that resembles Hannah Arendt's description in *The Human Condition* of the Greek polis, wherein the quality of debate differs from that of the private household. In the Greek world, the household was subject to the absolute rule of the household head, whereas the polis offered a site for contesting speech and action. "The *polis*," writes Arendt, "was distinguished from the household in that it knew only 'equals,' whereas the household was the center of the strictest inequality. To be free meant both not to be subject to the necessity of life or to the command of another *and* not to be in command oneself."[8] For the Greeks it was the public realm, not the private, that constituted the sphere of freedom and individuality. Arendt goes on to discuss the blurring of the public and private in the modern period, which has produced a social sphere she sees as constraining individual action and producing an ever-increasing conformity. That Welty's ladies of Victory debating the best life choice for Lily Daw are operating in the political realm, however, rather than the social, is evidenced by the existence of opposing conceptions of right action that are debated and enacted in an extrafamilial civic space. What is anomalous for Welty's Victory in comparison with the Greek polis is that the matter subjected to public debate (Lily's future) seems trivial and particular, rather than serious and communal.

Many critics have written that the *Curtain of Green* fiction reflects a modernist vision, that the seventeen stories are populated with an array of psychically wounded, self-conscious, cut-off-from-the-world characters.[9] Tom Harris in "The Hitch-Hikers," the stranger in "The Key" who tries to bridge a chasm between a deaf-mute couple and his world, Howard in "Flowers for Marjorie," who is both starved and surfeited by the gaudy, empty commercial world he can't escape—these and others are rather familiar wanderers, lost souls who have neither physical nor spiritual security. The stories are also responses in a specific historical context to one particular time and place, as Welty notes in her introduction to *The Collected Stories of Eudora Welty.* They de-

8. Hannah Arendt, *The Human Condition* (1958; rpt. Garden City, N.Y.: Doubleday Anchor, 1959), 30. In chap. 2, "The Public and the Private Realm," Arendt offers a full discussion of the Greek concept of the division between the polis and the household.

9. See, for example, Danièle Pitavy-Souques, "A Blazing Butterfly: The Modernity of Eudora Welty," *Mississippi Quarterly* 39 (1986): 537–60; Michael Kreyling, *Eudora Welty's Achievement of Order* (Baton Rouge: Louisiana State University Press, 1980), 3–15; Kreyling, "Modernism in Welty's *A Curtain of Green and Other Stories*," *Southern Quarterly* 20 (1982): 40–53; Barbara Fialkowski, "Psychic Distances in *A Curtain of Green*: Artistic Success and Personal Failures," in *A Still Moment: Essays on the Art of Eudora Welty,* ed. John F. Desmond (Metuchen, N.J.: Scarecrow Press, 1978), 63–70.

pict an impoverished, poorly educated, agrarian, small-town populace of 1930s Mississippi, a cast that steps almost directly from the photographs and articles of Welty's WPA work as a "junior publicity agent" traveling all eighty-two counties of the state. As snapshots of Mississippi people and places and as constructions of literary modernism, the world of these stories is mostly one in which political talk and action rarely occur. Sister in "Why I Live at the P.O." inquires into the operative conditions for justice—fairness, impartiality, reciprocity—but her auditor is wordless and no debate ensues. "Lily Daw" and "Petrified Man" are rather exceptions in the *Curtain of Green* collection, posing as they do public discussions (on the street and in the beauty shop) of what constitutes right action. More typical are "The Whistle," in which a desperate farm couple try to save their tomato crop by covering the tender plants with their very nightclothes, and "Death of a Traveling Salesman," Welty's first published story (1936), in which R. J. Bowman's lonely death and the nearly silent presence of the backwoods couple mark the Mississippi hill country as utterly remote from political life.

With a few exceptions already noted, Welty rarely entertains the possibility of political discourse in these early stories. Emancipatory strategies of speech possession and empowerment are revealed as available in a potential or chrysalis stage, as Patricia Yaeger observes of the character Ruby Fisher in her commentary on "A Piece of News," or even in a realized, albeit monologic, stage such as Dawn Trouard persuasively argues for Ruby Fisher,[10] but sustaining, confirming, negotiating, contestatory speech is far less present in most of these stories than is a muted spirit of endurance (Phoenix Jackson), a display of performative speech (Powerhouse), or utter self-silencing (Clytie).

And yet when Welty comes a generation later in her full maturity to

10. See Yaeger, *Honey-Mad Women: Emancipatory Strategies in Women's Writing* (New York: Columbia University Press, 1988), 114–23, and Trouard, "Diverting Swine: The Magical Relevancies of Eudora Welty's Ruby Fisher and Circe," in *The Critical Response to Eudora Welty's Fiction,* ed. Laurie Champion (Westport, Conn.: Greenwood Press, 1994), 335–55. Trouard writes that "Welty creates men who function as props in Ruby's little theater, and the reader's pleasure, as well as Ruby's, emanates from her ability to determine her own pleasure, the delight of self-absorption" (344).

the writing of *Losing Battles* (1970), returning to a hill-country farm similar to the one she first wrote about in "Death of a Traveling Salesman," she creates a parliament of vigorous voices, freely speaking, debating issues of authority, and legitimacy, and the boundaries between self, the nuclear family, and the larger group, debating, that is, the nature of justice and the knowledge most worth knowing. In fact, the novel is remarkably classical in its affirmation of the possibility of sustaining and renewing group life through the agency of human speech. If one is to appreciate fully the connection—and contrast—between the Welty of "Death of a Traveling Salesman" and the Welty of *Losing Battles*, one must gain an understanding of her views of the South— her views of politics, race, religion, and poverty, for example—as well as an understanding of the influence of literary modernism upon her writing.

Born in 1909, Welty grew up in a Mississippi dominated by a political and governmental system organized upon racial segregation. Open public debate exhibiting differing views about what constitutes, say, fair and equal treatment, or political legitimacy, or—more radically— racial justice, was not audible in the civic life of Jackson. The racism was, of course, exacerbated by the poverty, which Welty saw at close hand during her travels in the 1930s. She told Jonathan Yardley, and has often repeated in interviews, that the experience was pivotal in her growth as a writer. "It was a matter of getting to see something of the state. . . . I went to every county seat. . . . It was a—I almost said "heart-opener"—a real eye-opener. My feelings were engaged by the outside world, I think for the first time. . . . I never had really understood what was going on in the world until I saw it by myself. I'd always been sheltered, traveling with my father. I was shown the Grand Canyon, but that's not the same as seeing one family, living by the side of the road. That was when I really started writing stories."[11]

What she saw was often wrenching poverty and what she heard from Mississippi political leaders as Roosevelt's New Deal programs began to take effect was often complaint that the national relief programs were subverting the going wage for farm laborers and disturbing

11. In *More Conversations with Eudora Welty*, 6.

the political-social-racial system.[12] Ironically, even as they com-
plained, the politically powerful planters in the Delta became the
major beneficiaries of the New Deal in Mississippi. In fact, as historian
James C. Cobb notes, the New Deal gave a tremendous boost to the
state's economy, bringing to "the poorest state in the Union" its major
source of income in 1934. Writing of the Delta region in the Depression era, Cobb observes that some "slender benefits" of federal aid did
trickle down to the African American farm laborers, but that it was
the planters to whom the federal funds mainly flowed. They received
government crop subsidies, protection against risk, and assistance
with machinery purchases, while enjoying the advantage of a cheap
labor pool that federal aid helped support.[13]

In the 1940 story "Keela, the Outcast Indian Maiden," first submit-

12. For a succinct overview of economic and political conditions in Mississippi
    and the South, see *Mississippi: Conflict and Change,* ed. James W. Loewen
    and Charles Sallis (New York: Pantheon Books, 1974), 236 ff. A much more
    detailed discussion of general economic conditions may be found in Gavin
    Wright, *Old South, New South: Revolutions in the Southern Economy since
    the Civil War* (New York: Basic Books, 1986; rpt. Baton Rouge: Louisiana
    State University Press, 1996), 198 ff., and a more detailed social history in Jack
    Temple Kirby, *Rural Worlds Lost: The American South, 1920–1960* (Baton
    Rouge: Louisiana State University Press, 1987). For an excellent treatment of
    the conditions of life of black tenant families during the years 1890–1940, see
    Neil R. McMillen, *Dark Journey: Black Mississippians in the Age of Jim Crow*
    (Urbana: University of Illinois Press, 1989), especially chap. 4, "Farmers with-
    out Land." Also consult vol. 2 of *A History of Mississippi,* ed. Richard Aubrey
    McLemore (Jackson: University Press of Mississippi, 1973), for relevant and
    wide-ranging topical essays. Undoubtedly among the most authoritative and
    interesting sources of information about the Mississippi Welty came to know
    during her years of work with the WPA and afterwards are the author's own
    collection of photographs in *One Time, One Place* (New York: Random
    House, 1971), and the WPA guidebook, *Mississippi: A Guide to the Magnolia
    State* (New York: Viking Press, 1938). An excellent scholarly source of infor-
    mation about Welty's Mississippi is Albert J. Devlin's *Eudora Welty's Chroni-
    cle: A Story of Mississippi Life* (Jackson: University Press of Mississippi,
    1983); see especially the opening chapter.
13. James C. Cobb, *The Most Southern Place on Earth: The Mississippi Delta and
    the Roots of Regional Identity* (New York: Oxford University Press, 1992),
    196–7.

ted for publication in 1938, Welty portrays an onlooker, Steve, who has witnessed an act of oppression, carried to the point of torture and enslavement, visited upon a black man, small of stature and crippled, who is "saved" by a tall white man from Texas.[14] The restorative act is private and personal. Its outcome is neither monument nor legislation but rather Steve's anguished remembering and confessing his sense of guilt to Little Lee Roy, the victim, and to the impassive Max, Steve's guide in Cane Springs, Mississippi.

Instructively, in this story Welty substitutes the evangelical site of personal confession of sins for a public or political space of redress of civil grievance. Indeed, the story points up conditions of political life in the South that Welty came to know during these early years: a contaminated political space that allowed for little or no free discussion of societal relations; a religious space congenial to fundamentalist belief; private responsibility for one's salvation; and confessionals that occurred in dramatic moments of strong emotion or duress, such as one might experience in revival meetings or, as Welty describes in *One Writer's Beginnings*, religious gatherings held in the city auditorium, led by celebrated evangelists like Gypsy Smith or Billy Sunday. Although in the story of Keela Welty does not explicitly attribute Steve's motive for expiation to a religious conversion, there is ample evidence among historical studies of southern culture that religious belief contributed extensively to public ethical practice. Feelings of remorse for one's own guilt and for society's sins against another was an acknowledged, even familiar, motivation for political reform. Morton Sosna is one of many historians who has observed, for example, the importance of evangelicalism to southern liberalism. "Religion played a dominant role in the career of many," he writes, "and one is struck by the number of white Southern liberals who pointed to simple Christian pieties as the essential element of their thinking." Southern religion scholar Samuel S. Hill finds a marked "religious momentum" in the region's culture beginning in the 1870s and 1880s, although he notes that evangelical Protestantism had achieved dominance by 1830. Hill writes

14. See Noel Polk, *Eudora Welty: A Bibliography of Her Work* (Jackson: University Press of Mississippi, 1994), 366–7, for information about the publishing history of "Keela."

that evangelicalism was "relatively inert for half a century," but from the late nineteenth century to the present "it has been busy and aggressive, converting the lost, purifying an imperfect church, and going forth to transform the world."[15]

Since the church and the courthouse were perhaps the two most public sites available for adult social exchange in Mississippi, it would be useful here to look briefly at the relation of religion to politics in the decade of the thirties and in the preceding period, the years of Welty's childhood. Of particular interest is the role of the Methodist Church in efforts to improve the work and living conditions of the poor and needy, specifically, the home missions effort of Methodist women. Welty herself grew up going to the Methodist church, as she tells Patricia Wheatley in a 1986 interview taped for a BBC documentary, although hers was not, she notes, a particularly religious household. "My mother was brought up in the Methodist church, and my father, too. His father led the choir in the Methodist church in Ohio in his little town. And I was brought up going to the Methodist Sunday School, for which I'm glad, and learned the Bible, which I love to read."[16]

As one learns from John Patrick McDowell's *The Social Gospel in the South,* the women's home mission movement provided the most accessible avenue for southern Methodist women to participate in public social action. Their starting point, as McDowell notes, was the home and the family, their "desire to see stable, moral homes among the poor as well as the rich, and among the unchurched as well as the churched" their major motivation. The women involved in home mission work came, as Methodists, from "a religious tradition that emphasized the importance of ethical activity and the possibility of human improvement." McDowell cautions that one should not view the Methodist women's home mission work as overturning the wide-

---

15. Eudora Welty, *One Writer's Beginnings* (Cambridge: Harvard University Press, 1984), 32–3; Morton Sosna, *In Search of the Silent South: Southern Liberals and the Race Issue* (New York: Columbia University Press, 1977), 173; Samuel S. Hill, ed., *Varieties of Southern Religious Experience* (Baton Rouge: Louisiana State University Press, 1988), especially "Conclusion," 226.

16. Patricia Wheatley, "Eudora Welty: A Writer's Beginnings," in *More Conversations with Eudora Welty,* ed. Prenshaw, 130.

spread view that southern religion "focused primarily on individual salvation and personal morality," but he argues for an acknowledgment of their contribution to political and social reform in the South.[17]

Among the reform activists from Mississippi during this period were two women who did indeed get their start in politics in Methodist home missions: Nellie Nugent Somerville and Ellen Woodward. Both women furnish instructive examples of how socially constructed gender roles framed the "political sphere" for women, even for such activists as Somerville and Woodward. Implicit in much of their work and in their statements about their motivation for public service is the assumption that the purpose of political action is the establishment of justice in the personal, familial, and domestic realms, a view anticipating and closely paralleling Welty's political thought.

Born in 1863, Somerville, a devout Methodist, organized and served as president of a church home mission group when she was thirty-three. Later, despite what historian Anne Firor Scott describes as the obstacle of Mississippi's being "probably the most unpromising state in the country for a suffrage organizer," Somerville became an active suffragist leader and, later, in 1923, the first woman to be elected to the Mississippi legislature.[18] Ellen Woodward was active at the federal level in the Roosevelt administration, directing women's work relief under three successive New Deal agencies from 1933 to 1938, then joining the Social Security Board, and retiring as director of a division of the Federal Security Agency in 1953. According to her biographer, Martha Swain, Woodward's social conscience "in all probability" developed from her experience in the Methodist church and from the influence of knowing and working with Nellie Somerville, though as Swain also notes, "What is remarkable about Woodward is that her advancement was based almost entirely on her own self-education in

17. John Patrick McDowell, *The Social Gospel in the South: The Woman's Home Mission Movement in the Methodist Episcopal Church, South, 1886–1939* (Baton Rouge: Louisiana State University Press, 1982), 144–8.

18. Anne Firor Scott, *Making the Invisible Woman Visible* (Urbana: University of Illinois Press, 1984), 169–70. See also Marjorie Spruill Wheeler, *New Women of the New South: The Leaders of the Woman Suffrage Movement in the Southern States* (New York: Oxford University Press, 1993), 53 ff.

public affairs."[19] Both women justified much of their political activity as a defense of women and the family, which was, as already noted, a traditional stance for women and also consistent with their religious belief and church work. One must acknowledge, however, that even allowing for their political origins in home and church, these two political figures were surely "exotic plants" among southern women, to use Scott's apt phrase describing Somerville.

Despite the evidence that some religious organizations did offer access to public involvement and that a few exceptional political figures—female as well as male—did question the social arrangements of a segregated, paternalistic society and status quo politics, one must still conclude that the possibilities for public exchange of open speech and action in socially conservative Mississippi were to a great extent constrained, if not truncated or vitiated, for white women and, especially, for African American men and women.[20] Welty's *Curtain of Green* stories largely reflect this time and place through mute presences or monologic voices. As her experience and literary power grew during the 1940s, '50s, and '60s, she suggested in her fiction that public venues were not only deformed spaces but were remote and beyond one's power to affect or even were empty, inconsequential spaces. To an extent she seems to be anticipating the postmodern, postcolonial configuration that has come increasingly to characterize the political thought of the 1990s, that is, that the world is moving toward a two-tier system comprising the global and the local.

    Especially during the years of World War II, precisely the period dur-

19. Martha H. Swain, *Ellen S. Woodward: New Deal Advocate for Women* (Jackson: University Press of Mississippi, 1995), 10, x.
20. For discussions of implicit and explicit manifestations of the repression of white women in southern society, see discussions by Anne Firor Scott, *The Southern Lady* (Chicago: University of Chicago Press, 1970); Anne Goodwyn Jones, *Tomorrow Is Another Day: The Woman Writer in the South, 1859–1936* (Baton Rouge: Louisiana State University Press, 1981), especially chap. 1; and Louise Westling, *Sacred Groves and Ravaged Gardens: The Fiction of Eudora Welty, Carson McCullers, and Flannery O'Connor* (Athens: University of Georgia Press, 1985), especially "The Blight of Southern Womanhood," 8–35.

ing which Welty was trying to launch her literary career, the public consciousness was focused upon global warfare. As a woman whose brothers and friends were engaged in the life-threatening, heroic enterprise of combat, Welty took in the war as a deeply personal experience but at a remove from any direct agency she might bring to it. For her, the unity of the nation in support of the conflict placed it beyond politics. In a 1980 interview she told Charles Ruas that "everybody honestly believed we were trying to save the world from Nazism. . . . It was a very pure kind of wish to accomplish this victory, and we were in it heart and soul." A little later she added, "It was a terrible time to live through. I couldn't write about it, not at the time—it was too personal. I *could* write or translate things into domestic or other dimensions in my writing, with the same things in mind."[21] The domain she had knowledge of and dominion over—and thus could employ as a venue for investigating "the same things" (e.g., the terror of warfare)—is the domestic sphere. World War II was personally close, via her connection to military men, and mythically remote. This "public world" upon which the world's eyes were focused was not an available, viable "public world" for her.

In the last several decades much feminist critical attention, including Welty criticism, has been given to the many ways in which society genders human action, usually in a hierarchy that privileges male values. A recent formulation of such a gendering of "necessary oppositions" within the world and within the self is given by the European intellectual Tzvetan Todorov in *Facing the Extreme,* an examination of moral values manifest in the camps of Nazi victims. Todorov writes of Europe's disposition over the centuries to create gendered separate spheres to embody traits necessary to society's well-being. "To men, then, the world of work, politics and public affairs, heroic virtues, and the morality of principles; to women, the domain of human relations, the private sphere, ordinary virtues, and the morality of sympathy." Todorov sees and names the pernicious effect of such division and calls for a different paradigm. The complete moral being may not be the individual, he notes, but, metaphorically, the couple. So as not to

21. Charles Ruas, "Eudora Welty," in *More Conversations with Eudora Welty,* ed. Prenshaw, 66.

be misunderstood, Todorov adds the disclaimer, "Needless to say, when I speak of the couple I am not speaking of the heterosexual paradigm only or of a relationship that is necessarily stable or permanent."[22]

Welty well understood the damage to the psyche of rigid gender roles and stereotyping, as she shows in fiction that we are increasingly coming to read for its radical transformations of notions of "masculine" and "feminine" as well as "public" and "private." Peter Schmidt and Rebecca Mark, among many, have shown in recent studies of Welty how forcefully she challenges conventional patterns of gender relations, especially as these are manifest in Western heroic-quest narratives, and how insistently she exposes negative stereotypes that operate upon women, suggesting new definitions of heroism as feminine. Similarly, Ann Romines, Gail Mortimer, and others have instructively inquired into the consequence for the developing writer of a childhood and young adulthood that was experienced within a highly gendered society.[23]

Among many useful examinations of Welty's approaches to the dis-

22. Tzvetan Todorov, *Facing the Extreme*, trans. Arthur Denner and Abigail Pollak (New York: Holt-Metropolitan Books, 1996), 293–4. Among many critics who precede Todorov in analyzing gendered cultural conventions, see especially the responses of twentieth-century female artists to such conventions: Teresa de Lauretis, *Alice Doesn't: Feminism, Semiotics, Cinema* (Bloomington: Indiana University Press, 1984), and Rachel Blau DuPlessis, *Writing Beyond the Ending: Narrative Strategies of Twentieth-Century Women Writers* (Bloomington: Indiana University Press, 1985).

23. Rebecca Mark, *The Dragon's Blood: Feminist Intertextuality in Eudora Welty's "The Golden Apples"* (Jackson: University Press of Mississippi, 1994), especially 3–30; Peter Schmidt, *The Heart of the Story: Eudora Welty's Short Fiction* (Jackson: University Press of Mississippi, 1991), 53 ff; Ann Romines, *The Home Plot: Women, Writing, and Domestic Ritual* (Amherst: University of Massachusetts Press, 1992), especially 192 ff.; Gail L. Mortimer, *Daughter of the Swan: Love and Knowledge in Eudora Welty's Fiction* (Athens: University of Georgia Press, 1994), especially 1–42. For an examination of the influence upon Welty of a regionally gendered South and North, see Peggy Whitman Prenshaw, "The Construction of Confluence: The Female South and Eudora Welty's Art," in *The Late Novels of Eudora Welty*, ed. Jan Nordby Gretlund and Karl-Heinz Westarp (Columbia: University of South Carolina Press, 1998), 176–94.

placement of stereotypical male fields of action upon female fields is Albert Devlin's recent study of the relation of *Delta Wedding* to the wartime context in which it was written. Devlin argues that Welty's choice of the "benign year" of 1923 as the novel's temporal setting served not only to distance the action from the savagery of the war but to echo "in its own refined way . . . Welty's considered response to the bristling historic present." Drawing upon many sources, most notably Welty's letters to her literary agent Diarmuid Russell, quoted by Michael Kreyling in *Author and Agent*, and the text of the novel itself, Devlin persuasively argues that *Delta Wedding* and the drawing of the character Ellen Fairchild in particular embody a response to World War II that is directed not toward the world's political stage but toward "the solitary human heart," the venue offering the "only hope of correction." Acknowledging that Welty largely omits a contextualizing sociopolitical history of the Mississippi Delta in the 1920s, Devlin writes: "History itself is diminished as a primary category of experience, and fiction too is relieved of any need to act '*as a means*' (as G. E. Moore put it). . . . To test the efficacy of 'human understanding' against the present 'outrage' is the urgent mission that Welty gave to Ellen Fairchild, and it allowed neither of them any unbridled wandering in the field of Delta history."[24] In tracing the course of the composition of *Delta Wedding*, the progression of thought that gave it form, Devlin points up Welty's disposition to see politics as most vitally—and effectively—conducted at the site of the local and particular, the environs of the free individual engaging the immediate surround.

A number of critical analyses of *Delta Wedding* have enlarged our reading of the novel as an interrogation of cultural definitions of "public" and "private" and of "what counts" in our cultural valuing of the "heroic" and the "domestic."[25] Most recently, Susan Donaldson has

24. Albert J. Devlin, "The Making of *Delta Wedding*, or Doing 'Something Diarmuid Thought I Could Do,'" in *Biographies of Books: The Compositional Histories of Notable American Writings*, ed. James Barbour and Tom Quirk (Columbia: University of Missouri Press, 1996), 252, 260.

25. See especially Louise Westling's "The Enchanted Maternal Garden of *Delta Wedding*," in *Sacred Groves and Ravaged Gardens*, 65–93; Ann Romines, *Home Plot*, 211 ff.; and Suzan Harrison, *Eudora Welty and Virginia Woolf: Gender, Genre, and Influence* (Baton Rouge: Louisiana State University Press, 1997), 22–47.

discussed Welty's placing the ostensible hero, George Fairchild, on the back stage of the action while giving over the narrative consciousness to the women who surround him. Effectively, the foreground figure and the background players swap places, a reversal, notes Donaldson, that "highlights and problematizes the relationship between public and private, the world of historical action and the world of domesticity—or, one might say, the frontlines and the homefront."[26]

One infers from the portrayal of George Fairchild and many other "vaunting" heroes of Welty's fiction that she somewhat suspects public heroism to be tainted by a kind of theatricality that necessarily accompanies it. This is, of course, precisely the view held in *The Optimist's Daughter* by Laurel Hand, who objects to the community's effort to aggrandize her father as a public hero during the ceremonies attendant upon his death. The image of the public sphere that is projected again and again by the fiction is one that partakes of hyperbole and, often, insincerity or even sham.

Welty's photographs likewise expose the ineffectuality of "official" public speech to communicate much of anything trustworthy or meaningful to the public. In an image entitled "Political Speaking" in *One Time, One Place,* the speaker is entirely absent from the scene and the audience is revealed as inattentive, even bored. Centering the photograph is a parked car, site of the only animated conversation seeming to take place, that of a standing woman speaking to the driver of the car. In an adjacent photograph, "Political Speech," the viewer's eye is directed to the sleeping figure of a young girl, whose whole body is turned away from the speaker. Again, Welty frames the image so as to cut the political speaker entirely from view. Indeed, as Harriet Pollack has pointed out, in these images and in another from *Photographs* entitled "Political Speech, Tupelo, 1930s," one finds group scenes that withhold or deny any sense of a focal center.[27] Welty's visual messages unmistakably deconstruct the grandiose claims of political speech.

26. Susan V. Donaldson, "Gender and History in Eudora Welty's *Delta Wedding,*" *South Central Review,* 14 (1997), 5.
27. Eudora Welty, *One Time, One Place,* 66–7; *Eudora Welty Photographs* (Jackson: University Press of Mississippi, 1989), no. 62; Harriet Pollack, "Photographic Convention and Story Composition: Eudora Welty's Uses of Detail, Plot, Genre, and Expectation from 'A Worn Path' through *The Bride of the Innisfallen,*" *South Central Review* 14 (1997): 29.

Welty's stated reservations about the claims of public politics do not preclude our acknowledgment of her sharply aware consciousness of public life—what I would call a political consciousness—although perhaps they do help explain why that consciousness is manifested so obliquely in her work. She has frequently voiced her wariness about the enervating effect of the political when in works of fiction it is allowed to encroach upon the quieter workings of more private terrains. A reading of the two volumes of collected interviews, however, reveals that she has long regarded herself as a liberal Democrat and spoken of herself as an admirer of Adlai Stevenson, a foe of Nixon's politics, and a possessor of Michael Dukakis and Clinton-Gore bumper stickers.[28] She was an unflagging supporter in the 1980s of Mississippi's progressive governor, William Winter, who was also one of the members of the task force on race relations named by President Clinton in 1997. She is a careful news watcher, an avid follower of the PBS Jim Lehrer News Hour (formerly McNeil-Lehrer). Her interest in such overt political activity notwithstanding, one must infer from her essays and interviews that she regards her citizen's voice as singular, slight, and largely ineffectual in setting or effecting social policy. But increasingly it would seem that she has come to think of that ineffectuality as no great loss, that finally the private and local sphere, which is also (as she has repeatedly said) the habitation of fiction, is the place where informed and persuasive deliberation occurs, where speech legitimated by authority of experience and identity can be spoken and heard—the site, finally, where meaningful action can occur.

In her article "Women's History and Political Theory: Toward a Feminist Approach to Public Life," Sara M. Evans has traced changing conceptions of "public life" in the United States over the past two centuries, discussing many of the points I have been dealing with here. In her call for a feminist reconception of public life, she says attention must be paid first of all to the relationship between public and private. She notes that liberal theory of the nineteenth century, which amplified the public sector of governance to include the private sector of

28. For a quick guide to Welty's discussion of these subjects, one may consult the indexes to *Conversations with Eudora Welty* and *More Conversations with Eudora Welty*.

civil society, still was predicated, as in classical theory, upon an assumption of domestic life, the sphere of women, where life's essential needs were to be provided for. In her thought-provoking article, Evans suggests infinite ways in which the private and personal *are* political, and she insists that political history be redefined to represent "the dynamic relation between public and private life."[29] Evans focuses on women's organizations—voluntary associations, missionary societies such as the Methodist home missions discussed earlier, and reformist crusades growing from commitments to a social gospel—but I take her point also to elucidate Welty's defense of the local, the private sphere, as a site of "political" consequence.

Let me briefly reiterate my points about the evolution of Welty's political views. In the 1920s and 1930s authentic public political exchange was largely unavailable to Mississippians, especially to white women and blacks who were constrained by their "place" in the societal hierarchy, and the effect was usually cooptation or isolation of the individual, a condition Welty frequently represents in her early stories. Her witnessing a World War in the 1940s, McCarthyism in the 1950s, and the violent resistance to the civil rights movement in the early 1960s all greatly lessened whatever trust she had had in the political macrocosm and bolstered her belief in the microcosm as the only efficacious, viable sphere of human understanding and negotiation. As she worked on the writing of *Losing Battles* over fifteen years, from "a long story about the country" completed by spring 1955 to the publication of the novel in 1970,[30] Welty came to see in the rural story a possibility of— and human habitation for—active debate and discussion of topics that were in the last analysis not merely private needs but also political issues.

29. Sarah M. Evans, "Women's History and Political Theory: Toward a Feminist Approach to Public Life," in *Visible Women: New Essays on American Activism,* ed. Nancy A. Hewitt and Suzanne Lebsock (Urbana: University of Illinois Press, 1993), 119 ff., 126–7.

30. See Polk, *Welty: A Bibliography,* 122–4, for a summary of the composition history of *Losing Battles.* See also Suzanne Marrs, *The Welty Collection: A Guide to the Eudora Welty Manuscripts and Documents at the Mississippi Department of Archives and History* (Jackson: University Press of Mississippi, 1988), 40 ff., for an annotated listing of draft manuscripts of the novel.

When Judge Moody's black Buick breaks in upon the family scene in *Losing Battles*, its wreck calling upon everyone to take notice and try to "save" the assaulting vehicle, the Bannerites do not retreat into some quiet Promethean myth of heroism and renewal, as do the young farmer Sonny and his pregnant wife in "Death of a Traveling Salesman" in their response to R. J. Bowman's similar intrusion upon a rural family scene. Indeed, the vehicles and the accidents are nearly duplicates—Bowman's car, like Judge Moody's, hangs "on the edge of a ravine that fell away, a red erosion." In the novel the Beecham-Renfro clan vigorously dispute the standing of the judge in the court of the Banner front porch, charging him, a Ludlowite, with a barbarian's ignorance of the rightful claims of justice in Banner. In fact, *Losing Battles*, Welty's longest work, embodies an intricately detailed inquiry into the nature of justice, that ubiquitous, time-honored topic of political discourse.

One of the numerous family members attending the reunion celebrating Granny Vaughn's birthday and grandson Jack's release from Parchman penitentiary is Aunt Cleo, recently married into the family and endlessly curious about their history. "What I mainly want to hear," she announces early in the novel, "is what they sent Jack to the pen for."[31] The ensuing replies pose an opposition of two modes of justice: that grounded in constitutional law, which in the novel has been administered by Judge Moody from his courthouse in Ludlow, and that grounded in mediational law, which takes account of the specific conditions and context in which wrongdoers, victims, and crimes are considered in their singularity, an application of law considered by the family to be fair and just.

There have been many differing approaches to naming and understanding the opposing sides Welty has created in this novel. Michael Kreyling has written of myth versus history, with attention especially to the role of the schoolteacher Julia Mortimer. James Boatwright has analyzed speech versus silence, and Susan Donaldson has examined opposing modes of discourse, the spoken and the written, an opposition I have also discussed in addressing the contest between orality

31. Eudora Welty, *Losing Battles* (New York: Random House, 1970), 21.

and literacy in *Losing Battles*.[32] Despite a tendency to admire Miss Julia's societal meliorism, readers generally acknowledge Welty's balancing of claims by the Julia/Judge side and the Beecham/Renfros, finding the family's arguments for justice fully as commanding as those of its educated, progressive adversaries. Indeed, the family's hero, Jack, seemingly constrained by poverty and political powerlessness, is arguably the most humane and caring character in *Losing Battles*.

Ruth Weston has argued that Welty's portrayal of Jack gives evidence of a "gender role reversal" that extends even further the novel's reversing and balancing of a traditionally valued public or "heroic" sphere with that of a devalued private or "ordinary" sphere.[33] Noting the depiction of Jack as a "wonderful little mother," Weston observes that Welty deflates Jack's "masculine vaunting and blind optimism" but not his "feminine" nurturing traits. Weston's commentary here calls to mind Todorov's metaphor of the couple as an image of the linking of "necessary opposites" within human society. "As elsewhere," she writes, "Welty emphasizes human limitations by pairing two 'halves' that together constitute one whole human character—here, Jack and Gloria, a nurturing, family-oriented father and an independent, authoritative mother."[34] The hierarchical pattern of public over private and male over female is thus dramatically reversed.

Similarly, the judge's secure, publicly powerful position as objective dispenser of justice, removed from contingent and extenuating circumstances, gives way under the pressure of his own vulnerability

---

32. See Kreyling, *Eudora Welty's Achievement of Order*, 140 ff.; James Boatwright, "Speech and Silence in *Losing Battles*," *Shenandoah* 25 (1974): 3–14; Susan V. Donaldson, "'Contradictors, Interferers, and Prevaricators': Opposing Modes of Discourse in *Losing Battles*," in *Eudora Welty: Eye of the Storyteller*, ed. Dawn Trouard (Kent, Ohio: Kent State University Press, 1989), 32–43; Peggy Whitman Prenshaw, "The Harmonies of *Losing Battles*," in *Modern American Fiction: Form and Function*, ed. Thomas Daniel Young (Baton Rouge: Louisiana State University Press, 1989), 184–97.

33. For an enlightening discussion of the "heroic" and the "ordinary" as contrasted, gendered virtues, see Todorov, *Facing the Extreme*, 107 ff.

34. Ruth D. Weston, *Gothic Traditions and Narrative Techniques in the Fiction of Eudora Welty* (Baton Rouge: Louisiana State University Press, 1994), 152.

to time and chance. With his car wrecked and perched precariously on an embankment in Banner territory, he has to turn to a "human chain" for rescue. Although he rejects the family's insistence upon *understanding* (mediation) as a basis for justice, he nonetheless accepts their forgiveness for his transgression against Jack. The family likewise makes concessions: they admit him to the reunion as an equal and listen to what he has to say.

In this late novel of her career, Welty turns outward to the world and explores its multiple displays of human needs and possibilities. Unlike *The Optimist's Daughter*, which represents more of a journey inward for Welty, this lengthy dialogic novel brings the moral-private realm of society into direct contention with the political-public realm. Embattled, the family not only hold their own against Judge Moody and his Ludlow courthouse, but stand their ground against the accumulated power of Julia Mortimer, the correspondingly embattled teacher, adversary of ignorance, righteous reformer-crusader committed to bringing in a modern social gospel, or, perhaps more properly, a secular humanism for the purpose of improving her country charges' minds and lives. What Welty manages to do with extraordinary skill in *Losing Battles* is dramatize an almost idealized political occasion on which the stump speakers—whether young or old, male or female—have knowledge of the subjects debated and full standing in the forum of exchange. Indeed, as Suzan Harrison observes, the voices are principally female.[35] The speakers, who have differing conceptions of rights, responsibilities, boundaries, and justice, each possess the rhetorical ability to express themselves with force, the memory to call upon relevant precedent, and, most significantly, the freedom to speak. It is a polis in action.

For Welty, legitimate political speech, as distinguished from propaganda, demagoguery, fatuous display, intimidating threats, inspired revelation, or guilt-ridden confession, reflects the complexity and relatedness of human action. For her, the site where such speech is most likely to occur is a local, even private, habitation, and in this it is like fiction. Political debate subjected to the testing and tempering of a

---

35. Harrison, *Eudora Welty and Virginia Woolf*, 108.

home place may thus achieve validity and persuasiveness in much the same way that Welty describes as the way of art in "Place in Fiction:" "the art that speaks most clearly, explicitly, directly and passionately from its place of origin will remain the longest understood."[36]

In a 1978 interview, Jan Gretlund asks Welty a series of questions about her political interests, to which she responds with a discussion of her enthusiasm for the candidacy of Adlai Stevenson in the 1950s and of her efforts to stay informed about political issues and to vote. But she adamantly reiterates her disapproval of a writer's undertaking to crusade in fiction. "I think it's wrong when somebody like Steinbeck crusades in his fiction. That's why Steinbeck bores me so. The real crusader doesn't need to crusade; he writes about human beings in the sense Chekhov did. He tries to see a human being whole with all his wrong-headedness and all his right-headedness. To blind yourself to one thing for the sake of your prejudice is limiting. I think it is a mistake." Welty then adds a quick afterword that points up her self-exclusion from those who would "write politics": "There's so much room in the world for crusading, but it is for the editorial writers, the speech-maker, the politician, and the *man* in public life to do [emphasis mine], not for the writer of fiction." I think we see in Welty's response here her equation of "political" thought and action with a kind of rigidity, a blindness to all but one's own position, a firmness of purpose that is a prejudice and is self-limiting—the conditions she characterizes as "crusading." By contrast, an arena where open discussion occurs, where multiple options for action are considered, where the complexity of knowing the good and acting upon it is fully revealed is, for her, not a "political" arena. Distrusting the arena of politics as a location for ascertaining justice and right action, she looks rather to the "moral" arena for an understanding of life as it is—and as it should be. Replying in a mid-1970s interview to a question posed by Bill Ferris, "Do you feel the artist has a political role to play in a society?" she demonstrates a wariness about what she regards as the intellectual and psychological narrowness of politics, as well as the propensity of politics to turn all too readily into propaganda:

36. Eudora Welty, "Place in Fiction" (first published in 1955), in *Eye of the Story*, 132.

I don't believe that a work of art in itself has any cause to be political unless it would have been otherwise. I think there are places for political outspokenness, but in my mind, it should be done editorially, and in essays and things that are exactly what they seem. But I think a work of art, a poem or a story, is properly something that reflects what life is exactly at that time. That is, to try to reveal it. Not to be a mirror image, but to be something that goes beneath the surface of the outside and tries to reveal the way it really is, good and bad. Which in itself is moral. I think a work of art must be moral. The artist must have a moral consciousness about his vision of life and what he tries to write. But to write propaganda I think is a weakening thing to art.[37]

Welty's assumptions about what constitutes political action—that is, what the word "politics" denotes for her—are perhaps most clearly illustrated in the 1966 story "The Demonstrators." The main figure of the story, Dr. Richard Strickland, attends a dying young black woman, Ruby Gaddy, who has been stabbed by her jealous common-law husband, Dove Collins, himself wounded in turn by her and also dying. On the night of the story the physician moves among the black and white citizens of Holden, Mississippi, sensitively registering all the human connections that make moral—and political—decisions so difficult. He thinks of a young civil rights worker who in a newspaper piece has forcefully made a case against white oppression, but with clarity bought at the cost of truth telling:

"Speaking of who can you trust," [he had said to the young man,] "what's this I read in your own paper, Philip? It said some of your outfit over in the next county were forced at gunpoint to go into the fields at hundred-degree temperature and pick cotton. Well, that didn't happen—there isn't any cotton in June."

"I asked myself the same question you do. But I told myself, 'Well, they won't know the difference where the paper is read.'"

"It's lying, though."

"We are dramatizing your hostility," the young bearded man had

37. Jan Gretlund, "Seeing Real Things: An Interview with Eudora Welty," rpt. in *Conversations with Eudora Welty*, ed. Prenshaw, 226; Bill Ferris, "A Visit with Eudora Welty," ibid., 165.

corrected him. "It's a way of reaching people. Don't forget—what they *might* have done to us is even worse."[38]

In this story Welty dramatizes the complicity of everyone in what is a familiar human drama of self-serving and self-protection, of violence, betrayal, grief, bitterness, just old recalcitrant human perversity. Holden's county newspaper runs the Gaddy-Collins murder on the back page, with the subhead "No Racial Content Espied," advertising white innocence while indulging in titillating gossip: "TWO DEAD, ONE ICE PICK, FREAK EPISODE AT NEGRO CHURCH." Both the civil rights paper and the county paper are stating and defending their political positions, unwittingly demonstrating the narrowness of each point of view. And even the kindly Dr. Strickland's sense of connectedness with the black household he attends is exposed as inextricably linked to the privileged affluence of his family in this segregated southern town. Hand-me-down dresses of his mother's, sister's, wife's fly out from Ruby Gaddy's front porch, where they hang, starched, reflecting the moonlight like ghostly presences.

Nonetheless, it is clear in this story, as in *Losing Battles*, that the moral position Welty endorses is a respectful listening to the position of the other and a willingness to engage it empathetically. Jack Renfro is the hero of *Losing Battles* because, unlike his wife Gloria, who wants to withdraw to a private sphere and concentrate on her nuclear family's self-interest, he is willing to listen to all the others' stories—cases, if you will—and to put forward his own. What he counsels is a reasoning and sympathetic arena for Banner.

In "Must the Novelist Crusade?" Welty quotes E. M. Forster's "Only connect," calling the phrase "ever wise and gentle and daring words [that] could be said to us in our homeland quite literally at this moment." The homeland about which Welty writes in both the essay and "The Demonstrators"—Mississippi in the 1960s—was not congenial to the kind of piety of human connection she espoused. And it is telling that, several paragraphs later, it is the relation of a writer to Czarist Russia that comes to mind when she speaks of the role the artist can properly play in the support of such piety: "We are told that

38. Eudora Welty, "The Demonstrators," in *Collected Stories of Eudora Welty*, 617.

Turgenev's nostalgic, profoundly reflective, sensuously alive stories that grew out of his memories of early years reached the Czar and were given some credit by him when he felt moved to free the serfs in Russia. Had Turgenev set out to write inflammatory tracts instead of the sum of all he knew, could express, of life learned at firsthand, how much less of his mind and heart with their commitments, all implicit, would have filled his stories! But he might be one of us now, so directly are we touched."[39]

Welty suggests that the act of identification may give rise to civic virtue, and that such identification may be prompted by fiction. Following a long line of intellectual predecessors, she grounds right political action in moral virtue, and she then links these to the aesthetic, ever insisting upon the aesthetic realm as the legitimate home precinct of the writer. For her, being a writer is prepolitical, postpolitical, always and already political. In this view, she is quite close to Todorov, who pointedly discusses the relation of the political to the aesthetic in his 1996 review of J. M. Coetzee's collection of essays *Giving Offense: Essays on Censorship.* Toward the end of the review, Todorov remonstrates against what he regards as Coetzee's too-narrow understanding of the "political" and gives a spirited endorsement of the position that I have argued likewise constitutes Welty's political thought:

> Everything in this book reads as though Coetzee were defending himself against the charge of not having written more politically engaged work. His argument consists of saying that all engagement is futile, because the struggle against an adversary makes one like the adversary. This argument is wrong. But it is also, happily, unnecessary: Coetzee's position as a writer is above reproach. For the writer has no obligation, as a writer, to engage in political struggles. By means of his writing, he is already engaged, since his works help humanity to find meaning in existence, and no struggle is greater than the struggle for meaning. All true works of art create values, and in so doing they are political.[40]

Perhaps Welty, southern daughter of a bristling traditional society struggling to maintain itself, and Todorov, Bulgarian son of a truculent

39. In *Eye of the Story,* 156.
40. Tzvetan Todorov, "Tyranny's Last Word," *New Republic,* 18 November 1996, 33.

but dying Soviet Union totalitarianism, are similarly suspicious of defining politics as ideology and wary of political thought that codifies forces of necessity and coercion. In her writings and interviews, Welty shows unmistakably that what she regards as the politics of substance and courage, politics that is truly public, civil, and communal, is the human connection between freely operating individuals who confront issues that directly affect their lives. The domain where such connection occurs for Welty the writer, and also, I think, for Welty the human being, is typically personal, private, and interior. One thus finds no discrepancy between the title of "Must the Novelist Crusade?"—the writing that offers perhaps her most emphatic defense of the writer as a political (but not propagandizing) being—and the title affixed earlier to the same essay: "The Interior Affair."[41]

41. Noel Polk, *Welty: A Bibliography*, 381, notes that the Russell and Volkening file card for the essay bears the deleted title "The Interior Affair."

*Noel Polk*

## Engaging the Political

In Our Texts, in Our Classrooms

There is an odd and troubling moment in the movie version of John Grisham's *The Chamber.* Odd because I saw it on an evening when its showing was preceded by a preview of another film, *Ghosts of Mississippi,* about the murder of Medgar Evers and the eventual bringing to justice, thirty years later, of Evers's murderer, Byron de la—aptly nick-named "Delay"—Beckwith. Troubling because in *The Chamber* the lawyer grandson's most eloquent defense of his confessed and con-victed racist-murderer grandfather is that Mississippi's, and his fami-ly's, generations-old tradition of racial hatred had so conditioned him as to be itself responsible for Sam Cayhill's murderous behavior. He offers up Mississippi's tradition of violent racism as a "mitigating cir-cumstance" for his grandfather's actions—and by an unstated, a mind-less and slippery Hollywoodized nineties feel-good extension, as a de-fense for other perpetrators, for other individuals who have also been soldiers of that tradition's dark will, the ones who actually pulled the trigger, prepared the noose, sharpened the knife, planted the bomb. Clearly this tradition *is* a significant "circumstance," since who of us can escape the air we breathe? But neither Grisham nor the tearful au-dience address such questions as *how* mitigating this circumstance can or should be and, if it is mitigating, how many levels of cultural bureaucracy outward from the explosion or the lynching should the mitigation not just protect but absolve, especially now, this many years after?

Cayhill's defense is a highly sentimentalized version of the defense that many Nazis hid behind, a skewed version also of the recently pop-ular The Victim Ariseth defense, which the Menendez brothers, for ex-ample, tried unsuccessfully to use to exculpate themselves from their

admitted murder of parents they claimed were abusive; others—
women accused of murdering abusive husbands—have used this defense with better success. Grisham's Sam Cayhill thus makes self-
defense a cultural argument: We were in a war, we were under attack
and had to defend ourselves, he snarls at his defender grandson, explaining his actions in those awful years of the fifties and sixties in
Mississippi, when black and white citizens who challenged the prevailing ideologies paid such a heavy price—as did, to be sure, thousands of others throughout the South who did *not* challenge the ideological orthodoxy but were merely presumed to have done so or even
just accused of it.

The juxtaposition of *The Chamber* with *Ghosts of Mississippi* is all
the more troubling because Sam Cayhill, a dupe of the white Citizens'
Council and the Sovereignty Commission, is clearly based upon de la
Beckwith, Evers's finally convicted murderer, or at least the plot is
based upon the occasion that his recent prosecution provided us all for
viewing, yet again, all the old bad stuff, for reopening all the old
wounds and confronting, again, the old shame and the despair. The
film troubled me too because Gene Hackman, who plays Sam Cayhill,
is a fine actor who *humanizes* the crusty old racist murderer; as Cayhill gets closer and closer to his grandson we discover—surprise!—that
he too has feelings, a good deal of remorse (which is of course at first
hiding under that remorseless pusillanimous crust). We come to believe that he indeed *is* a victim of his culture's racial traditions. In one
quite moving scene Cayhill admits that for all the legacy of hatred of
black people he has grown up with, the only thing he's really ever
hated is himself: in this touching McPsychoanalytical moment we are
clearly supposed to feel sympathy for him. We understand, correctly,
that he is a very small operative, a soldier, in a larger ideological system that he has invested his life in and is willing to die for, believing
himself a martyr to a righteous cause, and willing to take the rap for
others whose bidding he has done. My personal sympathies with Sam
particularly trouble me because I've never had one iota of sympathy
with Byron de la Beckwith, and perhaps I should have. Though I know
the doctor who operated on Beckwith's heart, I've never been able to
believe that he had one.

The troublesomeness of the juxtaposition of *The Chamber* with
*Ghosts of Mississippi* becomes compounded in the context of the re-

cent blockbuster popularity of yet another film that originated in a Grisham novel, *A Time to Kill*, in which a do-gooding white lawyer convinces a Mississippi jury not to convict a black man who admits having killed the white men who raped and viciously beat his daughter. Clearly we, readers and moviegoers, are supposed to approve of this black man's actions; his white defense lawyer implicitly makes the same argument that Sam Cayhill makes during his own time of war: the law as presently constituted and enforced will not work *for me*, so I have to do the *right* thing in spite of the law. The film demands that we sympathize with him, and we do, for having no faith that a white court will bring white racists to justice. What the judge and the system do legally in *The Chamber*, the black man in *A Time to Kill* does illegally, though finally with that legal system's complete approval. In both plots the racist murderer and rapist get their deserved punishment, and racism generally gets a socko knockout punch as, in the ideologically pristine 1990s, they should—with a sentimental Hollywood leer toward the human tragedy of it all, regional redemption through racial reconciliation, etcetera etcetera etcetera.

In *The Chamber*, the system does the right thing, but in its own less-than-ideologically-pure terms and for its own less-than-ideologically-pure reasons. The governor of Mississippi tells Sam Cayhill's grandson that he will give Sam a stay of execution if he, Sam, will name an accomplice who with Sam's testimony can be indicted. Sam himself, honorable to the last, refuses to cooperate, but the grandson discovers that accomplice through illegal access to the tightly locked Sovereignty Commission files (which access is provided by the governor's assistant, a charming and sympathetic African American woman!). The governor makes pragmatic rather than ideological use of that information, however: he uses Mississippi's past not to save a murderer from his just execution, not to bring to justice members of the Sovereignty Commission who orchestrated such murders as Sam Cayhill committed, but rather to further his own legislative agenda, which even seems to be mostly progressive.

The three films form a curious Mississippi trilogy. All are set in the state and were filmed at familiar locations: Parchman, Canton, and Jackson. All were filmed with the enthusiastic cooperation not just of the Mississippi Film Commission but also of movie fans who gawked at the stars, black and white, who mixed and mingled with them at local pubs during the filming, and who themselves tried out for small roles.[1]

Unlike 1988's *Mississippi Burning* (which some people still regard as an accurate depiction not just of the civil rights years but of present-day Mississippi), neither *The Chamber* nor *A Time to Kill* engages particularly in Mississippi-bashing; in neither movie nor book does Mississippi itself seem to be on trial, but rather racism itself. *Ghosts* in fact operates to purify Mississippi of its past: *poof!* all the bad stuff disappears in a rush of smiles and back-patting and deep feelings at justice finally accomplished.

The films are Hollywoodized versions of novelized versions of Mississippi history. *A Time to Kill* is set in a sort of undefined historical moment, neither completely now nor then: characters refer to 1985 as a date some time ago and black characters call white characters by their first names, all of which places the action in the late eighties or early nineties, but the racial mise-en-scène of Klan marches, National Guardsmen, and racial violence in the streets is straight out of the sixties (and, for crying out loud, in the Mississippi of *A Time to Kill* there is not a single air conditioner, the absence of which would put the setting chronologically no more recently than the early fifties). But the movie's premise, that an all-white jury would set a black killer free, is Hollywood drama, unlikely even in the Twilight Zone; historical verisimilitude simply cries foul.[2]

I worry that so much dramatic misinformation, perpetrated in the

1. By contrast, in 1949 when the moviemakers came to Oxford to film Faulkner's *Intruder in the Dust*, another novel about racial justice in Mississippi, local citizens also rubbernecked at movie stars and hoped to have bit parts—but only the white actors were allowed to stay in the local hotels and attend cocktail parties given by Oxford's white elite; black actors and crew members had to find housing in the homes of Oxford's black citizens.
2. The film is ideologically skewed in other ways, too. In the final scene with his lawyer, the one just before the trial's summation, the black murderer accuses the lawyer of continuing to think of him in terms of racial difference. The lawyer takes this accusation to heart. In his powerful closing argument, he paints a horrible picture of what the two white men did to the little black girl and then, as his closing dramatic shot, admonishes them to imagine that all that had been done to a little *white* girl. For all its touchy-feely good intentions, then, *A*

name of a feelgood appeal to nineties audiences, will sentimentalize the real horror out of Mississippi's history, rendering it ideologically acceptable in one sense and bland and impotent in another.

Perhaps it is not clear exactly what this little *discursus* on the movies has to do with my purposes here. As a native and present Mississippian, as one who has worked for over a quarter of a century on Mississippi writers, I am uncommonly—perhaps neurotically is a better word—sensitized to depictions of Mississippi and the South in the media. It is not true, as my colleague Neil McMillen claims, that my favorite film is *Song of the South,* but it *is* true that I often seem like a seismograph around depictions of the South: I go completely off the Richter scale when I hear such characters as Forrest Gump wisely declare that life is like a box of chocolates and when otherwise intelligent people find such outlooks charming-because-so-southern. Doubtless my reaction is indeed mostly neurotic, and it is certainly highly defensive. But it's also an amateur historian's wish to *get it right,* if only because the consequences of getting it wrong are pretty serious. I think all parts of the country should get their histories right, but for a variety of reasons it's particularly important for Mississippians, present and future. I do believe that the truth can and should make us free, no matter how terrifying truth and freedom can be. Most of these musings, then, are the tightly closed circle of my recent conversations with myself about what we as professors and readers do: about those aspects of my life as a professor in and as a citizen of my home state that interest me right now. Alas, it's also about those places as professor and citizen where I most often fall far short of what I'd like to be.

Though I am mostly interested in literature here, I begin with these fairly recent, highly popular, and historically charged films because they raise interesting and significant questions about the relationship between politics and art—or, more specifically, since I believe that history is a form of fiction, the quadrangulation between history, politics, and literature, and what teachers do, and in *how* and in *what forms* our history gets transmitted through the very institutions, our classrooms, that are the designated purveyors of that history.

---

*Time to Kill* resolves itself not because of the injustice done to blacks at all, but because of the specter of injustice to whites.

Those who don't believe that there is a direct relationship between literature, literary criticism, politics, the writing of history, and the ideological structures of our lives need only consider the virtually monolithic, hegemonic control that Nashville's Fugitives and Agrarians and their progeny have exerted not just over southern studies, but over American literary criticism in general, through its most influential gurus Cleanth Brooks and Robert Penn Warren. I was trained in this New Criticism, which believed, or at least taught in such trenches as my undergraduate institution, just outside of Jackson, Mississippi, that criticism's mission was to relieve the individual work of art of the subjective baggage of history and politics; it could deal only with the timeless, the Universal Human Condition that transcended the merely local and the temporally dynamic. The New Criticism taught me that art and politics were two different things, at best kinky and perverse bedfellows; literature was indeed vulnerable to invasions and sneak attacks from the other and capable of being not just vitiated but annihilated by such invasions, because under any form of contamination literature ceases to be literature and becomes propaganda. Politics should be kept out of literature, certainly out of literary criticism: thus I was instructed, by the same folks who *at the same time* were applying to federal agencies for funds to publish their literary magazines and who were also promoting William Faulkner as the foremost representative of American cultural values during the cold war. Since Faulkner was southern, they were therefore trying to make American values explicitly southern—explicitly agrarian, that is, and explicitly their own.[3]

Literature could take politics and power as subject, of course, and often did, but it could not, by its very nature as literature, presume to instruct, to argue a political position any more specific than humanism, which they of course taught was not a political position at all, even if for the New Critics' purposes "humanism" was rooted in Western, American, Southern, White, and Male values. Literature could not in any measure constitute any kind or degree of a call to action, to po-

3. See Lawrence H. Schwarz, *Creating Faulkner's Reputation: The Politics of Modern Literary Criticism* (Knoxville: University of Tennessee Press, 1988).

litical or social engagement, lest it lose its status as literature and become mere polemic. I never did figure out, as an undergraduate, that I could have asked what such a dictum might have meant for a good deal of Milton and Pope and Swift and many others. Criticism, of course, had to be "objective" in order to do its proper job.

In high school I was shielded from overt politics; from my reading lists I could not have been aware that *anybody* had written *anything* after 1850, much less that anybody in Mississippi had written anything, even much less that there were social and political traditions in Mississippi and the South that I would one day inherit. As an undergraduate I was thus appalled to be handed a modern canon filled with the ungodliest of racial problematics (gender too, though we didn't know that yet), and to be told that though *Light in August, Go Down, Moses, Native Son,* and *Black Boy* were accurate depictions of the racial tensions in my home state—according to these same Fugitives and Agrarians, the best art was invested in *place* and so was by definition accurate in its depiction of the real world—that were erupting in violence not more than seven or eight miles from where, in the sixties, I sat being instructed, they did not, could not, would never demand of me that I go to sit-ins or perhaps to jail, perhaps die as hero or martyr, to try to correct the very situation that those novels described. We were talking art, not politics.

Thus I was let off the hook as neatly and cleanly as the Fugitive-Agrarian New Critics let themselves off. I could be moved to tears over Joe Christmas and Molly and Lucas Beauchamp and Bigger Thomas and the young Richard Wright, and that was enough. I was reasonably content with this state of affairs, having an aversion to crowds that somebody might shoot at. I didn't have to *do* anything about it except analyze the novels' themes and structures, appreciate the power of the authors' words to make me *feel deeply*—which feelings allowed me to feel human and, well, "good about myself" for being able to experience sweet sweet catharsis anytime, every time, I picked up a book: I could read Sophocles while Antigone buried her brother outside my window and not have to decide whether to help her or not. Instead of helping me to *engage* the world I lived in, literary criticism told me that it was sufficient that I observe it, indeed even admonished me that to do otherwise was to violate the very spirit of literature. The aesthetics by which I was trained, then, forced me to an *an*aesthetic vision of the very world those works purported to describe.

We know better now, of course. We now know that the personal is the political, the political is the personal, and we know, thanks to the well-established tradition of such writers as Simone de Beauvoir, Germaine Greer, Michel Foucault, Roland Barthes, and many many others, that every act is a political act and that politics is the exercise of power in any form—in the community, in the family, in the classroom. We no longer permit ourselves to believe that politics is merely marching in the streets or manning the barricades, although now we indeed feel empowered by that very literature and our criticism to so march or get arrested or write letters to the editor or to challenge senior colleagues or deans who harass, whose hiring or promotion policies reward people for the wrong reasons, or to say No in Thunder simply because we have the right to do so. And we now understand that literature, in its constant concern with alienation and rebellion, is a political act, no matter how much we aestheticize it. We have become wise and sophisticated in our concern with the political consequences of literature to our culture and with the political and economic nature of the processes by which certain works and not others get written, published, edited and reedited, bound into influential anthologies, taught in our classrooms, then written about and discussed by us and our colleagues in journals and at conferences and in books like this one.

In fact, our renewed interest in the politics of the Nortonized canon, for example, has allowed us to see literature itself as a political consequence of decisions made, money spent, cultural and historic conditions in place long before any particular work gets even written, much less published and anthologized. The surprisingly public nature of the discussion of the literary canon suggests how sensitive an issue, how hot a button, the tradition the canon represents is, even to a citizenry many of whom have probably never even seen a Norton Anthology: for them, the fact that *some* folks in the academy—mostly feminazis and Indians and blacks and other antiAmurrikins—want to change it is enough to defend it. The discussions about the canon thus provide a useful vantage point from which to view not just the politics preceding the writing and the publishing, but also the politics of critical discourse, which too often coopts the literature to its own uses, so that in our reading and anthologizing, literature and the prevailing culture replicate themselves in each other. There are profoundly political reasons why "southern literature" exploded as an academic discipline in the years following World War II, profoundly political reasons, including his Jeffersonian independence and his very southernness, why Faulkner became the New Critics' idol during the cold-war years. There are also profoundly political reasons why Thomas Dixon's *The Clansman* could be a runaway national bestseller at the turn of the century but nowhere closer than a light year or two to the latest anthologies.

Like writers, critics are citizens, political creatures, and ideologues, too, and in reading and teaching our texts we too impose our own political agendas on the works we teach, and so on our students. This is less a matter of right and wrong than of inevitability; one of the many legacies of theoretical, especially feminist, criticism, is that now we old white guys are being asked to lay our ideological cards face up on the table, to admit that our presumptive objectivity is itself a political position, and to understand that we are most heavily invested ideologically precisely at those times when we believe ourselves most neutral. Ideological certitude is a form of fear, to be sure, and of despair; but it is also a form of pride, of hubris, one of the seven deadly sins, pernicious and deadly precisely because it cannot recognize itself for what it is. The illusion of objectivity is the most pernicious of ideologies, in political debate, on the editorial page, or in the classroom.

A good deal of southern literature, certainly of southern literary criticism, lives in bondage to the mantra "the literature of memory," a term central to the critical jargon. In the hands of critics and writers who are not careful, literature can become merely a part of those larger fictions out of which we constitute ourselves in the present moment, by constructing for ourselves a coherent and meaningful past—a past by which, in the name of which, we hope to control the future, to render it less mysterious and problematic and frightening. Our anthologies and our syllabi have thus been foot soldiers in the service of a set of values, a culturally-constructed past—a tradition, a *version* of history that is both self-serving and self-justifying in its efforts to be also self-evident.

Even though we now know how pervasive the political is, we literary critics are still uncomfortable with it: we acknowledge Ezra Pound's fascism, partly because he did us the good favor of going crazy, thus allowing us to sidestep the issue gingerly, but we have only begun to talk about or deal with the racism and anti-Semitism—not to mention the grotesque and truly abominable forms of sexism—in the works and lives of T. S. Eliot, Ernest Hemingway, and F. Scott Fitzgerald. As far as I can tell we have more or less healed over the controversy surrounding the discovery of Paul de Man's newspaper articles supporting Nazi Germany, having apparently decided that his support of Hitler does not affect what he has to say about language any more than Richard Strauss's deep involvement with the Nazis need affect how his music sounds. But novelists and poets whose politics feed directly into their language pose quite a different problem.

During the 1950s Faulkner made forays into the public arena. He wrote letters to editors, published essays in national venues, and made speeches to try to correct a racial situation he believed would lead the South into another civil war. For a period of about five years he rolled up his sleeves and duked it out with recalcitrant white folks whose capacity to act in their own best interests he vastly overestimated. The critical establishment, even the Faulkner field, is still *very* uncomfortable with this overtly political Faulkner, the nonartist. Instead of admiring him as a courageous citizen responding to the racial morality of his own fiction, we have rather patronized him in a variety of ways. He was a well-meaning but not very sophisticated political thinker or intellectual, we say; he didn't always say *exactly* the right things, the proper things a seventies and eighties and nineties liberal would say, and so he never really overcame his own inherent Mississippi-itis, genius though he was. He got the big head in 1950, we say, and began to assume that the Nobel Prize qualified him to speak and be heard on public issues; as a final swat upside that bigheadedness, we generously allow that the worst effect of his political engagement was that those efforts drained his artistic capacities, so that his post-Nobel fiction suffered a decline. Thus we offer him, willy-nilly, as both proof of and cautionary tale about the proper distance between art and politics, good New Critics at least on that score.

How is our aesthetic sense complicit with history and biography? Put another way, how political are our aesthetics? What does it mean for our reading of Faulkner, for example, to know that in addition to his other public statements supporting racial justice, in 1956 he also quite publicly said that he would shoot Negroes in the street to defend Mississippi from invasion from the North, or that in 1931, almost simultaneously with the publication of "Dry September" and only a couple of months before he began writing *Light in August,* two classic and powerful studies of the pathology of lynching, he wrote a long and mean-spirited letter to the *Memphis Commercial Appeal* in which he didn't exactly defend lynching but didn't exactly say that it was all that bad either?[4]

What does it mean to our reading of *Alice in Wonderland* to know that Lewis Carroll was a pedophile with a particular fondness for little girls? Knowing such things about our authors, how can we *not* read them into the fiction? How can we not see these biographical countercurrents erupting everywhere? How do we deal with them in our teaching? It is easy enough to say, with Gerald Graff, teach the conflicts. But the larger question might indeed be, why should we continue to canonize and teach them at all? But here we're back at the old debate about whether Hollywood creates or merely reflects our social problems.

Peggy Prenshaw's superb outline of Eudora Welty's political attitudes goes right to the heart of the problem as I would like to focus it here. During the civil rights years, and before and after, Welty was asked by numerous interviewers and midnight callers what, in fact, she as a Mississippian *was going to do about it.* What she did about it was just the opposite of what her contemporary in Oxford did. She continued to observe and to write fiction; in a 1965 essay in *Harper's* she asked the question directly—"Must the Novelist Crusade?"—and answered, resoundingly, No.[5]

Prenshaw describes a Welty convinced of the uncertainty about

4. James B. Meriwether and Michael Millgate, eds., *Lion in the Garden: Interviews with William Faulkner, 1926–1962* (New York: Random House, 1968), 257–66; Neil R. McMillen and Noel Polk, "Faulkner on Lynching," *Faulkner Journal* 8 (1992), 3–14.
5. Eudora Welty, "Must the Novelist Crusade?" in *Stories, Essays, and Memoir,* ed. Richard Ford and Michael Kreyling (New York: Library of America, 1998), 803–14.

making political judgments, of the ineffectuality of the citizen's lone
voice in public discourse, and of "public venues" as "empty or inconsequential"; a Welty "increasingly" coming to regard "that ineffectuality as no great loss" and to understand that "the private and the local
sphere, which is also . . . the habitation of fiction, is the place where
informed and persuasive deliberation occurs, where speech legitimated by authority of experience and identity can be spoken and
heard—the site, finally, where meaningful action can occur." Prenshaw quotes Jonathan Yardley, who wrote that "as a Southerner and a
woman," Welty was "constantly pressed for her opinions on race and
Women's liberation." The writer told Yardley, "I've never had any prejudice shown to me, so I have no bone to pick. I do think women should
be paid as much as men, which I don't suppose anyone would disagree
with. I don't see why, just because I write stories, that should give me
the authority about, say, what should happen about abortion. Maybe
I'm shirking responsibility, but I don't think so. Everything I feel is in
my stories."[6]

For her purposes, Prenshaw does not discuss the question of "Welty's construction of 'prejudice.'" That, however, is precisely the question I increasingly find myself asking. Without challenging Welty's
right to whatever attitudes she chooses, I'd like some discussion of
what she means when she says that she has never had any "prejudice"
shown to her. Her fiction is awash with evidence that she understands
very well how political structures work prejudicially against women.
Her autobiography, *One Writer's Beginnings*, is so replete with the
problematics of family politics that many scholars, reading backwards
into the fiction, have discovered a structural thematic that focuses directly on mother-daughter relationships, on a daughter's response in
acquiescence to the family or in rebellion against it.

In *The Golden Apples* and *The Bride of the Innisfallen*, Welty frequently returns to the very nearly ironic tableau of a newly unfettered
daughter or wife poised on the edge of a future that she can reorganize

6. Peggy Prenshaw, "Welty's Transformations of the Public, the Private, and the
   Political," in this volume, 32, 37, 23; Eudora Welty, *More Conversations with
   Eudora Welty*, edited by Peggy W. Prenshaw (Jackson: University Press of Mis-
   sissippi, 1996), 11.

to suit herself.[7] The hero of the earlier work, Virgie Rainey, has come home to work for a lumber company logging in Morgan's Woods, a wilderness that is geographically so near Faulkner's Big Woods that it seems likely to be the same metaphorical primeval forest. Virgie's work with the logging company is thus surely a sign of Welty's demythologizing of Faulkner's exclusively patriarchal sense of history. His Isaac McCaslin bemoans the passing of that wilderness; Virgie works to get it on out of the way, so that progress can occur and she can change along with the rest of the world and free herself of the ideological/political structures those masculine woods symbolize. At the end of *The Golden Apples* Virgie sits with her back turned deliberately to the MacLain County Courthouse, Welty's version of Faulkner's Yoknapatawpha County Courthouse, that preeminent symbol of southern patriarchy and political consciousness.

Thus there is plenty of the political in Welty's work, though to be sure more of the politics of family and gender than of race or other forms. But again without presuming to question her decisions about how she lives her life as a citizen, my question is, shouldn't understanding how these structures function in our daily lives lead us, and the author, to want to *do something about it?* Indeed, Carolyn Heilbrun, noting the latent and implicit anger that she found throughout *One Writer's Beginnings,* proclaimed herself upset with Welty precisely because Welty did not express her anger more overtly and directly, so that her readers at any rate could claim their sisterhood with the author and then translate her anger, and therefore theirs, into direct action that would allow them to change, to improve, the quality of their lives.

A New Critical purist, of course, would argue that changing either one's world or one's self is therapy's, not literature's, function. But for the life of me, as a teacher, a professor in *this* world, in *this* day and time, I do not know how I can teach *The Golden Apples, Light in Au-*

---

7. Dawn Trouard, "Welty's Anti-Ode to Nightingales: Gabriella's Southern Passage," paper delivered at first international Welty conference, "One Day up in Tishomingo County: The Southernness of Welty's Fiction," University of Burgundy, Dijon, France, 1992; Danièle Pitavy-Souques, *La Mort de la Méduse: l'Art de la nouvelle chez Eudora Welty* (Lyon: Presses universitaires de Lyon, 1992), 47.

*gust*, and *Go Down, Moses*, much less *Black Boy* and *Native Son*, without at least *hoping* that my students will not just be deeply moved by what they read but will take their deep feelings, and mine, to the next step, see the relationship between these dramatized socio-political problems and their own lives, and take whatever steps they can understand, by virtue of these books, to be essential to changing the way they live or at least understand their own lives, private or public. Prenshaw describes Welty's long novel *Losing Battles* as a staged debate precisely about such issues. It dramatizes, she says,

> an almost idealized political occasion when the stump speakers—whether young or old, male or female—have knowledge of the subjects debated and full standing in the forum of exchange. [They] possess the rhetorical ability to express themselves with force, the memory to call upon relevant precedent, and, most significantly, the freedom to speak. It is a polis in action.
>
> For Welty, legitimate political speech, as distinguished from propaganda, demagoguery, fatuous display, intimidating threats, inspired revelation, or guilt-ridden confession, reflects the complexity and relatedness of human action. For her, the site where such speech is most likely to occur is a local, even private, habitation, and in this it is like fiction.[8]

Surely such things must be constantly debated in various forums. But to what purpose does the debate rage if it doesn't finally make some difference in the polis? What would Plato or Aristotle have said?

Like Welty, Katherine Anne Porter, as Susan Donaldson has pointed out, also engaged the political in her fiction in radically subversive ways that nevertheless did not prevent her from accepting its accolades: she willingly became, as Donaldson puts it, "an imposing combination of perfect southern belle and grande dame, photographed in various poses of glamour well into her eighties." That is, subverting the culture in her fiction did not prevent her from becoming that very culture's darling. I use the word "darling" deliberately, to suggest that that culture, though admiring them indeed, patently patronized both Porter and Welty—both were, after all, merely women, merely white

8. Prenshaw, "Welty's Transformations," 41.

southern women, writing in Faulkner's shadow, and best known for their stories about mostly female space, female concerns. Porter was, Donaldson says,

> [f]or a good many readers and reviewers . . . an emblem of beauty, style, and aristocratic grace, the southern belle of the Southern Literary Renaissance, and it was often in those terms of beauty and style [i.e., rather than of emotional power, or political and cultural substance] that reviewers defined her art. She was proclaimed a stylist and a writer's writer, a gifted practitioner of the minor art of the short story, whose form was as feminine as its content. It was a characterization that Porter herself acutely resented, all too aware as she was that women writers were regarded as minor at best by the male movers and shakers of modern southern literature.[9]

Thus Porter, as Donaldson points out, though lionized by the great high muckety-mucks of southern culture, was ultimately patronized by them, and so ultimately "held captive by the audiences she hoped to dazzle and by the memories upon which those audiences insist."

Like Donaldson, I find it very interesting indeed that both Porter and Welty became interested in the Homeric figure of Circe at about the same time. Porter discussed her in an essay, and Welty made her the first-person narrator of the first short story she wrote after completing the final story of *The Golden Apples*, the one that finds Virgie Rainey heroically poised at the moment of complete freedom. After freeing her hero from her historical baggage, then, Welty significantly turns in her next story not, as politicized readers might expect or hope, to tell the heroic deeds of a female Odysseus, but rather to *listen to* Odysseus's stationary nemesis herself, the island-bound storyteller. Though *The Bride of the Innisfallen* is filled with women who have detached themselves, or are trying to, from traditional family environments precisely so they can tell their own stories, in "Circe" Welty confronts head-on the limitations of female empowerment. Circe does indeed have the power to turn men to swine, but her power is only over those who by chance wander onto her island—not exactly a mar-

---

9. Susan V. Donaldson, "Circe Revenged: Katherine Anne Porter and the Politics of Memory," unpublished paper quoted here with the kind permission of the author.

ket for porridge or for narrative likely to warm a Norton salesperson's heart—and, according to Trouard, part of the reason she turns the men to swine is that when they come they always insist upon telling *their* stories instead of listening to hers.

In all kinds of practical ways, Eudora Welty was right about the re-lationship between art and politics, no matter how much we—I—want our heroes to hold admirable and heroic positions, and no matter how defensive Welty seems to be about her position in the sixties. She is indubitably right to feel that *practically* she might have accomplished little through public intervention. Her example was Faulkner, after all, who ten years earlier had stepped from his modernist aesthetic di-rectly into the marketplace itself, to engage the polis in a debate about the disaster its ideologies were moving it toward and to convince it that it was in its own best interests to change. In one sense he accom-plished exactly nothing—unless you count as something making of himself an object of contumely from both sides, black and white, and reaping the contempt of a critical establishment that would grudgingly give the poor white Mississippi boy credit for *The Sound and the Fury* but not for taking political stands that might have gotten him killed. The sense in which he accomplished nothing was the artistic and po-litical sense, the public sense: it remains known only to his bones what he thought he had accomplished in the private sphere of his life as a citizen, whether he believed the time and energy he invested in the political battle was worth it. He may well have come to believe, with Eudora Welty, that an island in the wine-dark sea is the best place, the only place, where such discourse can take place. It is surely certain that Faulkner and Welty and Porter will all be remembered far longer for their fiction than for whether they did or did not try to inter-vene in political situations. And so maybe I've finally arrived back at where I started thirty-five years ago, reading and feeling deeply while blood flowed in the streets of Mississippi.

Or perhaps I have become what my pastor back in my hometown forty years ago warned me against as I prepared for college: beware, he said, of college professors (he meant Secular Humanists, but let that pass) who will tamper with your mind (he meant faith, of course, but let that pass too). I have thus, in his definition, become the enemy. Perhaps so: teaching something besides Odysseus's story is, or may be, a perilous enterprise, for us and for our students, because even the most ideologically innocent and neutral of my demands as a teacher is that they learn to think for themselves, that they learn not just that there might be other answers to old established—canonized—questions, but that there may well be other questions too. Thus I do not, as a teacher, spend my classroom time stamping out ignorance, as we often joke; rather, quite the opposite, I spend a good deal of time *creating* it, since part of what I do in the classroom, like the literature I teach, is to put my students in touch with all that they don't know. To say that it is my job to teach my students to think for themselves is the tawdriest of clichés, the stuff of which university and departmental mission statements are made. It is no less true for that. But to *think*, as I, the enemy, understand it, requires them to ask questions the answers to which may well rattle the ideological cages they have grown up in.

This is as it *has* to be, I say, and I say further that if I do not do so I am not doing my job properly. No one, not the most ardent and dyed-in-the-cotton redneck, would want yesterday's chemistry when it comes to his own health or well-being, or yesterday's physics when it comes to Star Wars or other late-breaking ways to shoot something. But we as a state and as a nation are being overrun by those who insist that we should be governed by yesterday's ideologies, ideologies put into place with the best of intentions and after lots of arm wrestling and negotiation by practical politicians like our Founding Fathers in order to deal with the world as they found it, and then sanctified by people who in the 1990s want to continue to deal with the world the Founding Fathers dealt with and not the radically different one we have today. We as humanists, as educators, are under the same mandate as our colleagues in science to bring to our students the latest, the best, even the most potent and potentially dangerous of the ideas our disciplines offer to help us understand ourselves as human beings— and not just so they can keep up with what's going on in the rest of the world. Since an important part of our discipline's business is to analyze individual human beings in all their complicated relationships with their culture, we must inevitably bring those ideas to bear upon our own lives: upon our own and our students' individual and collective histories, the "mitigating circumstances" that have made us who and what we are.

To be sure, it is no business of mine to be an advocate, though that is inevitable, even indirectly, when I believe something passionately. Nor is it my business to tell my students what to believe or think. It *is* my job to ensure, if I can, that whatever they believe they do not believe it in a historical vacuum that allows them to accept what their tradition has handed them as the truth, the whole truth, and nothing but. Whatever they believe, they must believe it according to a conscious moral choice, a choice that can only be made in the full and sympathetic knowledge of other possibilities. They must learn that it is much more important to discover what the real questions are than to figure out which answers to give; this is both the end of our teaching and the most perilous part of it, since those who ask real questions eventually arrive at answers that may well set them against not only the prevailing culture writ large, but also against that writ very particular—even against mom and dad, who may thus find themselves paying for the subversion of their own belief systems, political and often religious, paying for the very ideas that might radically disrupt their families because the ideas play havoc with their own ideological securities. As a consequence, in my teaching I often put myself and my university in a relationship ideologically antagonistic to the very people whose taxes pay my salary. This is, of course, the reason for tenure: so that I can say things in my classroom that will make those who pay my salary mad as hell, so that I can presume to know better than they what their children need in order to understand and improve their lives.

I am of course dramatizing. In fact most of our teaching involves more mundane matters like simply making sure that our students know the plot of the *Iliad*—who does what to whom and why—that they can spot iambic pentameter and even make subjects and verbs agree. The student who takes Quentin Compson's suicide as a model for behavior is a rare one. But how often have I talked to students who, after classroom discussions of Faulkner's and Welty's depictions of family dysfunction, will come to me after class—to me, only because they have to talk to someone immediately—and say, through tears in their eyes and in their hearts, *My daddy did that to me.* How often?

Often enough that I have a different narrative about the meaning of "family values" than the one so publicly told in recent days. Often enough to despise and repudiate a system that allows fathers to rape their daughters and professors to harass their students just because they can. I cannot "fix" their problems, but the books I teach can give them the courage to admit how their own traditions have violated them, so that they can begin to find the tools to fix themselves. A mind is not only a terrible thing to waste, it is an infinitely fragile thing to tamper with, and so we assume a fearsome responsibility as teachers: we accept this responsibility with love, with reverence, and with fear and trembling. It is a gross dereliction of our duties, an arrogant and contemptible violation of our own powerful political positions as teachers to try to depose, by ridicule or presumptive dismissal, the ideological structures by which our students have lived their two decades, no matter how wrong or problematical we believe them to be.

Thus Circe may be a monster and a genius for both Welty and Porter, but her powers are severely constricted by the isolation in which she holds herself. In fact she doesn't represent much of a threat except to *wandering* men; certainly there on her marginalized island she is no serious direct threat to those who form the establishment. And we, too, are likely to be ineffectual unless, Circe-like, we take advantage of the wanderers who, by the chance winds of scheduling or bad advisement, happen upon our marginalized island classrooms, and insist that for one semester at least they listen to Circe's story too, and not just their own.

They need Circe's story, the one that Odysseus doesn't want to hear and won't listen to. We must ensure that Circe, her story at least, will follow Odysseus back to Ithaca to bear witness to *her* version of their encounter, a version different from the one he is likely to tell his wife and his friends. It may be that her version of the patriarchal hero's quest is the one we need to hear most, since we know the dominant story so well, and it is our function as teachers to make sure that that other story gets told too—the African American and Asian and Native American story as well as the white one, the female as well as the male, the gay as well as the straight—to students and others who, ideologically dormant, might not otherwise hear the rest of the story,

Paul Harvey notwithstanding. Circe's story is precisely that counter-memory that will ultimately prevent our cultural memories from becoming what Michel Foucault calls a "unitary discourse"—that discourse that sanctifies racism and sexism and nationalism and lots of other isms, those traditions that insist that there is only one truth, one way of understanding the world; that insist upon order—*their* order—above all.

Only by hearing Circe's story too can they know the difference between tradition, which produces only answers, and history, which produces mostly questions. And only by knowing this difference can our students avoid becoming victims, too, of Grisham's "mitigating circumstance" and of what E. L. Doctorow calls "the violence inherent in principle"—the principle, whatever it is, to which tradition clings for its very life. It is not history but the unitary discourse of tradition that produces the Byron de la Beckwiths and the Sam Cayhills.

At the end of *Huckleberry Finn* Tom and Huck are pretending to free Jim from the prison they have put him in. Tom's game requires that they follow the rules, go by the cultural book. Like the escapees in Tom's romantic books, Jim is supposed to escape by digging himself out of his cell with a spoon. Jim tries valiantly, but when Tom sees that using the actual case knife will take so long that he will lose control of the game, he immediately points to a shovel and tells Huck to hand *that* spoon to Jim—a linguistic ruse whereby he can play the game by the rules and get on with it to his own satisfaction. Huck, of course, doesn't immediately understand, but we do. Tom, the representative of his culture, controls the rules, controls the language by which the rules get interpreted and *used*. As the one who controls the books, he also controls the story: he has the power to call a shovel a spoon if he wants, to tell the story he wants told.

One of the most important political acts we as teachers and writers can do is to demonstrate, through our literature and our criticism, the ideological processes whereby shovels become spoons, the machinations of power whereby some people and not others get to say whether a shovel is a spoon or not. My students in Mississippi and all students everywhere need to know their own states' histories, and their countries', in all their rich and terrifying complexity; they need to be able to be critical of any tradition, especially if it is their own, that denies multiplicity in favor of its own unity. They *must* know the difference between a shovel and a spoon, so that they can always tell when any-body—Hollywood or John Grisham, president, governor, or even pro-fessor—is shoveling the shit, no matter how much it looks and tastes like sugar.

*Suzanne Marrs*

# "The Huge Fateful Stage of the Outside World"

Eudora Welty's Life in Politics

Stories written by the imagination for the imagination. Language ranging from the highly metaphoric to the taut and spare, from the lushly descriptive to the ungrammatically conversational. Plots conveying the mystery or wildness inherent in human experience. Characters, rich and poor, educated and uneducated, black and white, who share the author's respect and sympathy and who possess the complex, contradictory natures of actual people. The person who writes such a fiction is not likely to become a political activist, is not likely to accept political set speeches that undervalue the intellect of the electorate, to accept the stereotyping and even character assassination typical of political campaigns. Such a writer is Eudora Welty, and such scruples are certainly hers, yet Welty has from the start been absolutely aware of the importance of making political decisions, of voting for those candidates most likely to support the values she holds dear, and of acting in support of causes she esteems.

Throughout her life Welty has been interested in the political process—in the candidates who run for office, in the programs they espouse, in the methods they use to win or lose elections. She has never been a neutral party in this process—a lifelong Democrat, Welty has supported Democratic candidates and liberal causes from the beginning. But in the 1930s and 1940s, Welty's Democratic Party loyalties were divided. She was appalled by Mississippi's election of demagogues like Theodore Bilbo and John Rankin even as she rejoiced in the victories of Franklin Delano Roosevelt and Harry S. Truman. Of course, only rarely did Welty give public voice to these views. More typically she expressed them privately to friends and implicitly in her stories. In 1934, she was proud to see her friend Hubert Creekmore's anti-Bilbo letter published in *Time* magazine. In 1938, her story "The Whistle" indicted the evils of a tenant-farming system and in doing so suggested the importance of programs like the Farm Security Administration's Tenant Purchase Program. And in 1948 in a letter to her friend John Robinson, she celebrated Truman's victory over Dewey and the racist Dixiecrats as the "nearest to liberal choice."[1]

Welty, however, did not always keep private the expression of her political views. A notable exception is her December 20, 1945, letter to the *Jackson Clarion-Ledger,* complaining about the paper's coverage of Gerald L. K. Smith's visit to Jackson. Smith, who had been a devout disciple of Huey Long, in 1945 proclaimed himself opposed not only to "Stalinism," but also to "Internationalism and other forms of alienism" and sought to establish the basis for a Nationalist movement in the South. Knowing that Smith was, to use the words of Walter Goodman, "the country's noisiest anti-Semite," a man who had praised Hitler, had blamed Jews for the Great Depression and World War II, and had denied the reality of the Holocaust, Welty was offended by the newspaper's nonjudgmental coverage of Smith's speech. Recognizing the legacy of Nazism and the spirit that would eventually be called McCarthyism, Welty asked the editor, "Isn't there anybody ready with words for telling Smith that that smells to heaven to us, that we don't want him, won't let him try organizing any of his fascistic doings in our borders, and to get out and stay out of Mississippi?" She went on to ask, "[I]s there still nothing we can do to atone for our apathy and our blindness or our closed minds, by maintaining some kind of vigilance in keeping Gerald Smith away?"[2]

Welty concluded her letter by denouncing Smith's ideological pals: "we will get Bilbo and Rankin out when their time, election time, comes, God willing." Well might she have called for the defeat of Mississippi politicians Theodore Bilbo and John Rankin. Indeed, both rep-

1. Hubert Creekmore, "That Man Bilbo," *Time,* 22 October 1934, p. 2; Eudora Welty to John F. Robinson, Friday [November 1948], Eudora Welty Collection, Mississippi Department of Archives and History, Jackson.
2. "Bilbo and Rankin Get Blessings of Former Huey Long Chieftain," *Jackson Clarion-Ledger,* 20 Dec. 1945; Walter Goodman, *The Committee* (New York: Farrar, Straus, and Giroux, 1968), 181; Eudora Welty, "Voice of the People," *Jackson Clarion-Ledger,* 28 December 1948.

resented values that were anathema to her. Elected to the United States Senate in 1934, Bilbo sought "to send blacks 'back to Africa,' opposed anti-lynching and anti-poll tax bills, and spent much of his energy preaching race hatred and white supremacy." In a stump speech during his 1946 campaign, Bilbo was in rare form: "Do not let a single nigger vote. If you let a few register and vote this year, next year there will be twice as many, and the first thing you know the whole thing will be out of hand." Attitudes like Bilbo's were especially shocking in the wake of a war ostensibly fought against Nazi Aryanism. Equally repugnant to Welty were the policies of Congressman Rankin. Rankin, who served in the House of Representatives from 1921 until 1952, was a rabble-rousing member of the House Un-American Activities Committee. An anti-Semite in the Gerald Smith mode, Rankin taunted his Jewish colleagues in the House, equating them with Communists. In addition, he sought to block Chinese immigration into the United States and opposed any political measures that might move African Americans toward equality. When the American Red Cross sought to cease labeling blood as "black" or "white," Rankin exploded; this idea, he contended, was put forth by the "crackpots, the Communists and parlor pinks . . . [in order] to mongrelize the nation."[3] Welty must have cringed at such comments, comments that denied the validity of the American war effort. Her public call for the defeat of Bilbo and Rankin is testimony to her extreme disgust with their values. In her home-town newspaper, the usually circumspect Welty thus made a forceful and impassioned political statement, a statement for openness, toler-ance, and freedom, both of speech and of belief.

This public statement of 1945 prefigured Welty's active participa-tion in the presidential election of 1952, a participation not in spite of her stance as fiction writer, but because of it. In New York City in the fall of 1952, she canvassed for Adlai Stevenson and sold tickets for Ste-venson fund raisers, returning home in time to vote for the Demo-cratic candidate. For Welty this was a moment of convergence; Steven-son brought to the public stage the very values that animated her

3. James Loewen and Charles Sallis, *Mississippi Conflict and Change*, rev. ed. (New York: Pantheon Books, 1980), 239; Theodore Bilbo, cited ibid.; *Dictionary of American Biography*, s.v. "Rankin, John."

fiction. She admired his forthright nature, his acceptance of diversity, his keen intellect and complexity of thought, and his use of the English language. As a result, Welty for the first and only time in her life actively joined a political campaign.

The defeat of Stevenson was a bitter pill, but her loyalty to the candidate and her hope that he might one day lead the country were unquenched. She expressed that loyalty openly one more time, this time in print when the *New Republic* requested that she and other writers send New Year's greetings to Governor Stevenson. In her message, Welty told the governor that in his campaign his supporters saw "their chiefest inner convictions translated for the time being to the huge fateful stage of the outside world" and that Stevenson "had got up and represented those convictions and brought them to bear on the scene, life-size and first-hand." In writing about inner conviction translated to the huge fateful stage of the outside world, Welty might well be describing her own attempts in fiction. In *One Writer's Beginnings*, she notes that "the outside world is the vital component of my inner life. My work, in the terms in which I see it, is as dearly matched to the world as its secret sharer. My imagination takes its strength and guides its direction from what I see and hear and learn and feel and remember of my living world."[4] This "charged dramatic field of fiction" converged with the huge fateful stage of the outside world in the election of 1952 so that Eudora Welty supported a candidate she characterized in her New Year's greeting as having "intelligence . . . charged to communicate, . . . shaped in responsibility and impelled with learning and curiosity, [and] . . . alight with imagination." Stevenson, Welty saw, was concerned with communication and alight with imagination, and such concern and such imagination, she felt, made not merely for great literature, but also for credible political leaders, for effective political communication, and for innovative political policies.

Stevenson, as Welty recognized and admired, possessed the courage of his convictions, and during the campaign his convictions had led him to challenge directly and forcefully demands for the suppression

4. Eudora Welty, "What Stevenson Started," *New Republic*, 5 January 1953, 8; Eudora Welty, *One Writer's Beginnings* (Cambridge: Harvard University Press, 1984), 76, 102.

of dissent or for partisan advantage. As David Halberstam reported, Stevenson "went before the American Legion, a citadel of jingoism and political reaction, and told the audience that McCarthy's kind of patriotism was a disgrace." The American Legion was not alone in hearing such frank comments. Stevenson biographer Jean Baker observes:

> In his childhood Adlai Stevenson had learned the virtues of self-criticism, and so throughout the campaign he offered the language of business to labor, remarking that "goons and violence and property damage are as wrong and as intolerable in labor disputes as anywhere else." In New Haven he promised an audience of loyal party men that he would support only worthy Democratic candidates. In New Orleans he spoke on civil rights and tidelands oil. At a town hall luncheon in Los Angeles, he informed party activists that the people got the kind of leaders they deserved. "Your public servants serve you right; indeed they often serve you better than your apathy and indifference deserve."

Stevenson was a rare candidate who sought to challenge his listeners, not pander to them. That such a candidate went down in defeat raised for Welty a crucial question: "how soon and how fully can we accommodate greatness—honor it, not punish it, because it *is* greatness," she asked.[5]

For Welty, Stevenson's greatness lay in his recognition that political situations were too complex for simplistic answers. For example, the war in Korea was central in the mind of the electorate in 1952, but Stevenson offered no easy answers for this problem. A speech he gave in Louisville, Kentucky, is typical. There, as Baker reports, "he offered his special brand of the politics of unresolved modern dilemmas: 'I promise no easy solutions, no relief from burdens and anxieties, for to do this would be not only dishonest; it would be to attack the foundations of our greatness.' It was typical of Stevenson that he carefully and thoughtfully dissected the Korean War—its history, its manipulation by the Soviets (this was an era in which Americans misunder-

5. David Halberstam, *The Fifties* (New York: Villard Books, 1993), 236; Jean H. Baker, *The Stevensons* (New York: Norton, 1996), 323; Welty, "What Stevenson Started."

stood the tensions among Communist countries and exaggerated the power of the Soviets), and its necessary resolution by military containment under the United Nations." Stevenson's discussion of the multifaceted and perhaps impenetrable nature of reality held vital appeal for Welty, whose character Virgie Rainey knew that "all the opposites on earth were close together" and who herself would later write: "Relationship *is* a pervading and changing mystery. . . . Brutal or lovely, the mystery waits for people wherever they go, whatever extreme they run to."[6]

Finally, Stevenson's love of language, of its imaginative and precise use, set the note of the campaign in which Welty had so ardently participated. According to Baker, Stevenson paid more attention to the written text of his speeches than to their effective delivery. When his advisers argued that his defects as an orator limited his appeal to voters, "Stevenson's reaction was expectable: 'If they don't like me as I am, *tant pis*! I won't pretend to be anything else.'" Concern for language defined Stevenson. As Baker notes, "Intent on creating carefully crafted political essays graced with complex vocabulary—the language of the university, the Washington-based institutes, and the nation's best writers . . . , Stevenson paid no attention to the important consideration of advancing himself as a future president. Always the presentation of his words was secondary to the words themselves."[7] Such a stance clearly made Stevenson a writer's candidate.

If public and private thus converged for Welty in the campaign of 1952, if the fiction writer found her most interior values being championed on the "huge fateful stage of the outside world," she herself championed those values on a somewhat smaller Mississippi stage in the 1960s. That stage was literally located in the Christian Center of Millsaps College, and there Eudora Welty on April 18, 1963, and December 2, 1964, made powerful yet complex statements in favor of civil rights.

6. Baker, *Stevensons*, 333; Eudora Welty, "The Wanderers," in *The Collected Stories of Eudora Welty* (New York: Harcourt Brace, 1980), 452; Eudora Welty, "Writing and Analyzing a Story," in *The Eye of the Story: Selected Essays and Reviews* (New York: Random House, 1978), 114.
7. Baker, *Stevensons*, 325, 320.

When Welty came to the podium in 1963, she came with a background of interracial relationships more diverse, extensive, and empathetic than most white Mississippians possessed. During her student days at Columbia University and later during visits to New York City, Welty had often gone to Harlem: she loved to hear jazz played at the Cotton Club and Small's Paradise, and she had been thrilled to see an African American production of *Macbeth* directed by a young Orson Welles. In Jackson, Welty had frequented music stores in the black business district so that she could buy what were called "race records," and she had moved easily in and out of black neighborhoods, homes, and churches, photographing many a black Mississippian. Sometime in the 1940s, her editor John Woodburn introduced Welty to Ralph Ellison and took her to dinner at the Ellisons' New York apartment. It was her first social contact with African Americans, and she and Ellison became friends.[8]

Moreover, late in the 1950s Welty, often in the company of Millsaps history professor Ross Moore and his wife, began to attend events at Tougaloo Southern Christian College, an African American institution just north of Jackson. She also gave at least two lecture/readings there, one of which was sponsored by the Social Sciences Forum. According to John Quincy Adams, Tougaloo's Professor Ernst Borinski had designed the forum as part of an effort to provide a "model of an integrated society," and Millsaps professors of history, sociology, and political science had been frequent speakers. The invitation for Welty to speak about her work was a very unusual one for the Social Sciences Forum—her fiction and her creative process had little to do with the social sciences—but simply by addressing the group Welty was issuing an implicit call for integration. In fact, the lecture came only five months after a 1958 furor about the Millsaps College Religious Forum, which had dared to invite integrationists to speak, and her lecture seems almost to have been a response to the clamor raised by local newspapers, a clamor that had prompted Millsaps to close its public events to African Americans and to discourage its professors from teaching or speaking at Tougaloo. Welty clearly regretted that Millsaps

8. Welty has discussed this and other biographical information with me in many conversations since I first met her in the summer of 1983.

would no longer provide a "model of an integrated society," but she participated in such a model at Tougaloo, even though speaking at Tougaloo involved some personal danger. By 1958, white visitors to Tougaloo might have expected to have their visits monitored by the State Sovereignty Commission or its informers. Welty's friend Jane Reid Petty recalls that she and others often carpooled when going to Tougaloo, varying the car they took as often as possible so that the sheriff, whom they suspected of recording the tag numbers of white visitors to Tougaloo, would not see a pattern in their visits. Though the possibility of harassment loomed in the offing, neither Welty nor her friends were deterred from this activity.[9]

Despite a history of refusing to capitulate to racist pressure, Welty must have been keenly aware that her April 18, 1963, appearance at Millsaps occurred at a particularly tense moment in the history of both the state and the college. In the fall of 1962, there had been riots and two deaths at the University of Mississippi when James Meredith had arrived to enroll. In December a black boycott of downtown Jackson stores had begun and would be the source of much hostility for more than six months. In January 1963, twenty-eight young white Methodist ministers caused outrage in the white community when they published a *"Born of Conviction* statement . . . , in which they asked for a free and open pulpit in the racial crisis and full support of the public schools instead of the private schools that were being established to maintain segregation."[10]

At Millsaps there was tension as well. Both faculty and administration overwhelmingly supported efforts for integration, but the administration in particular feared both violence and the loss of its financial base if integration came to the school. Nevertheless, on January 24,

9. Social Sciences Forum Announcements, Tougaloo College Archives, Tougaloo, Mississippi; John Quincy Adams, Papers and Audio Tapes, Faculty Papers, Series F, Millsaps College Archives, Jackson, Mississippi; Laura G. McKinley, "Millsaps College and the Mississippi Civil Rights Movement" (honors thesis, Millsaps College, 1989), 5–6; "Millsaps President and Wright Protest," *Jackson Clarion-Ledger,* 9 March 1958, section A; Jane Reid Petty and Patti Carr Black, conversations with the author, March 1997.

10. W. J. Cunningham, *Agony at Galloway* (Jackson: University Press of Mississippi, 1980), 8.

1963, the Millsaps faculty voted 36-22-1 to support the twenty-eight Methodist ministers who had signed the *Born of Conviction* statement. The Millsaps resolution read, in part: "We are concerned . . . that encroachments upon the liberties of ministers to speak freely their sincere interpretations of the Christian gospel constitute but one manifestation of those evil tendencies which would deny men freedom in every sphere. Such tendencies are a constant threat, not only to a free and valid church, but also to a democratic society." Nor was this the end of consternation felt by Millsaps faculty over the racial situation in Mississippi. On April 2, 1963, a professor and several African American students from Tougaloo College were turned away from a play at Millsaps, and on April 11, the Millsaps AAUP chapter passed another controversial resolution, this time asking the college president to appoint a committee to study the possibility of integrating the Millsaps student body.[11] A week later, it was time for the college to host the Southern Literary Festival, which was directed by Millsaps English professor and Welty friend George Boyd, one of the signers of the AAUP resolution. The college thus faced a dilemma—whether to abide by its policy of segregation, so recently enforced, or to allow open admission to Eudora Welty's April 18 address because it was sponsored by the Southern Literary Festival rather than Millsaps.

Early on that day, officials from Millsaps called upon Welty to discuss the prospect of an integrated audience—they feared conflict. Welty, nevertheless, asked that her lecture be open to all, and it was. That lecture, published almost a year earlier under the title "Words into Fiction," seems detached from any sort of political situation. In it, Welty acknowledges that a reader may have a conception of a novel that differs from that of the writer, but she contends that this difference "is neither so strange nor so important as the vital fact that a connection has been made between them." The novel, she argues, is "made by the imagination for the imagination." After delivering this address, however, Welty went on to show her audience the political

11. Minutes of faculty meeting, 24 January 1963, Series B, Millsaps College Archives, Jackson, Mississippi; H. E. Finger Jr. Papers, Administrative Papers, Series A1, Millsaps College Archives, Jackson, Mississippi; Adams, Papers and Audio Tapes.

import a work made by the imagination for the imagination could have—she read her story "Powerhouse" to the interracial audience, which included a contingent from Tougaloo Southern Christian College.[12]

Written in 1940 and inspired by a Fats Waller concert Welty had attended, "Powerhouse" is the story of an African American pianist and his band playing at a segregated dance; it focuses on the white audience's simultaneous fascination with and repulsion by the band leader, Powerhouse, and on the band's ability to find intermission conviviality and refreshments only at a black café. In reading this story at the festival, Welty took a considerable risk. "The point of view of this story," she has noted, "is floating around somewhere in the concert hall—it belongs to the 'we' of the audience," and that audience is a racist audience. Powerhouse, on the other hand, is drawn from Welty's own experience as a writer. Welty has said that she is driven by "the love of her art and the love of giving it, the desire to give it until there is no more left," and Powerhouse is a performer who "gives everything."[13] Thus the narrative voice located in the story's white racist audience might have offended black listeners at Millsaps even as the author's clear identification of Powerhouse as representative of artists like herself might have offended whites. But Welty trusted in the ability of her listeners, and she might well have expected the story to bring together the two factions attending the lecture and reading.

In "Powerhouse," Welty suggests that a shared act of imagination can bridge, if only momentarily, the separateness between individuals. Though neither the whites at their dance nor the black citizens Powerhouse encounters at the World Café in Negrotown consciously recognize themselves in his lyrics or tall tales, this "inspired" musician, this "fanatic," gives his white audience "the only time for hallucina-

12. Eudora Welty, conversation with author, and R. Edwin King, conversations with author, 20 March 1997, 7 April 1997, 19 June 1997; Eudora Welty, "Words into Fiction," in *Eye of the Story*, 144, 145; Jerry DeLaughter, "Miss Welty Opens Literary Festival," *Jackson Clarion-Ledger*, 19 April 1963.
13. Eudora Welty, William E. Massey Lecture III, 6, Welty Collection, Mississippi Department of Archives and History, Jackson; Welty, *One Writer's Beginnings*, 101; Welty, "Powerhouse," in *A Curtain of Green* (New York: Harcourt Brace, 1941), 257.

tion" and leaves his black audience in a "breathless ring." At the dance he sends "everybody into oblivion" and at the World Café everybody "in the room moans with pleasure." The song that closes the story seems particularly relevant to this issue of communication and imagination. "Somebody loves me," Powerhouse sings and then concludes, "Maybe it's you!" Maybe, just maybe, Powerhouse will have a deep and lasting effect upon a member of his audience—the probability seems slight. Still, the story's very existence suggests that it is possible for a shared act of imagination to extend beyond the moment of performance. A Fats Waller Jackson concert, made by the imagination for the imagination, brought forth a complex, enduring, and imaginative response from Eudora Welty, a young white woman living in the Deep South.[14]

More than twenty years after writing this story based on the Waller concert, Welty read it to her 1963 Millsaps audience, black and white, as if to proclaim the destructiveness of segregation and the enriching effect of imagining oneself into other and different lives. Combining her story with a lecture about the power of the imagination to unite reader and writer was a political act for Welty, an act of courage and vision, an act that built upon the integrated readings she had earlier given at Tougaloo College. And Welty's presentation at Millsaps did unite, however briefly, black and white Mississippians. John Salter, the professor who led the Tougaloo contingent on April 18, reported, "Eudora Welty gave an excellent lecture, including a reading of one of her short stories—which we could follow as she read since we had brought along several copies of her work. When the evening was over we walked slowly outside. A group of Millsaps students came up and indicated that they were quite glad that we had attended. Other than that, no one appeared to notice us, and that, in its own small way, marked a significant breakthrough in Mississippi." Welty's part in this breakthrough won her the enduring respect of Tougaloo chaplain Edwin King, who attended the event along with Salter and black students from Tougaloo, and of Anne Moody, one of those black students, who in a February 1985 appearance at Millsaps recalled how important

14. Welty, "Powerhouse," 254, 265, 269.

it had been for her to hear Welty read.[15] Nevertheless, despite Welty's actions in support of integration and despite the standing ovation she received from blacks and whites at the festival, Millsaps College would less than one month later turn away African Americans who sought admission to a theatrical production by the Millsaps Players.

Off the Millsaps campus, infinitely more-virulent acts of racism soon occurred. On May 28, a faculty member and some students from Tougaloo were beaten and one student arrested when they attempted to integrate the lunch counter at Woolworth's variety store. On June 12, Medgar Evers, field secretary of the Mississippi NAACP, was assassinated. And on June 18, John Salter and Edwin King, leaders of the Tougaloo contingent that sought to integrate Millsaps and Jackson's commercial establishments, were almost killed in a suspicious automobile accident. In the wake of these events, Eudora Welty courageously published "Where Is the Voice Coming From?"—a devastating portrait of the racist mindset.

Even before Welty's story was in print, her friend and agent Diarmuid Russell expressed concern about violence in Jackson and about Welty's safety. Welty, on the other hand, was afraid not for herself, but for her mother. For months she had been consumed with anxiety about her mother's health and spirits, and that anxiety coupled with alarm for her mother in the local climate of hatred prevented Welty on one occasion from undertaking what would have implicitly been a symbolic act in support of integration. In late July 1963 (the time frame that seems most likely), she decided at the last minute, after much agonizing and with deep regret, not to be interviewed by Ralph Ellison on national television. She worried that a nationally televised appearance with this fellow writer, an African American man, would create a good deal of white hostility in Mississippi, hostility that she feared would be deflected from daughter to mother. She worried that such hostility would affect her ability to hire desperately needed caregivers for her mother, who in August was coming home from a five-

15. John R. Salter, *Jackson, Mississippi* (Hicksville, N.Y.: Exposition Press, 1979), 102. Edwin King arranged for Moody to speak at Millsaps, attended the lecture with her, and told me of her comments about Welty's importance to the Tougaloo contingent (19 June 1997).

month stint in a convalescent facility, and that it might affect the quality of care her mother would receive in the future. Although she and her mother had long been of one mind on the issue of civil rights, Welty sought to ensure that she alone would pay the price for their shared convictions. A desire to shelter her ailing mother from a volatile environment of racial tension and especially from white recrimination governed her decision, as she confided to Reynolds Price, not to be interviewed by Ellison. Ellison for a brief time was understandably mystified by Welty's decision. Shortly after the cancellation, Ellison told Price how open and outgoing Welty had always been with him, and he worried that he might have in some way unwittingly offended her. Price explained Welty's situation to him and also told Welty of Ellison's worries. According to Price, Welty then wrote to Ellison to explain her deep-seated apprehensions for her mother, and the Welty/ Ellison friendship endured.[16]

Welty's relationship with the state of Mississippi, however, seemed in danger. On August 14, 1963, and again on August 28, she wrote her friend and former *Harper's Bazaar* fiction editor Mary Lou Aswell about the impossible, but desirable, prospect of moving her mother and herself away from Mississippi and its racist political leaders. And in the following spring, Welty continued to worry about the effect of social unrest upon her mother. In March 1964, she wrote to Aswell about her anxieties. She wanted, she wrote her old friend who had settled in Santa Fe, to move her mother to "some convalescent home in that part of the world." The fact that her mother was fifty miles away back in a Yazoo City nursing home, that Yazoo City was "reputed to be now the headquarters of the Ku Klux Klan," that "our state is now authorized to . . . arm the highway patrol," and that violence might

---

16. Diarmuid Russell to Eudora Welty, 17 June 1963, restricted papers, Welty Collection, Mississippi Department of Archives and History, Jackson. Welty's 1963 correspondence with Russell and with Mary Lou Aswell (restricted papers, Welty Collection, Mississippi Department of Archives and History, Jackson) suggests a late July decision by Welty; Reynolds Price, conversation with author, 25 October 1998. According to Price, the *Paris Review* intended to publish the interview with Ellison. Instead Hildegarde Dolson conducted the *Camera Three* television interview, and the *Paris Review* decided against publication. The interview aired on Sunday, August 18, 1963.

prevent her from reaching Yazoo City and her mother played heavily upon Welty's mind. Recalling riots both black (Jacksonville, Florida) and white (Oxford, Mississippi), Welty wrote that she wanted to "bring my little mother to some safe spot where she won't hear of this even."[17]

But Welty did not leave Mississippi or the South; neither did she abandon a public stance in favor of an open society. Late in 1964, she returned to the Millsaps College Christian Center, this time as the college's writer-in-residence. Though she did not on this occasion have to request unrestricted attendance—Millsaps now welcomed all to its public events—she once again spoke during particularly tense times.[18] The previous summer had seen the murders of three civil rights workers in Philadelphia, Mississippi, the fire-bombing of forty black churches, and the white Citizens' Council's intimidation of whites known to have "moderate" sensibilities, intimidation that had not ceased.

In her December 2, 1964, lecture, titled "The Southern Writer Today: An Interior Affair," Welty delivered comments that she would later publish as "Must the Novelist Crusade?" Here, she ostensibly rejected a political purpose for fiction, arguing that "there is absolutely everything in great fiction but a clear answer," that fiction is concerned more with the complexities of human experience than with proposing solutions to human difficulties. Welty followed the address with a reading of "Keela, the Outcast Indian Maiden," which, appropriately, examines the complexities of human relationships. The story describes a crippled black man who was once kidnapped into carnival work as a geek called Keela, the Outcast Indian Maiden, and who, notwithstanding the horror of his past, feels nostalgic about the carnival experience, in which he was noticed, as now within his own family he is not. The story further deals with the guilt felt by Steve, the carnival barker, and with his inability, nevertheless, to overcome the separa-

17. Eudora Welty to Mary Lou Aswell, 14 August 1963, 28 August 1963, [24/25 March 1964], restricted papers, Welty Collection quoted by permission of Eudora Welty.
18. Finger Papers, 9 August 1963. Sara Ann Weir covered this lecture for the Millsaps College paper. See "Miss Welty Tells Position of Southern Writers Today," *Purple and White*, 8 December 1964.

tion of race, and finally, the story depicts a bystander's courting of detachment from the horror and guilt Keela represents.

Complex though it is, however, "Keela" makes an important political statement: the dehumanizing nature of racism is infinitely more grotesque than a carnival sideshow. Certainly, Steve recognizes that by acquiescing to this evil, he has become part of it: "'It's all me, see,' said Steve. 'I know that. I was the one was the cause for it goin' on an' on an' not bein' found out—such an awful thing. It was me, what I said out front through the megaphone.'" On the other hand, his acquaintance, Max, the owner of Max's Place, represses any guilt that might be his: "'Bud,' said Max, disengaging himself, 'I don't hear anything. I got a juke box, see, so I don't have to listen.'"[19] Max, in his disengaged state, might be speaking for many white Mississippians in 1964—they did not want to recognize their own complicity with evil, they did not want to accept the guilt they shared with Steve. But in reading this 1940 story to her 1964 audience, Eudora Welty called attention to that guilt. She did not ask that her audience become political activists, but she did ask, implicitly, that they refuse to be part of racist activities, that they recognize the humanity and complexity of all individuals. Millsaps College had already recognized the wisdom of positions like Welty's—within three months it announced that African American students were welcome to enroll at the college.

It is important to recognize that Welty's call for nonracist behavior was not a call to crusade, for she herself had chosen not to take to the streets. In a June 1965 letter to Mary Lou Aswell, Welty pondered her lack of stridency in the civil rights movement and concluded: "I'm to blame, I suppose, for not dashing into it and doing some of the shrieking, but I don't really think so, because it would not mean with me any change of heart. I've always felt as I do now, and I hope my feeling has been all the time in my work."[20] Welty's belief in the power of fiction was more important to her than public pronouncements. Even the

19. Eudora Welty, "Must the Novelist Crusade?" in *Eye of the Story*, 149; Eudora Welty, "Keela, the Outcast Indian Maiden," in *Curtain of Green*, 77.
20. Eudora Welty to Mary Louise Aswell, 8 June 1965, restricted papers, Welty Collection quoted by permission of Eudora Welty.

aborted Ellison interview was to have focused on fiction, and certainly, in her public appearances at Millsaps, Welty had demonstrated how effectively her short stories expressed support for the civil rights movement.

As one who did not march on Washington, organize voter registration drives, or challenge Mississippi mores on national television, Welty continued to find meaningful ways to act against racism, speaking at the 1965 Southern Literary Festival, supporting interracial audiences and casts at New Stage Theatre from its planning stages in 1965 to the present day, describing the segregationists' benighted resistance to change as part of her 1966 story "The Demonstrators"—a story Jesse Jackson in a letter to the *New Yorker* praised as "true and powerful"—and inaugurating in 1967 a series of Wednesday programs open to black and white at Jackson's St. Andrew's Episcopal Cathedral.[21]

21. Tragic circumstances prevented Eudora Welty from being present on January 25, 1966, opening night at New Stage Theatre. Her mother died January 21 and her brother Edward, January 26. Although she could not attend the opening, which she had helped to make possible, Welty's public and private support for the theater never faltered and has continued to this day. In its early days, New Stage encountered white opposition to its racial policies. A bomb threat on opening night occurred even though no African Americans were in the cast; the fact that tickets were available for both blacks and whites, as Jane Reid Petty and Patti Carr Black told me in March 1997, was enough to generate the threat. (Both Petty and Black were among the founding members of the theater.) The theater continued its open-door policy nevertheless, and African Americans, though relatively few in number, were in its audiences from the inaugural year onward. The regular appearance of African Americans in casts began in 1969, making New Stage the first theater group in Mississippi "other than academic departments" to have both integrated audiences and casts (Martha H. Hammond, "Dialogue: New Stage Theatre and Jackson, Mississippi" [Ph.D. dissertation, University of Southern Mississippi, 1994], 196).

In 1970 when gunfire from the state highway patrol and the city police took two lives at Jackson State College, a black Jackson State student who was then a cast member of *The Ponder Heart* resolved to continue in her role, living with a white cast member for the run of the show (Hammond 181). Frank Hains, the director of the play, devoted a regular *Jackson Daily News* column to his deep sorrow at the violence that had just taken place, to the decision of Florence Roach to continue in her role, and to the play's relevance to this

Welty's speech at the April 1965 Southern Literary Festival, held in Oxford, Mississippi, in honor of William Faulkner, is particularly instructive. Robert W. Hamblin has discussed the powerful statement for civil rights implicit in Robert Penn Warren's festival address, an address made twenty-four hours after a mob had harassed the Tougaloo College delegation that had hoped to participate in the festival. Hamblin might also have cited Welty's remarks, for they reiterated her faith in fiction's power to expose and combat racist hatred. In the midst of a wide-ranging discussion alluding to many Faulkner texts, Welty called the audience's attention to the brutal murder of Joe Christmas, "waiting with his hands in chains, 'bright and glittering,' . . . as Percy Grimm arrives with his automatic." Later she noted that Faulkner's characters "are white, Negro, Indian, Chinese, Huguenot, Scotch, English, Spanish, French, or any combination of these, and known always or at any point of their time on earth from birth till death and in between." And she added that these characters constitute "a population that has *reality* as distinguished from *actuality:* they are our hearts made visible and audible and above all dramatic; they are

Jackson crisis. *The Ponder Heart,* he wrote, though it seems far removed from questions of "race relations or problems of the day," actually has "everything to do with them." This play, he continued, is "all about love and Uncle Daniel's unbounded love for all the world—and it's a reflection of the great love of humanity which lifts its author, Eudora Welty, into a state of grace few achieve on this earth." Hains thus proclaimed in print the role New Stage Theatre hoped to play in defining race relations, and human relations more generally, in terms of love, not hate and violence, and identified Eudora Welty as a person living and writing by such a code. See "On Stage—Eudora Welty's 'Ponder Heart': A Message of Love Needed Now," *Jackson Daily News,* 17 May 1970, section C4.

Welty sent Mary Lou Aswell a xeroxed copy of Jackson's handwritten letter to the *New Yorker,* and this copy is included in the Aswell papers at the Mississippi Department of Archives and History.

In 1967 at St. Andrew's Cathedral, organizers wholeheartedly supported open admission to the series of readings, lectures, concerts, and plays, and they hoped African Americans would attend. As it turned out, however, Welty read to an all-white audience (personal conversation with Ann Morrison, chair of the 1967 Wednesdays at St. Andrew's programs, September 1999).

ourselves translated, and, at times, transmogrified."[22] Welty thus suggested that race is as artificial a concept as nationality and that to whatever race or nationality Faulkner's characters belong, they represent our common humanity.

Such local actions were tremendously significant. As David Chappell notes in his book *Inside Agitators: White Southerners in the Civil Rights Movement,* white southerners who "were sickened by segregation" together with white southerners who "found it terribly inconvenient in practice" provided the civil rights movement with a strategic "moral and political resource." Knowing of the existence of such whites, he writes, "gave millions of black southerners, despite a dispiriting history of crushed hopes and broken promises, confidence in their ability to win—not simply confidence in the righteousness of their cause but in the usually unrelated prospects of that cause for victory in the real world."[23] Eudora Welty, one of those white southerners who was sickened by segregation, thus played her own small but crucial and courageous role in the move toward integration. By repeatedly refusing to comply with racism in her private life and by locally encouraging others to refuse as well, she became one of many who helped to create a climate for change and for progress.

Most particularly, Eudora Welty had in her 1963 and 1964 Millsaps lecture/readings experienced the same sense of convergence that she had known in 1952. In 1952 she had found the fiction writer's values and the public domain pulled together by Adlai Stevenson, and she actively supported the convergence he represented. In the sixties, however, Welty herself pulled the private and public together. She pulled together aesthetic and political concerns, stories from the past and contemporary conflicts, fiction and politics, and she sought to part the curtain that divided Mississippi's blacks and whites. Since that time, Welty's public political statements have been relatively few. For many

22. Robert W. Hamblin, "Robert Penn Warren at the 1965 Southern Literary Festival: A Personal Recollection," *Southern Literary Journal* 22 (Spring 1990), 53–62; Eudora Welty, untitled speech, p. 7, Southern Literary Festival, 23 April 1965, Welty Collection, Mississippi Department of Archives and History, Jackson, Mississippi.

23. David L. Chappell, *Inside Agitators: White Southerners in the Civil Rights Movement* (Baltimore: Johns Hopkins University Press, 1994), xxv.

years after William Winter's election as governor of Mississippi, Welty continued to sport a Winter bumper sticker on her car; in 1988 a full-page ad in the *New York Times* contained Eudora Welty's signature in support of the word *liberal*; and in 1992 a Clinton-Gore bumper sticker greeted those who knocked on her front door both before and long after election day. The convergence of public and private has continued to be a factor in Eudora Welty's life, but it was most ardently felt and acted upon in 1952 and 1963–64. For Welty, Stevenson's campaign for the presidency and the civil rights struggle of the sixties were causes that transcended the writer's need to be a "privileged observer."[24]

24. Welty, *One Writer's Beginnings*, 21.

*Suzan Harrison*

## "Racial Content Espied"

Modernist Politics, Textuality, and Race in Eudora Welty's "The Demonstrators"

Is Eudora Welty a political writer? Only ten years ago, most critics agreed that Welty eschewed the political in favor of the personal, choosing to focus on the interior worlds of individual and family rather than on larger social issues. In her valuable and highly influential early study of Welty's fiction, Ruth Vande Kieft made the claim that "Eudora Welty's stories are largely concerned with mysteries of the inner life," and many critics followed suit. For example, D. James Neault argued that Welty's fiction focuses on "the interaction of a single consciousness" rather than on "historical effect or social consciousness." Critics tend to read even her works that include historical figures in terms of interiority rather than society. Michael Kreyling says of her Natchez fiction, "Starting with the Trace of history, Welty pushes through to the Trace of self." Feminist critics marked the first exceptions to the tendency to see Welty's fiction as apolitical. As early as 1979, Peggy Whitman Prenshaw's essay "Woman's World, Man's Place: The Fiction of Eudora Welty" explored Welty's resistance to traditional patriarchal social structures. Since then, numerous excellent studies have explored the gender politics of Welty's fiction. But the political dimensions of her work not overtly related to gender have not received much critical attention until quite recently.[1]

1. Ruth Vande Kieft, *Eudora Welty*, rev. ed. (Boston: Twayne Publishers, 1987), 14; D. James Neault, "Time in the Fiction of Eudora Welty," in *A Still Moment: Essays on the Art of Eudora Welty*, ed. John F. Desmond (Metuchen, N.J.: Scarecrow Press, 1978), 35; Michael Kreyling, "The Natchez Trace in Eudora Welty's Fiction," *Southern Quarterly* 29 (1991): 169; Peggy Whitman Prenshaw, "Woman's Place: The Fiction of Eudora Welty," in *Eudora Welty: A Form of*

Indeed, the most sustained negative criticism of Eudora Welty's fiction has to do with what some readers perceive as Welty's lack of attention to contemporary social and political realities. In particular, readers have challenged her treatment (or neglect) of racial issues. Diana Trilling set the tone for this sort of criticism in her 1946 review of *Delta Wedding,* which she called a "narcissistic Southern fantasy," complaining that "instead of the trenchant and objective commentator we hoped [Welty] would be, [she is] just another if more ingenious dreamer on the Southern past." In a 1973 article, "Blacks as Primitives in Eudora Welty's Fiction," John R. Cooley argued that "although Welty's nonfiction shows the sympathy and understanding of a southern liberal regarding civil rights and racial injustice, the black portraits in her fiction are sadly thin, unconvincing physiognomies. She is content to sketch in these black portraits in hyperbolic fashion, relying heavily on eccentricities." Welty is among the women writers who Richard H. King claimed in 1980 "were not concerned primarily with the larger cultural, racial, and political themes." More recently, Carolyn Heilbrun has argued that "the nostalgia and romanticizing" in which Welty indulges in *One Writer's Beginnings* are dangerous because they "mask . . . unrecognized anger" and allow readers to read her fiction for "what she can offer of reassurance and the docile acceptance of what is given" and to ignore the political dimensions of her work.[2]

The view of Welty as an apolitical writer is reinforced by her own 1965 essay "Must the Novelist Crusade?"—which she wrote in response to the external pressure she felt during the 1960s to "do something about" the racial situation in the South. The piece outlines her argument against the "crusader-novelist," one who writes fiction to prove a point, who replaces "climax" with "judgment," "distort[s] a work of passion for the sake of a cause," and creates, instead of a work

---

*Thanks,* ed. Louis Dollarhide and Ann J. Abadie (Jackson: University Press of Mississippi, 1979), 46–77.

2. Diana Trilling, "Fiction in Review" (review of *Delta Wedding*), *Nation,* May 11, 1946, 578; John R. Cooley, "Blacks as Primitives in Eudora Welty's Fiction," *Forum* 14 (1973): 20; Richard H. King, *A Southern Renaissance: The Cultural Awakening of the American South, 1930–1955* (New York: Oxford University Press, 1980), 8; Carolyn Heilbrun, *Writing a Woman's Life* (New York: Norton, 1988), 13–5.

of imagination, "a piece of catering." I believe it is a mistake, however, to read "Must the Novelist Crusade?" as Welty's manifesto for the separation of fiction from the political realm. While she clearly rejects one particular paradigm of the relationship between fiction and politics, she does not thereby deny fiction's connection to the world of social interaction, ethics, and value judgment. As I have argued elsewhere, crusading is not a useful metaphor for describing the political dimensions of Welty's fiction. Engaging in "conquest, conversion through coercion, ideological rigidity, and violent erasure of difference," crusaders are not condoned in Welty's work, and "Must the Novelist Crusade?" makes clear that Welty rejects ideological fiction motivated by hatred, self-justification, self-defense, rebuttal, and apology. Yet numerous passages in this and other essays and interviews demonstrate Welty's belief "that morality as shown through human relationships is the whole heart of fiction, and the serious writer has never lived who dealt with anything else." "I was always writing about justice and injustice," she claimed. "No writer can write without moral commitments and moral feelings at the very root."[3]

So perhaps the question should not be *is* Welty's fiction political, but *how* is Welty's fiction political? How does her work engage the political issues of injustice, morality, and human relationships? Several recent studies suggest that the political dimension of Welty's fiction may lie in the style of the stories, in her play with the structure and process of storytelling. Susan Donaldson locates a political Welty in her feminist aesthetics, in which "questioning, openness, and transformation constitute both subject and technique." In contrast, Linda Orr sees Welty as practicing a highly problematic politics of "seduction and southern equivocation" in her denial of "the duplicity of the southern story." For Rebecca Mark, Welty's feminist intertextuality is political, allowing the fiction to transform "Western narratives of rape,

3. Eudora Welty, "Must the Novelist Crusade?" in *The Eye of the Story: Selected Essays and Reviews* (New York: Random House, 1978), 148, 149, 157; Suzan Harrison, " 'It's Still a Free Country': Constructing Race, Identity, and History in Eudora Welty's 'Where Is the Voice Coming From?' " *Mississippi Quarterly* 50 (1997): 646; Jeanne Rolf Nostrandt, "Fiction as Event: An Interview with Eudora Welty," in *More Conversations with Eudora Welty*, ed. Peggy Whitman Prenshaw (Jackson: University Press of Mississippi, 1996), 30.

domination, and victimization of the feminine by the masculine into narratives of engagement, battle, confrontation, fertility, sexual exchange between masculine and feminine, finally challenging the very viability of the two terms." Barbara Ladd, too, views Welty's intertextuality as political. Arguing against the critical tendency to read the Welty canon as ahistorical, Ladd examines the intertextual relationship of *The Golden Apples* with Faulkner's *Go Down, Moses* to show how Welty's rewriting of Faulkner works "to relocate, to center, the woman's voice with respect to official History, to make the Historically invisible woman visible, to make silence speak—and speak in ways that undermine the ideologies of gender, particularly the ideologies of gender and authorship."[4] In an effort to further explore the political dimensions of Welty's work, the present article will focus on "The Demonstrators," an elusive, ambivalent, and contradictory exploration of the construction of racial identities in the context of the American civil rights movement. In its play with the form of the short story, the reading strategies we bring to texts, and textuality itself, this story is a valuable text for looking at the ways in which for Welty stories themselves are always political.

Welty wrote "The Demonstrators" during a politically charged time. By November 1966, when the story first appeared in the *New Yorker*, the racial situation in the South in general and Mississippi in particular had become increasingly complicated, volatile, and violent. Any hope for an easy transition from the segregated society of the Jim Crow era to an integrated national identity had been assaulted by the spread of violence. Between 1963 and 1966, Byron de la Beckwith was tried

4. Susan Donaldson, "Meditations on Nonpresence: Re-Visioning the Short Story in Eudora Welty's *The Wide Net*," *Journal of the Short Story in English* 11 (1988): 76; Linda Orr, "The Duplicity of the Southern Story: Reflections on Reynolds Price's *The Surface of Earth* and Eudora Welty's 'The Wide Net,'" in *Eloquent Obsessions: Writing Cultural Criticism*, ed. Marianna Torgovnick (Durham: Duke University Press, 1994), 74n37, 67; Rebecca Mark, *The Dragon's Blood: Feminist Intertextuality in Eudora Welty's "The Golden Apples"* (Jackson: University Press of Mississippi, 1994), 6; Barbara Ladd, "'Too Positive a Shape Not to Be Hurt': *Go Down Moses*, History, and the Woman Artist in Eudora Welty's *The Golden Apples*," *Bucknell Review* 39 (1995): 81.

twice for the murder of Medgar Evers, each trial ending in a hung jury. The year 1964 juxtaposed the youthful hope and enthusiasm of Freedom Summer with the murders of young civil rights activists Michael Schwerner, James Chaney, and Andy Goodman. Progress toward civil rights in the courts was countered by a widespread program of Klan terror, including fire bombings of black churches, Jewish businesses and temples, and the homes of civil rights workers and African American leaders.

In an 1978 interview with Tom Royals and John Little, Welty described "The Demonstrators" as "a reflection of society at the time." "I was writing," she continued, "about where I was living and the complexity of those changes. I think a lot of my work then suggested that it's not just a matter of cut and dried right and wrong—'We're right—You're wrong,' 'We're black, you're white.' You know, I wanted to show the complexity of it all." But the world of the story—the fictional town of Holden, Mississippi—is divided into black and white; as we discover on Dr. Richard Strickland's journey back into the center of town after treating Ruby Gaddy, the black and white districts of Holden are separated by the railroad tracks, which are traversed by "a grade crossing with a bad record."[5] The doctor's journey from the white section of town where he lives and works into the black district is, as Suzanne Ferguson points out, represented by a marked shift in imagery and syntax: "As the doctor moves out of the refined world of the retired schoolteacher, Miss Pope, in which his broken marriage is a solecism punishable by a whipping, the syntax loosens, the imagery becomes more sensuous, and metaphors and similes begin to appear. . . . Suggestions of a magical night journey are implicit . . . in . . . [the doctor's] ignorance of his goal, and the strangeness of his arrival." The words Ferguson uses to describe the changes in language and image—*loosens, sensuous, night, magical, strangeness*—echo the characteristics and associations traditionally projected onto the black Other by

5. Tom Royals and John Little, "A Conversation with Eudora Welty," in *Conversations with Eudora Welty,* ed. Peggy Whitman Prenshaw (Jackson: University Press of Mississippi, 1984), 259; Eudora Welty, "The Demonstrators," in *The Collected Stories of Eudora Welty* (New York: Harcourt Brace, 1980), 616. Hereafter cited parenthetically by page number in the text.

white culture: "the power of illicit sexuality, chaos, madness, impropriety, anarchy, strangeness, and helpless, hapless desire," in Toni Morrison's words.[6] Dr. Strickland's experience at Ruby's mother's house is one of radical otherness, charged with sexuality, violence, and exotic chaos; in the poorly lighted bedroom, where "the nipples of [Ruby's] breasts cast shadows that looked like figs" (610), observers answer his questions with questions of their own as guinea pigs run like "lightning" around the room and chickens roost in trees.

But Welty's story works to question this construction of the black Other through an emphasis on textuality. Embedded in the text is a parodic newspaper account—with a clearly political agenda—of the events of the narrative, and newspapers are mentioned multiple times throughout the story. In addition, intertextual references to epics and myths participate in the work's critical interrogation of racial constructions. In *Writing between the Lines: Race and Intertextuality*, Aldon L. Nielsen reminds us: "Just as the terms *black* and *white* serve, not, as observation will always confirm, to denote clearly demarcated differences in skin pigmentation, but to organize the meanings of human lives beneath constructed racial rubrics, so do language practices recognizable as racially motivated among native speakers serve to carve up territories of racial connotation rather than to reflect preexistent cultural facts."[7] "The Demonstrators" is a story about the power of stories to shape our interaction with the world, about the stories we construct to define national, cultural, and racial identities. Marked by a variety of racial constructions, it is a story about reading and writing race and about resisting and obstructing racial readings.

The story of Dr. Strickland's encounters with Ruby Gaddy and Dove Collins is framed by references to the aforementioned Miss Marcia Pope, "who had taught three generations of Holden, Mississippi, its Latin, civics, and English" (608). Author of white Holden's under-

---

6. Suzanne Ferguson, "The 'Assault of Hope': Style's Substance in Welty's 'The Demonstrators,'" in *Eudora Welty: Eye of the Storyteller*, ed. Dawn Trouard (Kent, Ohio: Kent State University Press, 1989), 47; Toni Morrison, *Playing in the Dark: Whiteness and the Literary Imagination* (Cambridge: Harvard University Press, 1992), 80–1.

7. Aldon L. Nielsen, *Writing between the Lines: Race and Intertextuality* (Athens: University of Georgia Press, 1994), 7.

standing of tradition and arbiter of its social relations, Miss Marcia can quote "great wads of Shakespeare and *'Arma virumque cano'*" (608). Welty's reference here to the opening line of Virgil's *Aeneid* invites multiple interpretations. "I sing of warfare and a man at war" might refer to the pervasive racism in the Jim Crow era, to the civil rights movement's war against segregation and racial injustice, to the white South's feeling of being embattled by the movement, to Dr. Strickland's weariness over his regional and personal divisions (he and his wife are separated), or to the violence between Ruby and Dove. Moreover, the *Aeneid* is an epic myth of national identity, calling our attention to the relationship between nation and text, to the role of narrative and myth in the construction and interpretation of national and individual identities.

Miss Pope considers herself to be self-sufficient—"only Miss Marcia Pope was still quite able to take care of herself" (622)—but there is ample evidence in the story that the traditional social order she represents is disintegrating. Bedridden, subject to seizures, and dependent on Dr. Strickland, she is an anachronism in the world represented in the next paragraph by the newspaper picture "of a young man burning his draft card before a camera" (608). Further evidence of social breakdown is suggested by the repeated pattern of marital failure in the story. What goes wrong in the relationship between Dove Collins and his common-law wife Ruby Gaddy is never revealed; it remains a mystery, a gap or absence in the text. But the effect of that failure is the dramatic mutual violence that kills both Dove and Ruby. The failure of Dr. Strickland's marriage to Irene Roberts results from the loss of a shared love and concern figured by their child Sylvia, "injured at birth" (616). Although "as yet it was not divorce" (617), there is little in the story to indicate any sort of reconciliation. The third failed marriage is recounted in the second paragraph of the embedded newspaper story: "Reputedly en route to see his fiancé," Billy Lee Warrum Jr. "was pronounced dead on arrival" (619), the victim of a motorcycle accident. These failed, destructive, or unconsummated marriages point to a loss of connection in the larger social context of the story—between Holden's black and white communities. In other words, the personal is political in this story, as the social and political disorder of the story's civil rights setting is manifest in the personal lives and relationships of the characters. As Albert Devlin observes, "in 'The Demonstrators' social disruption is revealed to be concurrent with personal, familial disorder."[8]

This disorder is evident in Dr. Strickland's inability to recognize Ruby Gaddy. The story positions Ruby as a text that Strickland cannot interpret because the expectations and strategies he brings to his reading—racially inflected strategies—interfere with his ability to see what is in front of him. Multiple references to newspapers reinforce the textuality of Ruby's body. Strickland approaches her along "a path of newspapers laid down on the floor from the doorway to the bed" (609); the walls of the room are "newspapered" (610); and Ruby's son sits "on a clean newspaper" laid on floor (611). While the surrounding of Ruby by newspapers prefigures her entrapment in the newspaper article later in the story, it also points to the significance of reading; the scene calls to mind an earlier Welty story in which newspapers are the vehicle for another Ruby's encounter with language. In "A Piece of News," Ruby Fisher's discovery of her name in a newspaper serves as a metaphor for the possibilities and dangers of a woman's relationship to language. As Patricia Yaeger says of this earlier story, it dramatizes both "one woman's victimization by masculine culture and texts" and her "real and potential pleasure in speech, her sense of discovering a verbal possibility that is submerged, repressed, embattled—but cherished by the narrator all the same."[9] In "The Demonstrators," published twenty-five years later, the politics of language are further complicated by issues of race and scientific authority, as the white Dr. Strickland, with the authority of his position as the town's physician, examines Ruby Gaddy's black body in the middle of the newspapered room.

Dr. Strickland tries first to read "the young, very black-skinned woman" in the "white dress" according to her position in white society: "A maid?" (609). When this strategy fails—"the white was not the starched material of a uniform but shiny, clinging stuff" (609)—he

8. Albert J. Devlin, *Eudora Welty's Chronicle: A Story of Mississippi Life* (Jackson: University Press of Mississippi, 1983), 143.

9. Patricia Yaeger, *Honey-Mad Women: Emancipatory Strategies in Women's Writing* (New York: Columbia University Press, 1988), 114.

reads her as "a patient," fragmenting and objectifying her, examining *"the* breast" and *"the* wound" (609; my emphasis). When this reading also fails to explain what has happened, the frustrated doctor resorts to the "who, what, when, where" of a news reporter:

> "Who did this to her?"
> The room went quiet; he only heard the men in the yard laughing together. "How long ago?" He looked at the path of newspapers spread on the floor. "Where? Where did it happen? How did she get here?" (610)

But, as the others in the room make clear, these are not the correct questions to ask in order to interpret the text of Ruby's body. "'Don't you know her?'" cry the women in the room, "as if he never was going to hit on the right question" (610). When he finally does recognize her, exclaiming, "Why, it's Ruby" (611), Welty's use of italics draws attention to the continued limits in the doctor's reading of her identity: "Ruby Gaddy *was* the maid. Five days a week she cleaned up on the second floor of the bank building where he kept his office and consulting rooms" (611). While this reading of Ruby's identity may be more accurate than his first, it is still reductive, once again defining her in terms of her position among Holden's privileged white populace.

The struggle over the interpretation of Ruby's identity positions her body as a site of conflict and resistance, as a politicized text. Diane Roberts claims that "representations of whites and blacks fuel a war over the body: the black body, the white body, the female body. . . . The black body in white America bears the marks both of desire and disgust."[10] Ruby's body is marked by sexuality ("the breast") and violence ("the wound below the breast") (609). Several images in this section of the story suggest that Ruby is vulnerable to further violence, that the doctor's misreadings are threatening to her. "Fastened around her throat" is a necklace like "sharp and pearly teeth" (610); the light is "like something that would devour her" (612). She is in danger of being consumed by the doctor's interpretation. But Ruby refuses to submit to the doctor's authority, refuses to be reduced to either maid

---

10. Diane Roberts, *The Myth of Aunt Jemima: Representations of Race and Region* (London: Routledge, 1994), 2, 9.

or patient, or even the Ruby Gaddy that Dr. Strickland believes he knows. She remains throughout the scene a mystery, never speaking, refusing to answer the doctor's questions, to submit to his misreadings; she responds instead with a "glowing look" (611), a luxurious sigh (612), "the unresponding gaze of ownership" (613), and "eyes . . . fixed with possession" (613).

In her resistance, her obstruction of the doctor's attempts to interpret her, Ruby's relationship to the doctor parallels the relationship between a Welty story and a reader that Harriet Pollack articulates in "Words between Strangers: On Welty, Her Style, and Her Audience." Pollack describes the fictional technique in particular stories as paradoxically inviting and obstructionist, "a richly articulate style that holds back initially as if she were reluctant to give her fiction to her audience." Pollack adopts the term "obstructionist" from Welty's essay "The Reading and Writing of Short Stories" (first published in the March 1949 *Atlantic* and later revised and included in *The Eye of the Story* as "Looking at Short Stories"). In this essay Welty claims, "We have observed that the finest story writers seem to be in one sense obstructionists. As if they held back their own best interests—or what would be in another writer their best interests." Certainly "The Demonstrators" belongs to the category of Welty's fiction that Pollack examines in her article, those stories "which may delight readers . . . yet leave them intrigued, feeling as if perhaps they have missed something in their understanding."[11]

Furthermore, Pollack's description of the text-reader relationship is also valuable in understanding the complex interaction between Ruby and Dr. Strickland and in theorizing the political dimensions of Welty's fiction. Pollack argues that "Welty's style demonstrates . . . the primacy of the text in the reading process."[12] During the interaction between Strickland and Ruby, the power shifts from the doctor, with his authoritative interpretive framework, to Ruby, the text he seeks to

---

11. Harriet Pollack, "Words between Strangers: On Welty, Her Style, and Her Audience," in *Welty: A Life in Literature,* ed. Albert J. Devlin (Jackson: University Press of Mississippi, 1987), 54; Eudora Welty, "Looking at Short Stories" in *Eye of the Story,* 105; Pollack, "Words between Strangers," 55.

12. Pollack, "Words between Strangers," 59.

interpret. As a physician, Dr. Strickland is accustomed to wielding authority over bodies; the body is his field of knowledge and power, the object to his subject. But Ruby resists his treatment, several times covering the wound with her hand, holding her breath when he uses his stethoscope, and pulling her hand away as he tries to take her pulse. Ruby is unwilling to expose herself to the doctor's scientific authority and objectifying gaze. She resists inscription into the white fictions that inform the doctor's reading of her and insists on her position as an embodied black subject.

Pollack's description of Welty's "healthy exasperation with wrong-headed readers" has its counterpoint in the exasperation of the women observing the doctor's treatment of Ruby.[13] "*Nothin'!*" they cry in answer to his question, "Ruby, this is Dr. Strickland. What have you been up to?" (611). They respond to the doctor's interrogation not by answering his questions, but by telling him whether he's asking the right ones:

"She married? Where's her husband? That where the trouble was?"
Now, while the women in the room, too, broke out in sounds of amusement, the doctor stumbled where he stood. "What the devil's running in here? Rats?"
"You wrong there." (611)

Dr. Strickland's "rats" turn out to be guinea pigs, "running underfoot, not only in this room but on the other side of the wall. . . . 'Catch those things!' he exclaimed. 'They lightning. Get away from you so fast!' said a voice" (611). Unlike the guinea pigs of medical research, controlled by and subjected to the intentions of human researchers, these creatures are wild and uncontrollable. Running in all directions, distracting and tripping the doctor, these guinea pigs are images of excess, indicating that there is much more going on in the scene than the doctor understands. "Race," notes critic Nielsen, "is excessive and unruly," and in this scene the guinea pigs serve, to use Lois Welch's term, as a "literalized metaphor" of that untamed excess of race that eludes and exceeds the doctor's desire to limit and control it.[14] The erratic,

13. Ibid., 70.
14. Nielsen, *Writing between the Lines*, 17; Lois M. Welch, "The Wilder Welty: Lizard Earrings and Literalized Metaphor," paper read at "Mississippi Home Ties: A Eudora Welty Conference" (Jackson, 1997).

wild, excessive motion of the guinea pigs destabilizes the scene and obstructs Dr. Strickland's desire for coherence and order, just as the scenes in the Gaddy household displace the authority of the doctor's disembodied white, masculine discourse.

"Welty's use of obstruction," writes Pollack, "could be a technique for shaping a responsive reader through her control of the textual experience. By composing texts that require attentiveness and yield best to rereading, she might invite a reader to practice self-correction." The many obstructions Dr. Strickland encounters move him to revise his reading of Ruby. The connection between Ruby's body and the text is emphasized: when Ruby begins to control her body, she also takes control of the narrative's focus. The doctor's emphasis shifts from what he is doing to what Ruby is doing, from himself as reader to Ruby as text: "'Why, she's bleeding inside,' he retorted. 'What do you think *she's* doing?'" (613). He acknowledges Ruby's autonomy and authority: "She knew what she had" (613). The obstructions have taught him, in Pollack's words, "to read for the sake of encounter rather than appropriation," and he is at this point able to recognize others in the house— "Oree, the legless woman" (614), the "tyrant" of the train station (614), and Lucille, who "was washing for [his] mother when [he] was born" (613).[15]

The description of the laundry the doctor sees as he leaves the Gaddy household echoes the interior scene's reversal of white culture's centrality and black culture's marginal, dependent position. "Flying around this house in the moonlight" are dresses he recognizes: "his mother's gardening dress, his sister Annie's golf dress, his wife's favorite duster that she liked to wear across the breakfast table, and more dresses less substantial. . . . With sleeves spread wide, trying to scratch his forehead with the tails of their skirts, they were flying around this house in the moonlight" (615). Circling the site of the black embodied subject, these flying dresses form a ring of disembodied white images, a reversal of the doctor's earlier perspective of Ruby as a black satellite to his own white community.

In Ruby's obstructionist textuality, Welty rejects and rewrites the patriarchal reduction of the feminine to a blank page passively await-

15. Pollack, "Words between Strangers," 59–60, 77.

ing the mark of the masculine pen. Textuality is not passive for Welty; instead, it is a site of potential resistance to privileged male—and, in this case, white—versions of story and history. Textuality is, of course, at risk of appropriation, misreading, and exposure, but it is also the site most open to rewriting the traditional constructions of the feminine or black Other and to revealing the operation of ideology in our culture's official stories and histories.

Ruby's textuality is not the only play with the politics of text and story in "The Demonstrators." In the remainder of the narrative, Welty explores a variety of ways in which fiction can exploit, rather than be exploited by, that politics. Driving home after his disorienting experience in the Gaddy house, Dr. Strickland experiences a modernist epiphany, a moment of illumination signaled in the text by the "long beam of electric light" (616) of a train passing through Holden. This epiphany works momentarily to resolve the contradictions, heal the social fractures, restore cultural unity, and replace the chaos of the earlier scenes with the order of art. At its center is a china cup that unifies past and present, black and white, suffering and comfort: "He had been carried a cup tonight that might have been his own mother's china or his wife's mother's—the rim not a perfect round, a thin, porcelain cup his lips and his fingers had recognized. In that house of murder, comfort had been brought to him at his request" (616). The moment of illumination engenders a "feeling of well-being" that "increased, until he had come to the point of tears" (616). Following it is a page and a half that describes the traditional, ordered Holden of the doctor's past and the disintegration of that community in the story's present. Dr. Strickland is Holden's only physician and the son of the town's previous doctor: "The watch he carried was the gold one that had belonged to his father" (616). By virtue of profession and history, he is among the town's economic and power elite. But as a result of the civil rights movement, Holden's social order has been disrupted by "the bitterness, intractability that divided everybody and everything" (617). The epiphany repairs the agonizing social rifts underlying that bitterness and intractability, so that "suddenly, tonight, things had seemed just the way they used to seem. He had felt as though someone had stopped him on the street and offered to carry his load for a while—had insisted on it—some old, trusted, half-forgotten family friend that he had lost sight of since youth. Was it the sensation, now returning, that there was still allowed to everybody on earth a *self*— savage, death-defying, private? The pounding of his heart was like the assault of hope, throwing itself against him without a stop, merciless" (617–8).

Had Welty ended "The Demonstrators" at this point, with the doctor's moment of revelation, we would have a traditional modernist story in which the unity and resolution of art replaced the fragmentation and disintegration of the social, cultural world. As Donaldson observes, Welty is often thought of as writing the type of modernist story "rendered whole and complete by the moment of illumination." But the narrative does not end with Dr. Richard Strickland's moment of illumination, and Welty uses the remaining third of the story not only to call such a resolution into question, but also to critique the politics of the sort of modernist aesthetic that would allow Dr. Strickland, Holden's well-meaning, compassionate white moderate to long nostalgically for "things" to be "just the way they used to seem" during the Jim Crow years before the civil rights movement. If, as Danièle Pitavy-Souques claims, the modernist "*need* to see the world familiarly is a result of the preoccupation with the self rather than the world," then Welty's story critiques the dangerous appropriation or exclusion of alterity necessary to make the world mirror the self.[16] Instead of a modernist story of cultural loss, "The Demonstrators," with its consideration of racial politics in the civil rights–era South, reveals the dangers inherent in the centralizing impulse of modernist nostalgia.

As the story continues after his epiphany, Dr. Strickland's feeling of comfort does not last; it "gradually ebb[s] away, like nausea put down" (618), and the description of the town belies the epiphany. The language describing Strickland's drive home is laced with images of emptiness, disorder, desolation, and lethargy, as Welty echoes the imagery of T. S. Eliot's poetry in order to question the politics of modernism. Holden is "lying out there in the haze of the long rainless fall" (615), recalling the drought of *The Waste Land:* "Here there is no water."

16. Donaldson, "Meditations on Nonpresence," 76; Danièle Pitavy-Souques, "A Blazing Butterfly: The Modernity of Eudora Welty," in *Welty: A Life in Literature,* ed. Albert J. Devlin (Jackson: University Press of Mississippi, 1987), 122.

The banks of the creek are littered with "narrow bottles . . . in which paregoric was persistently sold under the name of Mother's Helper" (615). A grass fire burns "sparkless and nerveless, not to be confused with a burning church, but like anesthetic made visible" (616), echoing the "patient etherized upon a table" of "The Love Song of J. Alfred Prufrock." Playing on the doctor's name, which itself suggests a waste land, Ruth Vande Kieft calls Holden a "small town in a stricken land." The description of the doctor's barren life associates him with the general misery of the land: "Now his father and his mother both were dead, his sister had married and moved away, a year ago his child had died. Then, back in the summer, he and his wife had separated, by her wish" (616). As Ferguson observes, this barrenness is evident in the prose itself. In the reflective passage summarizing the doctor's life, "not a single simile or metaphor occurs, in contrast to the previous section of description, in which they cluster, sometimes several to a sentence." Dr. Strickland is represented as impotent; he has not been able to save or even comfort Ruby Gaddy, and as his wife points out, he cannot face telling Herman Fairbrothers "what's the matter with him" (617). Even his epiphany, mixing as it does Eliot's "memory and desire," has failed him. As he drives on into the center of town images of emptiness multiply: the sign on the "shut down movie house . . . spelled out in empty sockets 'BROADWAY'"; "the flagpole looked feathery, like the track of a jet that is already gone from the sky"; and the water tank seems ghostly and impermanent, "pale as a balloon that might be only tethered here" (618)—images that find their counterparts in the sightless eyes and the "shape without form, shade without color" of Eliot's "The Hollow Men."[17]

Although Dr. Strickland experiences the profound sense of cultural loss that haunts *The Waste Land* and the rest of Eliot's early poetry, Welty's story is not a text that mourns that loss. Instead, it is a story that reveals the political dimension of such modernist angst. In *The Dragon's Blood*, Rebecca Mark demonstrates the ways in which in

17. T. S. Eliot, *Collected Poems, 1909–1962* (New York: Harcourt Brace, 1984), 3, 53, 66, 79; Ruth Vande Kieft, "Demonstrators in a Stricken Land" in *The Process of Fiction*, ed. Barbara MacKenzie (New York: Harcourt Brace, 1974), 143; Ferguson, "'Assault of Hope,'" 50.

*The Golden Apples* Welty is engaged in "parodying, battling, and above all transforming the subtext of masculine superiority" in modernist versions of the western heroic myth. As Mark argues, male modernist writers lament "the breakdown of the heroic narrative, a narrative that no longer . . . has the vitality to generate text."[18] In "The Demonstrators" Welty brings that critique of a patriarchal, elitist tradition to bear upon the politics of race in the civil rights era.

As Dr. Strickland comes upon the body of Dove Collins (Ruby Gaddy's husband, and owner of the wild guinea pigs) lying in the center of the empty town, the car headlights transform him from "prone and colorless" into "golden yellow" (618–9). The imagery here evokes the fertility myths so important in *The Waste Land:* "The man looked as if he had been sleeping all day in a bed of flowers and rolled in their pollen" (619). In the myth of the fisher king, some sort of violent treachery or betrayal has devastated both land and society, and a sacrificial reparation, a ritual death and burial, are required to restore the lost wholeness and renew fertility, communion, and order. In *From Ritual to Romance,* from which Eliot took his poem's title and some of its imagery, Jessie Weston describes several features shared by the many versions of the myth. She claims "that the main object of the Quest is the restoration to health and vigour of a King suffering from infirmity caused by wounds, sickness, or old age, . . . whose infirmity, for some mysterious and unexplained reason, reacts disastrously upon his kingdom. . . . [T]he misfortune which has fallen upon the country is that of a prolonged drought, which has destroyed vegetation, and left the land Waste." Several critics have interpreted the golden, pollen-coated Dove as a positive image of sacrifice necessary to redeem the ills of society, symbolized by the wasteland imagery. Ferguson reads Dove's dying body as an image of mythic sacrifice of the sort needed for restoration: "This culmination of the imagery of light in the story, with its magically beautiful simile, transforms the dying murderer, Dove, into a figure of myth or dream: a sleeping flower-god absorbing life from pollen." Vande Kieft calls him "the abstract self of Dr. Strickland's imaginings become visible."[19] Certainly his name, Dove, carries with

18. Mark, *Dragon's Blood,* 6, 21
19. Jessie Weston, *From Ritual to Romance* (New York: Doubleday, 1957), 20–1; Ferguson, "'Assault of Hope,'" 51; Vande Kieft, "Demonstrators in a Stricken Land," 147.

it associations of rescue and redemption, evoking the dove of Noah's ark and the doves of the annunciation and baptism of Christ.

I would argue, however, that if we accept an unproblematically positive interpretation of this image, we, following the doctor's lead, are in danger of reading to appropriate rather than to encounter. The "mythicized" image of Dove marks another obstruction in the text, a point at which, in Pollack's terms, Welty's fiction "elicits expectations that it promptly defies." The narrative impulse toward myth is countered at this point by a disruptive gesture that focuses our attention on Dove's black body inscribed by violence: "The man raised up on his hands and looked at him like a seal. Blood laced his head like a net through which he had broken" (619). The image of Dove as a golden fertility god is replaced by an image of blood and entrapment. Linda Orr notes that Welty often figures narrative as a web or net. In this case, we can interpret the net of blood as representing the repressive mythologies of racial identity, the myths of blood, by which white culture has sought to construct, control, and constrain black Americans. In *Reading "The Waste Land,"* Jewel Brooker and Joseph Bentley argue that through myth, "Eliot is trying to provide a means for the reader to transcend jarring and incompatible worlds, to move to a higher viewpoint that both includes and transcends the contemporary world." But as Rachel Blau DuPlessis explains, the modernist use of myth is problematic since "it is imbued with a nostalgia for center and order, for elitist or exclusive solutions, for transforming historical time into myth."[20] Breaking through this net of blood, Dove is no "golden god" or "abstract self" (a construction that has been used time and again to exclude alterity), but an embodied black self, vulnerable to the myths suggesting that black sacrifice is necessary to restore the fertility and vitality of the white southern community.

Welty reworks Eliot's dismembering and re-membering of the mythic male fertility figure to demonstrate the racial and gendered

20. Pollack, "Words between Strangers,"59; Orr, "Duplicity of the Southern Story," 62–3; Jewel Spears Brooker and Joseph Bentley, *Reading "The Waste Land": Modernism and the Limits of Interpretation* (Amherst: University of Massachusetts Press, 1990), 59; Rachel Blau DuPlessis, *The Pink Guitar: Writing as a Feminist Practice* (New York: Routledge, 1990), 152.

version of history in which it participates. "The Demonstrators" reveals that behind the modernist drive to displace the fragmentation of the present with the structure, coherence, and unity of myth lies the desire to replace historical difference with a mythologized Other. As every move toward myth in the story is obstructed by black embodiment, the desire for a fixed, mythic black Other is exposed as an avoidance of history, an avoidance particularly dangerous in the context of the civil rights movement by which black Americans sought to escape the confines of white mythologizing about race and gain access to historical agency.

Though the story works to critique traditional white constructions of black identity and the modernist desire for center and order, the embedded newspaper article, like the deputy sheriff's interpretation of Rider's actions in William Faulkner's "Pantaloon in Black," demonstrates the reification of binary racial identities. In a highly politicized parody of the white press's construction of race and racial unrest during the civil rights era, the *Sentinel*'s report of the event dramatizes the white town's resistance through the repeated claims that the event does not "carry racial significance" and "warrants no stir" (619). Caught in another textual net, Ruby and Dove (mistakenly identified as Dave in the story) are appropriated and misread in this article designed to reinforce the cultural myth of blacks as meaninglessly violent and whites as confused and blameless. "Well I'm surprised didn't more of them get hurt," reads a comment by the pastor of one of the town's white churches. "And yet they expect to be seated in our churches" (621). The county sheriff is quoted as saying, "That's one they can't pin the blame on us for. That's how they treat their own kind. Please take note our conscience is clear" (621). Reminding the reader once again of the politics of reading and the textuality of race, the article attempts to enact the process described by Frank Lentricchia in *Criticism and Social Change*: "to write is to know is to dominate." But Welty's story suggests that attempts to control and structure reality through writing are always subject to interpretation, appropriation, and rewriting. As Nielsen notes, "Writing, however, even the writing of racists, . . . that seeks to immure black experience within a silence beneath the imposed significations of white discourse cannot attain complete closure. It must be read, and thus it must open itself to rewriting by the other in whose place it would speak."[21] In the context of Welty's narrative, the newspaper article is revealed as a narrative construction of white identity rather than an accurate, objective description of black identity. In its evident desire to depoliticize the violence of Ruby and Dove's relationship, the article reveals the operation of politics in the official construction of events. The comment of the young civil rights demonstrator earlier in the story, "We are dramatizing your hostility" (617), seems superfluous in light of the *Sentinel* piece's vivid revelation of its white supremacist ideology. Welty's narrative works to obstruct the sort of appropriation that the *Sentinel* article dramatizes and that Dr. Strickland tries to impose upon Ruby Gaddy at the story's start. Situating the private quarrel between Ruby and Dove in the context of the civil rights movement, the story demonstrates the irony of the article's subhead, "No Racial Content Espied" (619).

At the end of the article, the narrator informs us that "the cook had refilled his cup without his noticing" (621). If, as seems likely, Dr. Strickland's cook is a black woman, then his failure to see her may suggest that despite what he experienced the evening before, he still fails "to see in time what it wouldn't . . . have occurred to him to look for" (617). The two "crusaders"—the young man burning his draft card and the young civil rights worker—enact public performances of political power, but they are not Welty's primary interest in this story. Instead, "The Demonstrators" explores the degree to which even private actions are politicized. Doctor Strickland's interaction with Ruby, Dove, the mayor, his estranged wife, and even the cook are all revealed to be political performances, implicating the performers in the culture's ideologies of race.

In her essay "The Duplicity of the Southern Story," Orr discusses her difficulties with the politics of Welty's fiction. Arguing that southern stories have participated in the hiding of that which is "unspeakable" in southern history, Orr objects that in Welty's stories, "despite whatever has gone on, all will be or remains well in the end. This reconciliation is not exactly a happy ending, but somehow the tensions,

21. Frank Lentricchia, *Criticism and Social Change* (Chicago: University of Chicago Press, 1983), 146; Nielsen, *Writing between the Lines*, 25.

conflicts, and hidden violence smooth over and allow nothing struc-
turally to shift." By the end of "The Demonstrators," however, something has shifted. While the story does not end with a damning exposure of the racist agenda of white-supremacist public rhetoric, the
closing paragraphs reveal the operation of racial politics in the private
and personal spheres. The story works to resist the sort of reconciliation and reduction to which Orr objects by calling our attention to the
politics of story. "You're not justified in putting a false front on things,
in my opinion. . . . Even for a good cause" (617), claims Dr. Strickland,
chastising a young civil rights worker for his paper's story of laborers
"forced at gunpoint to go into the fields at hundred-degree temperature
and pick cotton." "That didn't happen—there isn't any cotton in
June," chastises the doctor. But, as his wife points out, the doctor himself regularly participates in the same sort of falsifying: "*You* won't tell
Herman Fairbrothers what's the matter with him" (617). If, as Orr
claims, "a gap defines the South: between civility and violence, public
and private persona, not always or just the difference between the
truth and lie but between conflicting representations of history and
the self," I would argue that "The Demonstrators," with its exploration of the politics of textuality, tradition, and representation, works
to reveal rather than mask that gap and to explore the problematic stories it engenders.[22] All stories are suspect in Welty's text because they
are never pure, never free from personal and political agendas, but always complicitous. The closing words of "The Demonstrators," "or
such was her own opinion" (622), underscore the contingency of the
stories we tell ourselves and others.

22. Orr, "Duplicity of the Southern Story," 7–8, 53.

## Ann Romines

# A Voice from a Jackson Interior

## Eudora Welty and the Politics of Filial Piety

In the 1960s, large numbers of American women began to discover and acknowledge that the personal was political. Adrienne Rich wrote famously of the early sixties that she began then "to feel that politics was not something 'out there' but something 'in here' and the essence of my condition." For women writers in particular, the split between "private woman" and "public stage" that Mary Kelley has influentially anatomized in the careers of mid-nineteenth-century white, middle-class women writers seemed, a century later, to be part of a very distant past. Eudora Welty, however, resisted the prevailing rhetoric of the sixties and the stance of an activist writer like Rich. In 1970 she dismissed "Women's Liberation" as "noisiness"; in 1972 she added that "your private life should be kept private."[1]

As this collection begins to establish, Welty's published and public acts as a white southern woman writer *are* complexly, powerfully, and often effectively political—especially those that took place during the troubled years of the civil rights movement. In this essay, I want also to propose that the circumstances of the "private woman" Eudora Welty are deeply and importantly implicated in her short fiction of the 1960s, and that such implications extend the political impact of her career beyond her staunch support of liberal Democrats, her opposi-

---

1. Adrienne Rich, "When We Dead Awaken: Writing as Re-Vision," in *On Lies, Secrets, and Silence: Selected Prose 1966–1978* (New York: Norton, 1979), 33–49; Mary Kelley, *Private Woman, Public Stage: Literary Domesticity in Nineteenth-Century America* (New York: Oxford University Press, 1984), passim; Barbaralee Diamonstein, "Eudora Welty," in *Conversations with Eudora Welty*, ed. Peggy Whitman Prenshaw (Jackson: University Press of Mississippi, 1984), 36; Linda Kuehl, "The Art of Fiction XLVII: Eudora Welty," ibid., 81.

tion to racial segregation and other abuses of civil rights, and her advocacy of "peace, education, conservation, quiet"—the "causes" for which she attested support on a questionnaire.[2] A wider sense of the "political" will allow us to read both specific works and the entire shape of Welty's distinguished career—including its silences and absences—as illuminating and troubling texts of twentieth-century gender, race, and class politics.

Between 1955 and 1966, Eudora Welty was more housebound than she had ever been in her adult life. She was enmeshed in "troubles in the house," the long illnesses and deaths of her mother—for whom, as an unmarried and only daughter, she was primary caregiver—and her two brothers. During this period her responsibilities curtailed her earning power as well as her mobility. Her mother's illness was an extra drain on Welty's modest income, but, as she told an interviewer, she "couldn't leave home" to earn money in her usual way, through visits to distant colleges, because of the constraints of "illness in the house." In those same years, however, some of the largest dramas of U.S. political life were acted out closer and closer to Welty's Mississippi home, culminating in Medgar Evers's 1963 murder in Jackson. Many of the conditions of Eudora Welty's life in the early sixties seem to have conspired to insist that for her, too, politics was "in here" and "the essence of [her] condition." This is suggested by (among many other things) one of the titles she considered for what is perhaps the most overtly political of her works of fiction, the 1963 story based on Evers's murder, "Where Is the Voice Coming From?" One version of that story is headed, "A Voice from a Jackson Interior," suggesting that, in Welty's mind, politics might be closely linked with private spaces—in her case, a domestic Jackson interior.[3]

2. Diamonstein, "Eudora Welty," 38.
3. Jonathan Yardley, "A Quiet Lady in the Limelight," in *More Conversations with Eudora Welty,* ed. Peggy Whitman Prenshaw (Jackson: University of Mississippi Press, 1996), 8; Danny Romine Powell, *Parting the Curtains: Voices of the Great Southern Writers* (New York: Doubleday, 1994), 458; "A Voice from a Jackson Interior," Eudora Welty Collection, Mississippi Department of Archives and History, Jackson, Series 8, Box 14, Folder 2. Welty's partial solution to the dilemma of her intensified need for money and inability to travel was to

During the terrible decade that ended with her mother's and her brother Edward's deaths, within four days of each other, in January 1966—those protracted years of nursing, caregiving, and anxieties both personal and financial—Eudora Welty was a model of daughterly, sisterly devotion: the epitome of filial piety. As a daughter and sister myself, I can only hope to find the resources she marshaled, living through that harrowing time. In those years, Welty, who was in her vigorous late forties and early fifties, published only two stories, and those stories ended (to date) her career as a publishing author of short fiction—although she has continued to characterize herself as a "natural" short story writer and to speak of unfinished stories she hopes to complete and publish. Confronting those facts, I am tempted to join Welty's agent, Diarmuid Russell, in deploring her allegiance to filial piety. In 1960 and 1961, he wrote to her, "I still feel strongly you ought, willy nilly, to set aside time to write, something your own . . . to be committed to others wholly is not right." "You are doing all, and more, than your mother needs."[4]

Welty scholars have already begun to discuss the important ways in which her great fiction of the next decade, *Losing Battles* and *The Optimist's Daughter*, is animated by these troubling questions of filial piety. In this essay I want to suggest that the two sixties stories, "Where Is the Voice Coming From?" (1963) and "The Demonstrators" (1966, written in 1965), also evoke these questions, with an urgency that challenges the ideal of filial piety as trenchantly as anything Welty has written and frames it as an issue with deeply political repercussions. Both are stories of middle age, when many people (like Welty herself) encounter crises of filiality. In interviews and in her autobiography, Welty has returned to such issues; when asked if she felt torn between independence and family love, she replied (after nearly twenty years as sole survivor of her family of origin) in the present

---

teach her first writing workshop, at local Millsaps College. She solicited this job, even though she has said repeatedly that she is *not* a teacher, as her mother was before marrying. Thus an effect of this work may have been, once again, to intensify her bond with her mother.

4. Michael Kreyling, *Author and Agent: Eudora Welty and Diarmuid Russell* (New York: Farrar, Straus, Giroux, 1991), 200–1. In addition to the two short stories, Welty published *The Shoe Bird*, her only book for children, in 1964.

tense: "Oh yes, I still feel it. It haunts me. I think about how I could have managed it better."[5]

Filiality has at least two dictionary meanings: the relation of a child to a parent and the "sequence of generations." One classic response to human crises of filiality in the first sense is to turn to the second sense: to place (and re-place) oneself in a continuing sequence of generations, moving from the perspective of a child to that of a parent, a grandparent. For the male protagonists of "Voice" and "The Demonstrators," this is not an option; they are apparently childless, as are some of Welty's most intensely imagined female protagonists: Virgie Rainey, Laurel Hand, Julia Mortimer, Miss Eckhart. In fact, it is Miss Eckhart, of *The Golden Apples*, that Welty has named as the character with whom she feels "oddly in touch" and who comes closest to speaking for her, "the author, in person." Their commonality, she says, is their "love of . . . art." However, Welty and Miss Eckhart have another important and pertinent commonality that she did not choose to mention: they have both been single, childless, passionate middle-aged daughters, living in close filial relations with their disabled mothers.[6]

The sixties stories also draw on another close personal relationship, vaguely filial/familial itself: Welty's close ties to her home state. In interviews she tells again and again about accusing calls from the North during the civil rights movement: "Why aren't you going out there and writing about those devils you live with down there?" "Where Is the Voice Coming From?"—a response to Medgar Evers's murder—is written, extraordinarily, in the murderer's first-person voice. Welty described writing this political story in terms of near-familial intimacy: "I wrote from the interior . . . that world of hate that I felt I had grown up with and I felt I could speak as someone who knew it . . . really, I just wrote from deep feeling and horror."[7]

5. Hermione Lee, "Eudora Welty," in *More Conversations with Eudora Welty*, ed. Prenshaw, 149.

6. Eudora Welty, *One Writer's Beginnings* (Cambridge: Harvard University Press, 1984), 100–1. In a 1980 interview with Jo Brans, Welty described Miss Eckhart as being "trapped, you know, with her terrible old mother" (Prenshaw, ed., *Conversations with Eudora Welty*, 305).

7. Charles Ruas, "Eudora Welty," in *More Conversations with Eudora Welty*, ed. Prenshaw, 67; William F. Buckley Jr., "The Southern Imagination: An Inter-

\*   \*   \*

The narrator of "Where Is the Voice Coming From?" is a man who knows the markers of his hometown with the intimacy of total recall: he can recite every signboard on Nathan B. Forrest Road, from "Surplus and Salvage" to "Live Bait."[8] And he reads every class and economic signifier: the green (irrigated) July grass and paved street of black civil rights leader Roland Summers's home spell out his economic ascendancy over the lower-class and evidently unemployed white narrator, who is also competing with younger white males, the "babyface cops" (607) and the affluent "dern teenager[s]" (606) who drive their own cars, while he is in a truck he borrowed from his brother-in-law. Back at home after gunning down Summers, he is derided by the one person he tells, his wife: unimpressed and unfazed, she berates him for not waiting to shoot "somebody better" (605).

The story's pronouns offer important clues to this narrator's profound confusion about his relations with his community. "I," "we," "you," and "they" set up murderous oppositions. The unbearably hot local climate—92 degrees at 4 A.M.—establishes a communal "we" that the narrator shares with Summers even as he stalks him, hoping "one or the other of us wouldn't melt before it was over" (603). The narrator shoots Summers so that—for once—he can make clear distinctions between them: "*I'm* alive and *you* ain't," he declares to the corpse at his feet (604, emphasis mine). To the murderer's ambitious (and gainfully employed) wife, she and her husband are "we" only when community property is concerned; the lost gun is "*our* protection" but "*you're* the one they'll catch," she tells him (605–6, emphasis mine). The story is addressed to a white male collective "you" that shares the narrator's intimate knowledge of Thermopylae, including knowledge of how to find where "that nigger" Summers lives, even in the dark: "It's where you all go for the thing you want when you want it the most. Ain't that right?" (603). This *you* and *I* form a *we* on the basis of shared racial and sexual exploitation. Again and again, the nar-

---

view with Eudora Welty and Walker Percy," in *Conversations with Eudora Welty*, ed. Prenshaw, 101.

8. Eudora Welty, "Where Is the Voice Coming From?" in *Collected Stories of Eudora Welty* (New York: Harcourt Brace, 1980), 603, 604. Hereafter cited parenthetically by page number in the text.

rator deconstructs such collectivities as fast as he constructs them: "I don't owe nothing to Thermopylae. Didn't . . . [kill Summers] for you. . . . I done it for my own pure-D satisfaction" (605).

Why do I argue that this story raises questions of filial piety? Because the narrator, whatever else he may be, is a dutiful son. Standing over the corpse of Summers, he invokes his father to certify his victory: "There was one way left, for me to be ahead of you and stay ahead of you, *by Dad*, and I just taken it" (604, emphasis mine).[9] In 1963, many white Mississippians vehemently resisted the power of the United States government—largely represented by its male agents, headed by the president—to intervene in local matters. Thus Welty's narrator denies the authority of all other males over him, with one exception: as a good son, he acknowledges paternal power, saying, "Even the President . . . can't walk into my house without being invited, like he's my daddy" (607). In fact, another of Welty's several working titles for this story further emphasized father-son relations: it was "Ask Me My Daddy's Name."[10]

This murderer is also true to his country-family upbringing. He is not a native of Thermopylae, a rapidly expanding small southern city (based on Jackson). Unlike Roland Summers, a local TV celebrity, the narrator (like many country people Welty met in the thirties) has never been photographed.[11] But he has kept, treasured, and memorized an advertisement his mother placed in "our county weekly" when he once ran away, saying,

> "SON: You are not being hunted for anything but to find you."
> That time, I come on back home.
> But people are dead now. (607)

9. The possibility that this phrase may have had special import to Welty is suggested by the fact that, in the first typescript of the story in the Mississippi Archives (Eudora Welty Papers, Series 8, Box 14), she deleted the phrase "by Christ" and substituted "by Dad"—thus replacing the name of the son of God with the name of the human father.
10. Eudora Welty Papers, Series 8, Box 14.
11. See Hunter Cole and Seetha Srinivasan, "Introduction: Eudora Welty and Photography: An Interview," in Eudora Welty, *Photographs* (Jackson: University Press of Mississippi, 1989), xxviii.

The ad, which addressed the narrator only in the language of filiality, as SON, returned him to a place he knew how to find: "home." But now—parentless, childless and apparently without friends or love—this traditional white Mississippian conceives himself as homeless; this time, he will be hunted not as a loved and identified son, but only as the murderer of Roland Summers.

The final paragraph of the story is its most appalling, because it is so indelibly moving. In the empty house, the narrator takes down his "old guitar" that he has "held on to from way back when, and I never dropped that, never lost or forgot it, never hocked it but to get it again, never give it away, and I set in my chair, with nobody home but me, and I start to play, and sing a-Down. And sing a-down, down, down, down. Sing a-down, down, down, down. Down" (607).

Preserving a prized possession, playing a traditional ballad whose one word spells decline and fall, implicitly mourning his dead parents and invoking their authority, this bigot and murderer is a pious son.

"The Demonstrators" also has a pious white son at its center. According to the sign on his office window, Dr. Strickland's dead father is still a partner in his medical practice. Many of the doctor's patients are "inherited" paternal legacies, and he tells time by his father's gold watch. He behaves by the small-town standards of Holden, a cotton-gin town at the edge of the Mississippi Delta, whose inhabitants treat the sole doctor as community property as well as local deity. To both white and black patients, Strickland issues absolute orders and withholds and dispenses medical information entirely at his own discretion. He believes in his own authority, whether with the young white civil rights worker—to whom he makes confident ethical pronouncements—or his patients. When he finally recognizes a black patient, he names her solely by her relation to him—"the maid"—and announces (preposterously) to the watchers: "I know Ruby . . . and if the lights would come back on I can tell you the names of the rest of you and you know it."[12]

Obviously, Strickland is experiencing a power failure more disabling than the temporary electrical emergency. In the sixties of the

12. Eudora Welty, "The Demonstrators," in *Collected Stories*, 612. Hereafter cited parenthetically by page number in the text.

civil rights movement, his patriarchal flaunting is no longer convincing or authoritative, even in Holden. "Let me see you do something," screams Ruby's mother, whose daughter is slowly dying from a puncture wound. "You sure ain't your daddy!" (613). Wielding an archaic kerosene lamp in the dark, crowded room, this woman derides the doctor for his powerlessness to help her child. At the same time, even she—Strickland's opposite in race, class, and gender—recalls a time when (she implies) doctors *could* "do something." One such effectual patriarch was Strickland's "daddy."

Strickland also pays mental homage to his dead mother. He is reminded of her through the complex network of domestic servitude, for Ruby's mother (one of those whom he fails to recognize) was his mother's laundress. The starched dresses hanging in her yard become, for Strickland, maternal presences connected with the comforting water he commandeers and drinks from an ancestral cup. The house and the maternal imagery connect him to something he cannot consciously know or express: another kind of intimate and inaccessible knowledge that runs underfoot and in the interior walls, like Dove's uncatchable guinea pigs. Among these female African Americans whose work has surrounded him all his life, worn as closely as the garments Ruby's mother laundered, Strickland may assert that he "knows" them all, but his failed confrontation with the self-possessed gaze of the dying Ruby tells another story: "he stepped across the gaze of the girl on the bed as he would have had to step over a crack yawning in the floor" (614).

Such cracks, cuts, and fissures recur; they are the domestic, local, and political texture of the doctor's life. Strickland's marriage is severely cracked, if not broken, and the filial links between generations have been severed by the deaths of his parents and his daughter. Demonstrators spread Strickland's driveway with broken glass that slashes his tires—and with them any possible wish to bond with the young activists. Ruby's murderer and former lover—wounded by her—falls into another fissure, a deep creek gully, and is left for dead. But, with unexpected strength, the dying man hauls himself out of the ravine and onto a Holden street where he too confronts Strickland and asks for help—secrecy, healing, interracial collaboration—that the doctor is powerless to give. "Dove said: 'Hide me.' Then he hemorrhaged through the mouth" (619) and died.

When Strickland's wife left him, infuriated by his persistently authoritarian stance, she acknowledged his primary commitment, as a son, to preserving and occupying his father's place. (In fact, some of his patients confuse him with his father.) When he had perfunctorily "offered to be the one to leave," she had retorted, "Leave Holden without its Dr. Strickland? You wouldn't to save your soul" (617). However cutting, her remark shows considerable insight into her husband's condition. She recognizes that enacting the inherited role of "Holden's Dr. Strickland" has brought him to a state of spiritual crisis that perhaps can be cured only by leaving Holden, and filial duty, behind. Yet leaving is what her husband will not do, not even to save his soul.

As he turns his back on Ruby's deathbed, still acting the doctor's part although there is little a doctor can do for her, Strickland is sick, tired, and grieving for his dead child and absent wife. But his mind is flooded with images of a time when—as his parents' well-nurtured white child—his sense of power, place, and continuity was intact. He remembers starched laundry and "good" china and sustaining stories; when he sees cotton wagons they remind him of "the gypsy caravans or circus wagons of his father's, or even his grandfather's, stories" (615). Suddenly Strickland feels as though an "old, trusted, half-forgotten family friend" has "offered to carry his load for a while" and "that there was still allowed to everybody on earth a *self*—savage, death-defying, private. . . . The pounding of his heart was like the assault of hope . . . merciless" (618). This epiphanic episode proposes, in a rush of heightened rhetoric, a release from the straitjacket of filial piety and a return to things "the way they used to seem" (617–8), in which the burden of filial obligation is not repudiated (unthinkable for a Dr. Strickland) but permissibly shared by a supportive friend of his family. Such release permits the return of a powerful vision of private selfhood, like the "something your own" that Diarmuid Russell urged Eudora Welty to claim in the sixties. Strickland, who has recently endured familial deaths and marital separation, has been "putting down" his personal griefs, memories, and passions as he numbly fills his role as a public figure, the small-town doctor who is the site of so many other people's expectations and hopes. Only by suppressing his private self has Strickland been able to enact his filial piety as Dr. Strickland's son and heir, continuing his father's rounds. However, Strickland's passionate vision of renewed privacy has arisen out of the deeply problematic connections that he senses, helplessly, at Ruby's deathbed—and to accept it would endanger his already precarious performance as "Holden's Dr. Strickland." Thus the returning hope of such unbroken, uncontested self-possession is both thrilling and profoundly dangerous; it is an assault that shakes this white man's body. In a few minutes the intense, visionary moment ebbs away, like an episode of sickness, "nausea put down" (618).

For Strickland, there is no apparent way to cure his malaise by moving to another position in the filial "sequence of generations." His gesture of kindness toward a man young enough to be his son—the demonstrator—ends in estrangement. His dead daughter was "injured at birth" (616) (in what may have been another failure of medical authority) and was thus profoundly retarded. He cannot bequeath his father's timepiece to her. At the story's end, Strickland strains to establish the most tenuous of links with the dead child; he is "pretty sure" that she was aware of the birds he watches in his yard. And he returns to his accustomed, inherited role; oblivious to the cook who provides him with domestic service, he picks up his doctor's bag and resumes his rounds. He ultimately comes to view Holden as a network of interlocking needs in which no one—himself included—is "quite able to take care" of himself or herself alone, like a vision of filiality extended to the entire town. Is there a place in such a network for a "savage, death-defying, private" self, or is that self a sick, archaic fantasy of a racist individualism? The story leaves that question unanswered but powerfully present.

As I have tried to show, both "The Demonstrators" and "Where Is the Voice Coming From?" recount their protagonists' night journeys, travels in the dark that involve both murder and yearning for release from a daylight life that has become unbearable. These journeys are marked by carnivalesque reversals. In "The Demonstrators," Dr. Strickland—accustomed to a position "on top" of Holden's authority structure—finds himself helplessly in the dark, forced to implore a chorus of black women, so insignificant to him that he repeatedly forgets their identities, for the most basic of information. The unemployed white country narrator of "Where Is the Voice Coming From?"—a man near the economic bottom—effects a reversal, putting himself "on top of the world" (604) by murdering an ascendant black urban media hero. He identifies less with Roland Summers, returning home from a late meeting to be shot at his door, than with Summers's wife, waiting inside, "the woman. I doubt she'd been to sleep. Because it seemed to me she'd been in there keeping awake all along" (605). The narrator himself occupies the same position, waiting at home for his wife (who pays the bills) to return from her work. The very conditions that make him sensitive to the position of a black, housebound woman, waiting *inside*, have compelled him to murder her husband, who has been usurping the ultimate public and political space: the television screen.

As Lillian Schlissel observes, carnival has traditionally created sites for "breaking bounds," where people "wore different faces and lived different lives that needed no accounting."[13] Their carnivalesque night journeys put the narrator and Strickland in situations where they are dislodged from their customary social constructions and connect—however briefly—with Others, particularly blacks and women. But the fact that such moments occur under cover of darkness suggests that they are an enormous threat to the prevailing, daylight status quo. Particularly in the South, filial piety has traditionally been the essence of that status quo. The name of the father is the ultimate formulation of an ongoing white patriarchy, and both these men dutifully act, again and again, to preserve Daddy's name and place. The narrator's murder is committed "by Dad," and Dr. Strickland's name and work are literally indistinguishable from his father's. In the troubled, changing Mis-

---

13. Lillian Schlissel, with Byrd Gibbens and Elizabeth Hampsten, *Far from Home: Families of the Western Journey* (New York: Schocken Books, 1989), 234. Recent scholarship reflects controversy about whether carnival's social functions are conservative, reinforcing "social structure, hierarchy, and order through inversion," as argued by Victor Turner, or belong in an innovative, "productive category, affirmative and celebratory," as argued by Bakhtin (Mary Russo, "Female Grotesques: Carnival and Theory," in *Feminist Studies/Critical Studies*, ed. Teresa de Lauretis [Bloomington: University of Indiana Press, 1986], 214–15). See Russo for a pertinent discussion of carnival issues in relation to feminist theory.

sissippi of the sixties, both men take their stands by staying put, as their fathers' loyal sons.

In this essay, I have concentrated on a few telling similarities in two otherwise very different stories: two white male protagonists, both involved with murder and abuse, who are stuck in their own filial piety, as dutiful (and childless) sons, and also stuck in the loneliness of a middle age with no apparent supportive peers. Both men lack the "cohort" of contemporaries who, according to recent scholarship, are an important component of successful aging.[14] There is a no-exit quality to these stories that makes me wonder even more about the existence and the difficulty of the other sixties stories that Welty is said to have written but has not (yet) published.[15] Written at a time in her life that was almost entirely consumed by familial care, "Where Is the Voice Coming From?" and "The Demonstrators" offer an uncompromising contemplation of the possible costs and consequences of filial piety. With their emphasis on male protagonists and father-son relations, the two stories gave a woman writer, emotionally entwined with her mother at a time of mortal emergency, an opportunity to address issues of filiality from a stance that was not specifically autobiographical and *was* specifically political.[16] (After her mother's death, the prob-

14. See Mike Featherstone and Mike Hepworth, "Aging and Old Age: Reflections on the Postmodern Life Course," in *Becoming and Being Old: Sociological Approaches to Later Life*, ed. Bill Bytheway et al. (London: Sage Publications, 1989), and Betty Friedan, *The Fountain of Age* (New York: Simon and Schuster, 1993), 385.

15. In 1978, in an interview with Tom Royals and John Little, Welty said of "Voice" and "The Demonstrators" that "all of it was a reflection of society at the time it happened. . . . And I was trying for it in both those stories and in several others that I have underway here in the house that will be in my next book. They all reflect the way we were deeply troubled in that society and within ourselves at what was going on in the sixties. They reflect the effect of change sweeping all over the South" (Prenshaw, ed., *Conversations with Eudora Welty*, 259).

16. It is important to remember, however, that Welty herself had a close relationship with her father, who was her primary early adviser in her choice of profession. Also, she was the close sister of two brothers who lost their father as very young men. So the subject of father-daughter and father-son filial relations is not entirely without autobiographical associations for her.

ing of mother-daughter relations would return in a rush, in the rapid writing of *The Optimist's Daughter*.)[17]

As I think again about the shape of Eudora Welty's writing career, I see her 1960s contemplation of the politics of filial piety as facilitating much that came later. In some ways, twelve-year-old Vaughn of *Losing Battles* (the one character whose private consciousness Welty allowed her narrative to access) is the affirmative answer to Strickland's anguished question about the possibility of a private self, even in the filial claims and intrusive din of a "huge, soul-defying" family reunion. But that affirmation is set in the Depression thirties, probably the era of Strickland's and the murderer's own childhoods, not in the civil rights turmoil of the sixties. When Welty returned to that turbulent decade in *The Optimist's Daughter*, the turmoil was relegated to the farthest edges of her canvas. But Laurel Hand—again the childless survivor of beloved parents—works through the same issues with which the sixties stories' male protagonists wrestle. The ruthlessness of some of Laurel's choices (burning her mother's recipes, abandoning her breadboard, leaving her childhood home), which I have resisted for years, is easier to comprehend in the context of Welty's two previous sixties stories, when I compare the murderer's decision to hang on to a beloved relic of his personal history—the guitar—with Laurel's choice to let go, and to leave Mount Salus, as Dr. Strickland cannot leave Holden. Later, in *One Writer's Beginnings*, which most of us have read as a deeply (and some as an excessively) filial book, Welty describes her exploratory nonfiction meditation as a way to get beyond the filial in its meaning as a fixed and constraining sequence of generations. In this autobiographical book, she says she can "glimpse our whole family life as if it were freed of that clock time which spaces us apart so inhibitingly, divides young

17. According to Kreyling, Welty set aside her work on *Losing Battles*, to which she first returned after her mother's death, to rapidly "write, from start to finish, a new long story early in 1967." That story was published in the *New Yorker* in March 1969 and, in book form, became *The Optimist's Daughter* (Kreyling, *Author and Agent*, 204).

and old, keeps our living through the same experiences at separate distances."[18]

Welty's admirers customarily deplore the fact that she has published no fiction since *The Optimist's Daughter* in 1972—and indeed, the absence of any further published fiction may be an implicitly political decision in which issues of filial piety are intimately involved. When someone asked Eudora Welty if, in *The Optimist's Daughter*, she had "come to terms with death," she replied, "I suppose I had, but I was too young to come to terms when I wrote that. . . . You can come to terms, but you have to keep coming to terms because each loss is a new loss and a different kind of loss." Finally, I want to suggest that we may read many of the nonfiction texts Welty has published since her fiction ceased as a continual "coming to terms" with the evolving issues of filial politics plumbed in the sixties stories. For example, the 1930s photographs of *One Time, One Place* also address issues of race, class, and community—but Welty's 1971 introduction makes it clear that the "trust" between black subjects and white photographer that she sees in many of her photographs is not accessible in the present, thus emphasizing the futility of romantic longing, like Strickland's, for "the way it used to be" ("Demonstrators" 617–8). Welty's 1971 foreword for the *Jackson Cookbook* (which she valued highly enough to include in her volume of selected essays) is also revisionist; it places her in an ongoing, multiple, community cookbook culture that is more complex and fertile than a single filial line of domestic inheritance from mother to daughter. And her last published work, as coeditor of *The Norton Book of Friendship*, suggests friendship as another model of human relations to supplement—if never to supplant—the filial piety that she has rendered repeatedly, with such harrowing grace.[19]

18. Eudora Welty, *Losing Battles* (New York: Random House, 1970), 363; Welty, *One Writer's Beginnings*, 102. *The Optimist's Daughter* was originally conceived and published as a "long short story," Welty's favorite form.

19. Patricia Wheatley, "Eudora Welty: A Writer's Beginnings," in *More Conversations with Eudora Welty*, ed. Prenshaw, 142–3; Eudora Welty, "One Time, One Place," in *The Eye of the Story: Selected Essays and Reviews* (New York: Random House, 1978), 352.

*Rebecca Mark*

# A "Cross-mark Ploughed into the Center"

## Civil Rights and Eudora Welty's *Losing Battles*

In an interview with Eudora Welty shortly before the release of *Losing Battles,* Frank Hains reported that she was "a bit apprehensive that some of the reviewers may criticize *Losing Battles* because of her apparent lack of concern for the preoccupations of today; where, she fancies them saying, is her awareness of black versus white, the degeneration of the family, all the 'relevant' problems?" In 1972, when Charles T. Bunting asked her to comment on the "rather conspicuous absence of Negroes in *Losing Battles,*" Welty answered that she "didn't know an absence was conspicuous because I thought I had everything in there that mattered . . . northeast Mississippi is not a part of the state where there ever were any black people. . . . There is, all the same, a very telling and essential incident in *Losing Battles* . . . that involves a Negro as such. Perhaps you remember." Bunting did not respond. The incident to which Welty refers is Uncle Nathan's story. In *Losing Battles* Uncle Nathan murders Herman Dearman "with a stone to his head, and let 'em hang a sawmill nigger for it."[1] While this moment takes up no more than two or three lines in the novel, it is, as Welty states, a very telling and essential incident. If we explore the ramifications of this incident, we find a key to reading the whole novel.

Interestingly enough, reviewers and scholars did not criticize Welty for her seeming lack of concern for the central preoccupations of the

1. Frank Hains, "Eudora Welty Talks about Her New Book, *Losing Battles,*" in *Conversations with Eudora Welty,* ed. Peggy Prenshaw (Jackson: University Press of Mississippi, 1984), 26; Charles T. Bunting, "'An Interior World': An Interview with Eudora Welty," ibid., 48; Eudora Welty, *Losing Battles* (New York: Random House, 1970), 344. Hereafter cited parenthetically by page number in the text.

day. The thirty or so essays and book chapters that make up the critical canon on *Losing Battles* rarely approach political matters and certainly never discuss *Losing Battles* in terms of civil rights issues. This seems a bit strange considering that in 1970, when *Losing Battles* was published, racial issues in the South, particularly in Mississippi, dominated the local and national imagination. Since Eudora Welty had been virtually silent for fifteen years, there were many readers waiting to hear what one of the most famous contemporary writers would have to say about the violence in her state. Recent essays by Suzanne Marrs, Sharon Baris, Noel Polk, Harriet Pollack, and Peggy Prenshaw prove quite definitively that throughout her life, Welty has been a person of strong political convictions, a deeply committed Adlai Stevenson Democrat, and an advocate of the civil rights movement. Welty did not march or participate in sit-ins, but she did speak and attend lectures at a predominantly black college, she did send letters to the editor and sign her real name, and she did voice her concerns to family and friends. What remains to be demonstrated is the way in which she translated these beliefs into her fiction.

By refraining from seeking an activist subtext in *Losing Battles*, we accept the idea that the work of as sensitive and empathetic a writer as Eudora Welty would remain unaffected by the lynching of Emmett Till in 1955, James Meredith's fight to integrate the University of Mississippi in 1962, the murder of Medgar Evers in 1963, the murder of civil rights workers Chaney, Schwerner, and Goodman in 1964, the Jackson, Mississippi, lunch counter sit-ins, the economic stranglehold placed on black citizens by lack of equal education and job opportunity, and the raging debate over desegregation of the schools and the role of school busing in that debate. When we realize that Welty wrote *Losing Battles* during a fifteen-year period between the *Brown* vs. *Board of Education* ruling in 1954, which made segregated facilities illegal, and the Swann ruling of 1970, which enforced desegregation of the schools through federally mandated school busing, the problem becomes more complex. Add to this the fact that one of the central symbols in *Losing Battles* is a yellow school bus and the protagonist, Miss Julia Mortimer, is a teacher, and we might reasonably consider the possibility that Welty's story comments, however obliquely, on the political situation in her state.

In Jackson, Welty watched the unwillingness of the governing, legal, and civic bodies of Mississippi to conform to federally ordered desegregation. She lived through the formation of the white-supremacist Citizens' Council and the Sovereignty Commission, a white surveillance organization that spied on the activities of civil rights leaders and individual citizens and thwarted any and all attempts at desegregation, including establishment of health-care facilities, schools, and job placement services for African Americans. Mississippi was in a state of siege, and those who felt deeply—those with a heart, and a brain, and a conscience—were in terrible moral turmoil. Welty was so disturbed by the racial conflict in Little Rock, Arkansas, that on September 25, 1957, she wrote to Diarmuid Russell: "I feel like emigrating from the whole country."[2] This is the climate in which Welty struggled to compose *Losing Battles*. As the nation, and in fact the whole world, condemned Mississippi, many intellectuals and artists left the state. Welty stayed and dealt with the turbulence within and without in the best way she knew how, by writing a novel, a novel that is comic only insofar as it is satiric—a novel that is instead a deeply moving reclamation of the best of humanity and a powerful condemnation of the worst. While family issues, including the death of her mother and both of her brothers, did slow the writing of *Losing Battles*, it was not only the extreme difficulty of the personal but also the horror of the political climate of Mississippi that forced one of the most prolific writers of our day to struggle for a decade and a half to produce this text, which evolved from the somewhat straightforward story of Jack's homecoming in a 1955 short story manuscript to the complex drama of a 1965 manuscript and finally to the formidable epic of the 1970 published work.

Welty herself created the initial critical silence concerning political elements in her writing when she wrote her famous essay, "Must the Novelist Crusade?" Whether intended or not, the result of this essay has been to make politics and activism off-limits as topics for Welty critics. However, if we read "Must the Novelist Crusade?"—published in 1965—as a dialogic companion to *Losing Battles*, we find not an ar-

2. Michael Kreyling, *Author and Agent: Eudora Welty and Diarmuid Russell* (New York: Farrar, Straus, Giroux, 1991), 189.

gument for why the novelist should refrain from the activist arena, but instead a carefully detailed description of exactly how the novelist *can* contribute to social change. In "Must the Novelist Crusade?" Welty explains: "On fiction's pages, generalities clank when wielded, and hit with equal force at the little and the big, at the merely suspect and the really dangerous. They make too much noise for us to hear what people might be trying to say. They are fatal to tenderness and are in themselves non-conductors of any real, however modest, discovery of the writer's own heart. This discovery is the best hope of the ordinary novelist, and to make it he begins not with the generality but with the particular in front of his eyes, which he is able to examine." Welty develops these thoughts later in the essay: "A plot is a thousand times more unsettling than an argument, which may be answered. It is not a pattern imposed, it is inward emotion acted out."[3] These words show us how to approach *Losing Battles.* Its plot is unsettling, specifically because it is not an argument, but an inward emotion, full of particulars that must be understood and decoded. No simple polemic could do justice to the magnitude of change, the passion of despair and grief occurring in every arena of this writer's life at this time. She has left us a profound aesthetic record of her own heart in *Losing Battles.* We owe it to her to discover the intricate messages inscribed therein.

In order to interpret the political subtext of *Losing Battles,* we must read the book in the manner prescribed by Louis Rubin in his 1970 *Hollins Review* article: "Every line must be read carefully. It cannot be skimmed. . . . This means that you have to follow the conversations and note the narrative directions and take in every word, every phrase, holding it all in suspension, letting it accumulate. Many of us don't like to read that way; we haven't the patience to follow every footpath and byway in a novel that takes approximately the same amount of time to read as it does for the events themselves to happen. So we tend to go racing through, and we miss the detail and so the story." Literary critics brought up to think of close readings as apolitical have neglected this approach when looking at texts like *Losing Battles,* and so we miss the story just as Rubin predicts. Welty herself evokes Rubin's

3. Eudora Welty, "Must the Novelist Crusade?" in *The Eye of the Story: Selected Essays and Reviews* (New York: Random House, 1978), 148, 150.

careful reader when she writes, in "Words into Fiction": "Fiction is made of words to travel under the reading eye, and made to go in one sequence and one direction, slowly, accumulating: time is an element. The words follow the contours of some continuous relationship between what can be told and what cannot be told, to be in the silence of reading the lightest of the hammers that tap their way along this side of chaos."[4] "Words into Fiction" was first published in 1962, then reprinted while Welty was working on *Losing Battles*. It is as if she knew she would have to write these essays in order to help us read *Losing Battles*. Her words allow us to cross the bridge between what can be told and what cannot be told, a bridge as precarious as the Banner bridge, hanging suspended between the town of Alliance, representing the ability to form coalitions and create unity (in this context, to effect desegregation), and the town of Banner, representing the nationalist desire to fly the flag of one group to the exclusion of another (in this case, to maintain white sovereignty and segregation). The town names are not coincidences but clearly mark the central issue in the novel.

Welty knew she had to help her readers cross this bridge, to provide them with a map not as a literal representation but as a visionary diagram of the narrative terrain. This is the kind of map Welty includes in the first pages of the text, as well as the kind of map Julia Mortimer gives to Judge Moody, whose reaction is puzzlement: "'And it's a maze,' he said, squinting down at the old bill on which a web of lines radiated from some cross-mark ploughed into the center. 'Just a maze. There wasn't much right about her thinking any longer. I didn't try to go by it—but I lost my own way on Boone County roads for the first time I can remember. I could almost believe I'd been *maneuvered* here,' he said in grieved, almost hopeless, tones. 'To the root of it all, like the roots of a bad tooth. The very pocket of ignorance'"(303–4). The judge is right in assuming that he has arrived at the root of it all, but naming this root "ignorance" is too easy. Miss Lexie tells us that when she was caring for Miss Mortimer and would move her inside, the old schoolteacher would "'Shake—she'd shake that big oak door!

4. Louis Rubin, "Everything Brought Out in the Open: Eudora Welty's *Losing Battles*," *Hollins Critic* 7 (June 1970): 3; Eudora Welty, "Words into Fiction," in *Eye of the Story*, 143.

You ever see a spider shake his web when you lay a pine straw in it just for meanness? She could shake her door like a web was all it was. I felt sometimes like just everything, not only her house but me in it, was about to go flying, and me no more'n a pinestraw myself, something in her way'" (278). Miss Julia Mortimer is the spider shaking Judge Moody in her "web." The two images—the web and the maze—are symbolically in opposition to a linear narrative, which offers a definite conclusion or way out. A map requires a geographical reading, spatial and repetitive, rather than additive. One must look at the whole picture as well as the parts.

By examining this novel as both a maze and a web, we can begin to answer Bunting's disturbing question: Why didn't Eudora Welty write directly about racial issues? She appears to have virtually ignored African American people and civil rights activists in her novel. As she herself says, there were no blacks living in Tishomingo County in the 1930s, the time period of the novel. While this is not quite accurate, it is close: according to a Vanderbilt University study, they constituted as few as 9 percent of the population.[5] No other counties in Mississippi had as small a black population as Tishomingo. Why Welty would choose this particular county to write about at a time when race relations were so dominant, when she herself lived in a county 50 to 60 percent African American, is curious. She claims that she chose this area of the state because of the poverty, because she wanted to write about a group of people who had nothing. If this were the case, she could easily have written about many groups of African Americans anywhere in the state.

We might begin to unravel the problem if we remember that Welty wrote from the perspective of the white murderer in her most damning condemnation of white racism, "Where Is the Voice Coming From?" The desire of the small town of Banner to be left alone by the teachers and preachers and judges of the rest of the world mirrors the desire of the people of Mississippi in the 1960s to become a sovereign state separate and left alone by the laws and beliefs of the rest of the nation and the rest of the world. In "Where is the Voice Coming

5. Paul Breck Foreman, *Vanderbilt University: Mississippi Population Trends* (Nashville: Joint University Libraries, 1939), 5–7.

From?" the narrator and murderer of the civil rights leader muses: "But I advise 'em to go careful. Ain't it about time us taxpayers starts to calling the moves? Starts to telling the teachers *and* the preachers *and* the judges of our so-called courts how far they can go?"[6] In *Losing Battles*, the family members at the reunion do try to tell the teachers and preachers and judges exactly what they think. By delving deeply into the isolationist instincts of the people of Tishomingo County, by trying to show the world the workings of this community, and by including just the one horrifying incident of the hanging of a black man for a white man's crime, Welty may have felt she provided a more dramatic presentation of the insular beliefs of white Mississippi than if she had tried to portray African American characters. But this approach would only make sense if the rest of the novel were in some way related to the one "essential incident." I think if we read the text carefully we will see that everything—Jack's trial and return, Gloria's search for her parentage, Miss Julia Mortimer's dying wishes as voiced to Judge Moody, Jack and Gloria's love affair—relates to and comments on this essential incident.

We have often read *Losing Battles* against the historical backdrop of economic depression and dust-bowl starvation, but never against the backdrop of lynching. Although the majority of the lynchings in the United States occurred between 1864 and 1930, there were still many lynchings committed in Mississippi during the 1930s. Mississippi and Georgia led the nation in the number of African American men and women lynched between 1890 and 1940. Welty certainly heard echoes of those horrible deaths from the '30s as the Ku Klux Klan once again gained power in her state and Emmett Till, Medgar Evers, and three civil rights workers were murdered a short distance from her home. In the 1950s, one case in particular, the lynching of Emmett Till, shook the foundation of Mississippi society and awakened the whole nation to the need for civil rights action.

In Mississippi, the 1954 *Brown* ruling began a period of reactionary resistance. Shortly after the decision, Tom Brady sent out an inflammatory pamphlet called *Black Monday*, in which he wrote, "the fulmi-

---

6. Eudora Welty, "Where Is the Voice Coming From?" in *Collected Stories of Eudora Welty* (New York: Harcourt Brace, 1980), 607.

nate which will discharge the blast will be the young negro schoolboy.
. . . The supercilious, glib young negro, who has sojourned in Chicago
or New York, and who considers the counsel of his elders archaic, will
perform an obscene act, or make an obscene remark, or a vile overture
or assault upon some white girl.'"[7] As Stephen J. Whitfield describes in
detail in his book *A Death in the Delta,* only a year and a half later
(August 1955) two half-brothers lynched a fourteen-year-old teenager
named Emmett Till from Chicago who was visiting his aunt and uncle
in Tallahatchie County. Earlier that week Till had been accused of taking a dare from some of his Mississippi cousins and whistling at Roy
Bryant's wife at her corner grocery store. Normally such racially motivated crimes were hushed up because local African Americans did not
speak out for fear of reprisal, but Till's mother, Mamie Bradley, grief-
stricken and outraged, put Till's horribly mutilated body on display in
an open casket in Chicago, where over two hundred thousand predominantly African American mourners witnessed the horror of his lynching. People saw photographs of the body of this young boy, and condemnation of the crime poured in from all over the world. Because of
the intense publicity surrounding this case, many historians mark
Till's lynching as the catalyst that ignited the civil rights movement;
leaders from Martin Luther King to Rosa Parks cite Till's death as a
galvanizing moment. Although the murderers were caught and tried,
in the racist climate of 1955 Mississippi they were acquitted. The trial
brought hundreds of people, including reporters and politicians, to
rural Mississippi, and the acquittal brought infamy to the state as reporters and politicians around the world decried the failure of justice
in America.

While Till's death did not lead Welty to begin *Losing Battles*—
Michael Kreyling documents letters discussing the long story about
northeast Mississippi prior to August 1955—there is ample textual evidence that the events of 1955, particularly this horrific lynching, influenced the writing of the novel. Obviously, there is no direct parallel
between the two; Welty's novel is a fictional comedy, Till's death a

7. Tom P. Brady, *Black Monday* (Winona, Miss.: Association of Citizens' Councils, 1955), 12, 63–4, cited in Stephen J. Whitfield, *A Death in the Delta: The
   Story of Emmett Till* (New York: Free Press, 1988), vii.

horrible and very real tragedy. In suggesting that Welty was influenced by Till's murder, I do not want to belittle or diminish the reality of the historical events of Till's death. To even suggest such textual ghosts seems irreverent, but I offer the analysis as my way of saying that Welty knew all too well the horror and despair felt by Till's family and friends in the wake of his brutal death, even though she does not fictionalize the death or the trial, nor does she make any direct comparisons between the real people and the fictional characters. My purpose in pointing out the moments in the *Losing Battles* manuscripts and in the published version that echo back to the trial of Till's murderers is only to bring attention to the full extent of Welty's condemnation of white racism. Whereas in "Where Is the Voice Coming From?" Welty is direct in her historical allusions and in *Losing Battles* the allusions are embedded and transformed, her purpose in both texts is the same, to name and thus expose racist ideology.

The first section of *Losing Battles* tells the story of the return of the prodigal son Jack to an isolated community in Tishomingo County, Mississippi. Welty evidently drafted this first portion of the manuscript in early 1955 before Till's murder. It was simply the story of the son's return; Welty has never mentioned anything about a trial or the particulars of the incident that got Jack into trouble in the first place being part of this draft. The first extant partial draft of the novel, held by the Mississippi Department of Archives and History, is dated 1961; subsequent partial drafts are dated 1963, 1964, and 1965. Between Welty's first attempt at a story and the revisions of that story that she in the early sixties chose to save, there was plenty of time for the events of 1955 to act on her imagination, which we know to be powerfully resonant. Her works are intertextually laced with historical facts, literary and mythical allusions, moments from newspaper articles, popular fiction, and the music of the time. Historical facts, local events, and personal memories turn up in alchemically altered and thus coded yet recognizable new formations. In all of his histories Shakespeare freely appropriated even the most minute details from the written histories of the events he dramatized, but in the hands of his genius they loom large in new and symbolically altered forms, producing subtle political commentary, satire, and parody. I contend, as Sharon Baris has done in her work on *The Ponder Heart* and its allusions to the Rosenberg trial, that just such a form of coded commentary is in place in *Losing Battles*. What Welty does in this and other texts is filter historical events through the web of her genius so they are recognizable but no longer have the same meaning they had in their original historical context. In order to understand this kind of imaginative process one must put aside the conventional terms of literary criticism such as influence, allegory, comparison, and historical accuracy. The act of imaginative transformation that occurs in these texts is more subtle, more mysterious, and more chilling than we have yet fully understood.

The trial of Roy Bryant and J. W. Milam for Till's lynching was one of the most publicized legal events in history, and people from all over the world flooded into the tiny town of Sumner, Mississippi, to watch. In *Losing Battles* the Beechams and Renfros boast that there were people from all over the state at Jack's trial: "Even a few Ludlow folks was there, with nothing better to do, I reckon, than come to get a peep at a bunch of country monkeys" (52). Jack is on trial for roughing up Curly Stovall and ostensibly stealing a ring Curly had taken from Jack's sister Ella Fay in exchange for all the candy she had been eating. No one ever finds the ring. The whole thing starts as a prank and escalates. Till was on trial in a rural town in Mississippi for wolf whistling at Mrs. Bryant outside her grocery store. A young African American boy from Chicago, he did not know how dangerous this could be. Judge Moody makes "an example out of Jack" by sentencing him to Parchman for two years, a state penitentiary located surprisingly near the place Till was murdered. Milam and Bryant made an example of Emmett by beating and lynching him. The whole rhetoric of racist terrorism was designed to let the other African Americans know what would happen to them if they crossed the race line. The elements are all there—a prank, a country store, a redneck store owner, sexual overtones, a country trial, and, as I will explain, a ring—but the story is radically different. What we can begin to see is that the major difference is race—the fact that Jack and Curly are white whereas Emmett Till was black renders the fictional tale completely opposite the historical events. Unlike in "Where Is the Voice Coming From?"—where Welty enters the mind of the racist—in *Losing Battles* she focuses on a supposedly innocent white community and, by creating a play of symbols in which details from the national coverage of Emmett Till's murder mix with an entirely new set of narrative demands, exposes the racism at the root of it all. In both cases she allows the white reader to explore his or her own culpability, which might not be possible had she written directly on the subject of black/white relations. The angle she did choose creates a political critique that could not be achieved in any straightforward manner. If we have any doubt that this powerful political commentary is occurring in *Losing Battles*, a close reading of the text and the manuscripts should convince us otherwise.

In the narrative, the judge sends Jack to prison for roughing up the stereotypical fat redneck Curly by putting him in an oversize casket, pouring cottonseed meal all over him, tying him up with clothesline to prevent his escape, and stealing the safe that supposedly has the ring in it. Curly himself is far from innocent. He has chased the young schoolgirl Ella Fay all over the store—after much more than her money—and is known to have done this to many other young girls, usually in church. However, he gets off scot-free for chasing Ella Fay and taking her gold ring. Both Curly and Jack do much worse to each other and to the young girls than Emmett Till ever did to Mrs. Bryant, yet Jack is only sent to prison for two years and does not serve the whole sentence, and even so, everyone thinks this relatively light sentence is unjust. Ella Fay, who ostensibly gave away the ring in the first place and cried for her brother to come and protect her, receives no punishment except from her mother, who understands her culpability—a fact that becomes clearer when we realize that rings and broaches, such as the red broach in *Delta Wedding*, are symbols of women's sexuality in Welty's fiction. If we add to this the plot twist that has Ella Fay engaged to Curly by the end of the book, we see that Welty has revised the chivalric scene of the damsel in distress calling to her hero brother who will save her from being ravished by the evil lecher. Here, the white man is the lecher and the white girl is not innocent. The perverted chivalric myth of the helpless, vulnerable, virginal southern white lady formed the basis for the lynching of thousands of black men in Mississippi and throughout the South in the first half of the century and provided an excuse for men like Tom Brady to continue to preach segregation. In their politically motivated inflammatory "logic," contact between the races meant rape of white women. Throughout the rest of *Losing Battles* Welty makes it perfectly clear that the white women in the book are far from virginal. They all have active sex lives, including sex outside of marriage, and no one, even Granny, is exempt from sexual desire.

When Jack says he tied Curly up because he found the fellow "aggravating," the judge does not view this as a defense and sentences Jack to two years in the pen. This is a stern sentence for a prank, but Jack is back in the bosom of his family in less than the time prescribed—a much different story from Emmett Till's. Till's murderers also wanted to make an example out of their victim, but they are the self-appointed, and not the rightful, law. In a 1957 interview with William Bradford Huie, Milam and Bryant admitted killing Till and claimed that they did so for no other reason than that he had a picture of a white girl in his wallet and he had wolf-whistled at Mrs. Bryant.[8] They felt that he was aggravating, but more importantly, he had broken the race code. Till's prank—if it even occurred—ended in his being beaten, shot in the head, and thrown in the river to die. Milam and Bryant felt completely justified in their actions because he had threatened white womanhood.

Till's open casket galvanized the world against Mississippi. To have Jack stuff Curly Stovall into an open casket and leave him there on display as part of Gloria's lesson to her schoolchildren on the first day of class is to put the true culprit where he belongs and to teach Mississippi history in the way it should be taught. He is covered with cottonseed meal, representing the crop that was responsible for the development of slavery in Mississippi—and so it was the seed of racial injustice. Curly Stovall and all like him are put into coffins of their own making.

The one accusation against Emmett Till that anyone who lived through this moment in history remembers is the wolf whistle. While there are people whistling in *Losing Battles*, there is nothing that remotely resembles this moment. If Welty had mentioned wolves or whistles or anything close to them, her readers would have known the

---

8. Bradford Huie."The Shocking Story of Approved Killing in Mississippi,"*Look*, January 24,1956, 46.

source and suspected that she was weaving a fictional commentary about the lynching. I do not believe this was a connection Welty wanted to make openly. However, in the 1965 manuscript when she described the night that Stovall and Champion abduct Jack, she wrote:

"It wasn't without their portion of trouble they ever got those boys out of Banner, just the same," said Uncle Dolphus. "Had to chain 'em both together to drag 'em through the cemetery—that's where the marshal had his motorcycle hid."

"That Ernie's version and Ernie [later Etoyle] embroideries."

"And one of these days you'll cry 'Wolf! Wolf!' And something's going to pop *you* down its little red lane," said Aunt Birdie to the child.[9]

The published version reads:

"Curly knew better, that's why! So off Jack's carted to Foxtown and shooed in jail. And Etoyle said Homer warned him before they started that if he give any more trouble resisting arrest he'd get a bullet ploughed through his leg."

"Etoyle embroiders. What are you doing sitting down with company now, Etoyle Renfro?" asked Miss Lexie. (42)

The issue is not so much that Welty in the 1965 draft made reference to the common folk saying "don't cry wolf." What is noteworthy is that she used it at this moment in the text when the similarities between the fictional and real incidents are great—Till was also abducted from his home in the middle of the night and a young child was the only one who saw him being taken—and then cut it from the published version entirely. It is also interesting that Aunt Birdie says that Ernie (later Etoyle) will be popped, which means killed. Etoyle is an innocent child. The intensity of the outcry against Till's lynching was because he was an innocent child.

Till drowned with a ring on his finger that had his father's initials and the year 1943 printed on it. However, in the farce of a trial that followed his murder, the ring was discarded as evidence. In *A Death in the Delta*, Whitfield recounts the defense's strategy:

9. S44, Part I, 1965, Eudora Welty Collection, Mississippi Department of Archives and History, Jackson.

Strider, the Sheriff of Tallahatchie County, testified for the defense. Taking advantage of the fact that no witness had seen Till actually murdered, Strider claimed that all he knew about the body dredged up from the Tallahatchie river was that it was human. He speculated grotesquely that the notorious NAACP had plotted Till's so-called killing, and that Till himself was living happily in Detroit. One of the five defense attorneys, John Whitten, the chairman of the Democratic Party in Tallahatchie County as well as a first cousin of Mississippi congressman Jamie Whitten, was then faced with the inconvenient fact of Emmett Till's ring. It sufficed for Whitten to conjecture that some sinister group had planted it on the body, and in his summation he denounced such "rabble rousers." The attorney told jurors that he was "sure that every Anglo-Saxon one of you has the courage to free these men in the face of pressure."[10]

No one refuted this absurd claim and the defendants were acquitted and are still free today.

In response, Hodding Carter editorialized in the *Greenville (Miss.) Delta Democrat-Times*, a publication Welty most certainly was at least aware of: "The body was identified by relatives, was accepted by the boy's mother. . . . Had such a murder been planned to replace another body for Till's, . . . someone would have had to have been killed before the boy was abducted, the ring stolen from the young Till and placed on the dead person's finger. Without prior knowledge that Roy Bryant and his half-brother would kidnap Till, as they admittedly did, such a conspiracy defies even the most fantastic reality."[11] In *Losing Battles* Miss Beulah screams, "Oh the safe was on show, the coffin was on show, everything was on show but the ring! The only thing in the world that would have told the true story and spoken for itself! . . . That's missing!" (53) Miss Beulah refers not simply to the facts of the case but also to the intent of the case—Jack protecting his sister's virginity. This wrong-minded notion concerning male chivalry caused Jack's problem in the first place, but his predicament is nothing compared to the violence inflicted in the name of chivalry upon African

10. Stephen Whitfield, *A Death in the Delta: The Story of Emmett Till* (Baltimore: Johns Hopkins Press, 1988), 41.
11. Hodding Carter, *Delta Democrat-Times*, September 6, 1955.

American men, many of whom were killed by lynching throughout the century.

What is ironic about the whole ring story in *Losing Battles* is that there is evidence that Jack did steal the ring from Curly and that on top of this he kept it from his family and gave it to Gloria. After being gone for a period of time after the safe is overturned, he returns to propose to Gloria with a ring. Jack does not whistle at Gloria, the schoolteacher, but he goes much further. He not only proposes, but, given the date of Lady May's birth, most likely has sex with her that very afternoon, long before they are married. If an African American schoolboy had done this to a respectable white woman in the 1930s in Mississippi, he would undoubtedly have been killed. If anyone had known what Gloria did, she would have lost her job and been scorned. In the novel, however, no one thinks anything of Jack's indiscretions and no one accuses him of stealing. They assume that a normal young man needs this outlet. White men could be sexual, but not black men or white women. By focusing only on the lives of the whites, Welty draws a disturbing comparison and provides a mirror in which the white racist can see himself more clearly. Nothing except race—not money or social standing—lies between the fate of the poor white characters in Welty's story and the fate of poor black people in the state of Mississippi at this time, and yet when young white men—even poor white men—engage in pranks and sexual teasing they do not end up being lynched.

If democracy depends on education, it must also depend on having a legal system that enforces the law of the land. In Judge Moody's case he is enforcing the law over a relatively trivial incident. In Mississippi from the 1930s through the 1960s, the legal system did its job only in the best interests of white citizens. This fact became particularly divisive when federal law demanded equal opportunity of education through school busing. Desegregation in a racist society requires strict law enforcement, but in the 1960s—when Welty wrote most of *Losing Battles*—the legal system in Mississippi was allowing anarchy and rule by the masses.

As the law, both Judge Moody and Miss Lexie ("lex" means law) have neglected and abused education as embodied in the figure of Miss

Julia Mortimer. The judge cannot fathom what information Miss Julia wants to give him and avoids ever reaching her. He must sit in the school chair until the voices weave a tapestry in which justice means restraint, dignity, compassion, and empathy rather than violence, force, revenge, and mob rule. For the Beecham/Renfro gang, Judge Moody becomes the student, if not—thanks to Beulah, Jack, and Gloria—the victim of this reunion. At the same time, most of the clan has much to learn about justice. While the judge believes in the letter of the law, the family wants to go around the law, believing in the old model of revenge, the cause of mob rule during desegregation.

When Jack suggests that he will go and let Judge Moody know who helped him out of the ditch, the male cousins and uncles led by Uncle Curtis insist that more be done. "'You got to do more than announce yourself in this world, Jack,' said Uncle Curtis. 'We proved that in court. You're going to just about need to run headlong into the man and butt him with it like a billy goat, to make him pay you heed. But we'll be right behind you to a man. Won't we, sons?'" (84). Welty has made a choice, sending a band of men, boys, and dogs not after an African American man whom they are falsely accusing of rape or murder, as is usually the case, but instead after the judge, the symbol of law and order in a democratic system. Miss Beulah tries to cut through the talk and the increasing hysteria by feeding Jack, but before she can pop a life-saving biscuit in his mouth the cousins chime in:

> "Hey! Jack! Are we supposed to spend the whole day waiting on you to catch up at the table?"
>
> The men were all on their feet. At the same time the porch seemed full of liver- and lemon-spotted dogs. The barking had started over.
>
> "Nathan ain't going to go exactly into raptures over this!" Miss Beulah cried despairingly at them. "Remember I've still got one more brother to come!" (87)

For Miss Beulah to evoke the memory of Nathan, the brother who left to follow the calling of the Lord after killing Mr. Dearman "with a stone to his head, and let 'em hang a sawmill nigger for it" (344) is not only to remind the men pointedly where this kind of action can lead but also to say quite blatantly that they are resembling a lynch mob. But alas, it does no good.

Both Beulah and Gloria object to the tactics the men have planned. Gloria tells Jack, "The system you're trying won't work. . . . I wouldn't need to bring you down to earth if I wasn't your wife" (109). As Jack's wife, Gloria needs Jack on the earth, as part of the physical world, a fertility partner. Gloria tries to bring out Lady May, whose name designates her the archetype of the fertility goddess, but again, it does no good. The men are still dead set on mob action: "There was a general surge of men and boys departing from the house. Bird dogs, coon dogs, and squirrel dogs were jumping and pawing the air and racing for the gate, every one giving his bark" (93). What we hear in this passage is the rhetoric surrounding the creation of a mob that will literally take the law, represented by Judge Moody, into its own hands. By setting whites against whites Welty keeps the scene on the level of political commentary and satire, reminding us quite clearly that the racist battle in the courts has been created and perpetuated by Anglo-Saxon Americans.

At the moment in the narrative when the old ways of creating justice seem to be winning, Welty asserts the central image of the text, the school bus, and all that it symbolizes—education, desegregation, community understanding, and change. When the men try to decide how they will get to Banner Top, they gradually realize that the only vehicle that still runs is the school bus. When Elvie suggests that Jack drive it, Vaughn declares that Jack is no longer the driver, implying that a new hero, with different powers of regeneration, is coming to replace the old, and that in this new story the school bus is not meant for performative acts of vengeance. In case we have any doubt that Welty sees salvation through education, she reinforces this theme by crafting the plot so that the one who finally succeeds in interrupting the mob rule is Gloria, not merely in her role as wife and mother, but in her role as schoolteacher: "'Let every one of you come back to your seats,' came the uplifted voice of Gloria. 'I don't want man or boy to leave this house, or budge an inch till Jack gets back. This is Jack Renfro's own business. And nobody's coming with him but me and the baby'" (93). Gloria takes with her into battle both her school satchel and her baby. As Jack takes off to find Judge Moody, he is entering not a traditionally "masculinized" world of battle, revenge, and heroic hardship but a fertile world, of sex, family, and love. Looking after him

Aunt Beck says, "'Jack's going to make a wonderful little mother himself'" (94).

In the actual fray of battle, after they have reached Banner Top and Gloria has made love to Jack and Jack is still dead set on sending Judge Moody's car off the road, Gloria hands him the baby: "'If you can't be a better example to Lady May—hold her!' Gloria's arm circled up in a teacher's best gesture, and it threw her off balance" (119). As Jack falls off Banner Top, off "Lovers' Leap" as it is also called, with Lady May in his arms, trying to nurse at his chest and kicking him with her heels, he lands in a bed of yellow cosmos: "it might have been everything feminine laughing at him" (119). Gloria, on the other hand, lands in the ditch at the foot of the mailbox holding on to the image of Uncle Sam. In using her motherly sense and teacher's power Gloria is doing more to uphold the law of the land, the connection to a national, communal identity than is Jack, the quintessential hero. Willie Trimble sounds the death knell to family isolation, to the isolation of Banner from the rest of the world, when he constructs Uncle Sam mailboxes all up and down Banner Road. The written word, the letter, serves as a means of crossing over. Through the written word Julia Mortimer becomes a central character at the reunion, which someone terms her wake. Presidents and the concept of democracy are strong symbols in the novel; Miss Lexie tells Julia that if she has such terrible things to say about the human race she should send them to the president. Miss Beulah's profile is said to look like George Washington. The novel's political vision is an unmistakably maternal one, in which mothers are taking over as the founders of the country and the nation as a democracy is more powerful than the whims of individual clans. As long as the Beecham/Renfros try to create an isolated family unit, they face constant intrusion from the outside world.

When Gloria runs into the road, she crosses beyond gender stereotypes into a new realm in which action and motherhood are combined. Jack and Gloria reverse gender roles and dramatically redirect the plot. The offspring of their union, of the true merging of "male" and "female," the baby Lady May, becomes the hero of the moment. She forcefully knocks the breath out of Jack, making it impossible for him to speak, and the moment the judge's car goes around the bend, she takes off across the road. She runs in front of the car, and Gloria, as both sacrificial mother and heroic savior, throws herself on top of her. As for Jack, he spins around in a buffoon-like pirouette and falls down in his own ditch.

As Suzanne Marrs has informed us, this scene was a late addition to the novel, appearing first in the 1969 manuscript and, as she asserts, signifying the change from revenge to love as Jack's motivation.[12] Rather than picking Lady May up in her arms and running to the side of the road, Gloria forces the narrative to turn in the direction of love rather than revenge by lying in the road in wait for Judge Moody. Since he cannot hit Gloria and Lady May, he heads up Banner Top: "The car took the only way left open and charged up Banner Top in a bombardment of pink clods like thrown roses" (120). The car in this instant becomes the plot, with the only direction it can take being up Banner Top; like the hearse of a famous person, the car is followed by thrown roses representing the burial of the old heroic revenge narrative. Gloria and Lady May have changed the story so that Jack must be indebted to his enemy. Gloria is still the ultimate teacher, and she is not putting her life on the line for only one student, as it might appear; she is teaching to the whole community, the whole audience of this novel, the most important lesson of all: the essential distinctions between heroic action and communal action and between revenge and love. On a comic level it is understood that Gloria is in no need of being saved but that she must enact this moment in order to save Jack from himself. The "bombardment of pink clods like thrown roses" combines the conventional pink of little girls and femininity with the war imagery of bombardment. "Roses" and "pink" have won the novel's war. Upon Jack's return from the pen, Elvie had cried out, "You'll have to go back to driving the school bus!" and Welty had gone on to describe that vehicle: "Under the tree it stood headed downhill and first in line, with a chunk under the wheel. It was wrapped in dust as in a pink baby blanket" (88). By changing his motivation from revenge to love and gratitude, Jack at last earns the right to drive the school bus. Wrapped in pink dust like a baby's blanket, the bus is like a girl baby waiting to change the world. The bus is the hope of the future.

12. Suzanne Marrs, "The Making of *Losing Battles*: Jack Renfro's Evolution," *Mississippi Quarterly* 37 (1984): 469.

The metaphorically resonant introductory pages of *Losing Battles* end with the line, "A swollen shadow bulked underneath it, familiar in shape as Noah's Ark—a school bus" (4). To call a school bus "Noah's Ark" at any historical moment would be suspicious. To create this metaphor in Mississippi in the 1960s was explicit and courageous. The bus's being named "Noah's Ark" suggests quite directly that it is our only salvation from certain death by the flood of violence and ignorance. It also implies that, like Noah, we are going to save the human race if we get on this bus in fertile pairs of opposites and if we include all types of human beings. For Welty school-bus desegregation meant the symbolic fertility of mutual crossing over of different worlds—black and white, old and young, rich and poor, masculine and feminine.

The one moment in *Losing Battles* that Eudora Welty breaks the flood of dialogue to take refuge in the lyrical cadence of her own narrative, she turns to Vaughn and his silent reverie. To Vaughn, the voices he has been listening to all day are like the "rush of water—the Bywy on the rise in spring; or it might have been the rains catching up after them, to mire them in" (363). Vaughn's answer to this flood of talk is to pull the school bus out of the ditch and drive it home safely to be ready for the next day. Everyone else is talking; Vaughn is the only one acting. The bus is the savior, the ark. When it starts to run, it sounds like the "chirping of a frog," a symbol of water and fertility in a drought-ridden land. Vaughn must start the bus because "he so loved Banner School that he would have beaten sunup and driven there now, if the doors had any way of opening for him" (364). To Vaughn, the

> bus, as long as he held the wheel, held him all around, and at the same time he could feel that bus on its own wheels rolling on his tongue, like a word of his own ready to be spoken, then swallowed back into his throat, going down, inside and inside. . . .
>
> Before he left the bus here, ready and secret till morning, he made sure of the book he had been sitting on, the new geography that he'd traded out of Curly Stovall. He dragged it to his cheek, where he could smell its print, sharper, blacker, dearer than the smell of new shoes. (365)

Vaughn then notices the bell that gathers all the children to school and, finally, Grandma's loom: "There the loom stood, open to the

night like the never-closed-in passage itself. The moon picked out its
spider web. It looked as tall as Banner bridge, and better made, stretch-
ing from the old loom to the ceiling of the passage. His mother's
broom tore it down every morning, it was back new every night" (366).
With the images of the loom, the web, the maze, the bridge, and the
passageway, Welty connects all the forces of communion. Jack is a
farmer, but Vaughn is a farmer/scholar, a new breed of hero. Jack creates stories with linear temporal plots, but Vaughn loves spatial geography.

Conventional plot development presupposes a building toward a
point of climactic action and then a denouement moving quickly
toward a point of closure or a conclusion. The story of the rise and de-
scent of Judge Moody's Buick follows a schoolteacher's diagram of rising and falling action. The plot revolves around whether it will fall and
whether Jack has achieved his revenge. Balanced on a cross planted by
Uncle Nathan, which reads "Destruction is at Hand," the Buick, the
symbol of class privilege and power, waits in the balance. Obviously
on a purely comic level, Jack and the poor people of Banner whom he
represents get their revenge tenfold while claiming all the while to be
forever grateful and indebted to Judge Moody for saving Gloria and
Lady May's life. This episode would have made a humorous short
story, but as the backdrop to a multivocal novel it serves a more significant purpose: it allows Welty to parody traditional heroic narrative
and present a contrasting, largely feminist narrative structure—
namely the webbed map, the symbol of communal knowledge, responsibility, and education.

When the cyclone hits in *Losing Battles*, the schoolroom does not
fall because it is held up by the students. The schoolroom is not the
locus of education. Education takes place because of the students' desire to learn. During the cyclone, a school chair gets caught up in a
gust of wind and blown over to the Renfro home, an acknowledgment
that they have plenty to teach a body who wants to sit and listen, that
true understanding comes through listening to each other's stories. As
Miss Mortimer keeps telling the children throughout the storm, the
schoolroom is the best place to be. In comparison to education, religion is definitely the loser in Welty's fiction. As the members of the
Beecham-Renfro clan are talking about Julia Mortimer, we hear

Brother Bethune shooting at a tobacco can in the back of the house. Such is the nature of religious leadership, and Welty suggests that sectarian divisions are equally absurd. When Mr. Renfro recalls a tornado striking Banner, he says it "picked the Methodist Church up all in one piece and carried it through the air and set it down right next to the Baptist Church!" (238). If religion is going to serve any purpose at all, all denominations will have to learn to be neighbors. The Banner bridge might well be seen as a metaphor suggesting the need for such alliances. In the eye of the cyclone, as Mr. Renfro reports, "it didn't even wiggle." When Miss Mortimer decides to hold a spelling bee, "school children against the legislature—Miss Julia Mortimer's idea" (242), we hear again Welty's own heart, voicing the belief that school-children know more about the essential elements of education—how to spell, how to dispel ignorance and illiteracy—than legislators and it is time the legislators learned something from them.

By making the bus, the schoolroom, and the schoolteachers so important to the direction of the narrative, Welty has positioned herself firmly on the side of desegregation and busing, the debate that fueled the establishment of the Citizens' Council and the Sovereignty Commission and resurrected the rhetoric of white female virginity and the myth of the black rapist. By establishing femininity on the side of desegregation, by making Gloria and Elvie and Miss Beulah and new hero Vaughn leaders in the struggle against mob rule, she reasserts the position held by many liberal white and black women throughout the century who have argued that women should not present themselves as frail and helpless victims of sexual aggression who need to be saved by white male vigilantes but instead should actively resist that role. In their pamphlets, newspaper articles, and novels, Ida B. Wells and Lillian Smith held white women accountable for the terrible lies they told in order to escape social humiliation in the face of sexual indiscretion. Rather then be accused of having illicit affairs and unwanted pregnancies, white women often accused innocent black men of rape and watched as they were lynched or mutilated. When we read *Losing Battles* against this backdrop we find the story of Miss Julia Mortimer much richer and more politically significant.

Upon looking at the map, Judge Moody comments that nothing was right about Miss Julia's mind when she drew it. In one sense this was perfectly true. Pushed to the limit by her circumstance and by Miss Lexie, she was not doing anything "right" in the sense of proper or correct. Instead she was growing beyond the person they knew to a more self-aware, more communal view of herself. If the judge has been maneuvered here to the reunion, it is not to teach but to be taught. Beulah, whose name in the Old Testament means the promised land, puts him in the school chair. From mothers Beulah, Granny, and Gloria and all their relatives Judge Moody learns about a type of maternal knowledge, a way of negotiating difficult terrain that no law book could teach him. What Julia Mortimer might have realized in her dying days is that there is more than one kind of knowledge, just as there is more than one kind of ignorance. The maze or web, emanating from a central point but leading out in all directions, mirrors the surface structure of *Losing Battles*. The reunion is the point and the lines stroking out are all the lives and voices speaking. Miss Julia herself is a point, with all her students and all that she has taught them forming the lines in all directions. The maze or web insists on connection and is held together by the cross-mark ploughed into the center. What the judge almost grasps is what the text reveals—that Miss Mortimer's death and the family reunion occurring at the same moment force a kind of bringing together of groups that is essential to the revitalization of this poverty-stricken wasteland.

In the unveiling of the story, as they try to determine Gloria's parentage, Judge Moody, Gloria, and all the reunion participants are led through a maze of stories, primarily by Granny. It is a maze that has no exit, but one through which we must travel. What we know or we think we know are several "facts": Sam Dale Beecham suffered an accident when he was a little boy. A piece of coal landed in his lap and left him infertile. Sam Dale wrote Rachel Sojourner a postcard in which he mentioned getting a toy for "our baby." These are all stories that Granny and Beulah could be weaving to keep Jack out of trouble for marrying his cousin, or they could have actually happened. Welty makes sure we do not know. We are fairly certain that Sam Dale is not the father although most of the female contingent of the reunion try to force this identity down Gloria's throat. During the watermelon rape scene someone has just sung "London Bridge." London Bridge was not a bridge bringing together people of different backgrounds like Banner Bridge but a bridge where political dissidents were imprisoned; one verse says, "Take the key and lock her up." Because we know Gloria is being held prisoner by the Beecham clan, we know the parenthood of Sam Dale and Rachel Sojourner may very well be a fiction. They want to cut Gloria down to size as Miss Lexie does when she "fixes" her dress: they want her to be one of them.

Mr. Dearman seems to be the most likely candidate for Gloria's father, and everyone sees Miss Julia as her inspirational mother, but no critic has ever suggested that Julia Mortimer herself could be Gloria's physical mother. By considering Julia's maternity as one possibility in a multivariant text, we allow her sexuality and acknowledge her role as fertility goddess, as one who crosses over the bridge, rather than limiting her to the old-maid straitjacket. But even more importantly, we understand her position in a society that denies freedom of sexual expression and forces people into deceit and secrecy. Welty makes it obvious that Jack is a fertility consort. Rain does not come and the crops do not grow in his absence. But if Jack is the male element, then Miss Julia Mortimer is a fertility goddess in the crone aspect, ready to die in the fall (the novel is set in August) to return in the spring. What we must ask is what kind of fertility she will bring to this dying community. We know from Gloria's stories that Julia grows extraordinary roses and all types of flowers and sends seeds and peach trees out to the starving people throughout the county. She is the earth mother feeding the children the milk of her harvest. She keeps a herd of cows and milks them, and she is known for her "fruit bushes and flower plants for sale, and good seed—vegetables. She had a big yard and plenty of fertilizer. . . . She'd sell through the mail. She wouldn't exchange. But she'd work just as hard trying to give some of her abundance away" (243).

Referring to all Miss Julia's successful students, Judge Moody says, "They're all scattered wide, of course"(305). During Miss Lexie's story, Miss Beulah keeps asking Lexie if she threw the letters Miss Mortimer wrote and received into the pigpen. In "The Yule Boar" chapter of *The Golden Bough*, James Frazer notes that the pig was seen as a fertility corn spirit and that when the last sheaf was cut in the harvest it was called the pig and thrown in the pigpen.[13] The last writings of Miss Mortimer and the last letters sent to her are her final harvest. If we allow for the possibility that Julia had been fertile in her youth, then we can allow for the possibility that she is also connected with the crone aspect in her old age. As Mortimer she would be associated with Morrigana, the goddess who drives sailors to their deaths, and with Mort, the death element. In these manifestations Julia could have more to do with Mr. Dearman's, and by extension the sawmill black man's, death than first meets the eye. If she had to give up Gloria in order to keep teaching, then her passion for teaching becomes that much more powerful. If she had to murder or keep silent about a murder in order to keep teaching, she then becomes culpable in an intricate web of deceit and prejudice, part of the problem rather than above it and therefore able to teach a more personal and thus more powerful lesson. The fertility she would then bring to the community would be one of honesty and full disclosure, a type of disclosure that would help herself and her community to atone for the execution of the innocent black man. In this symbolic web we view her with a depth of awe, sadness, and understanding that we could not have felt before. The cross-mark on the map Julia gives to Judge Moody is literally "ploughed" into the center as if it is a seed planted that will sprout later in the story. If the cross-mark symbolizes not only the actual physical and sexual union or crossing of men and women but also the death and destruction of the crosses burned into people's lawns by the KKK, then sexuality and race are again juxtaposed.

Granny tells the reunion directly that she remembers Julia and Mr. Dearman riding out together:

> "And on moonlight nights like tonight,"said Granny, "they'd mount 'em the same steed and ride 'em up the road and down the road, then hitch the bridle to the tree. That's after I was safe under the covers and Mr. Vaughn had left off his praying and settled in to snore."
>
> "Who, Granny?" the aunts were all asking her.
>
> "Just told you. The schoolteacher. Ain't that who you're trying to bury?" she asked.

13. James Frazer, *The Golden Bough*, vol. 2 (New York: Avenal Books, 1981), 26–31.

"Miss Julia Mortimer? Granny!" Uncle Percy, Uncle Curtis, and Uncle Dolphus all exclaimed at her in shocked voices. Uncle Noah Webster asked, "Granny dear, are you telling us about Miss Julia Mortimer and a sweetheart?"

"Call him Dearman. That's his moniker," said Granny. (340)

We might give this story little credence because Granny has willfully been taking the reader down blind turns in the maze; however, earlier in the narrative, the judge has also intimated that there might be something between Dearman and Mortimer. Asked if he had been Miss Julia's lover, Judge Moody responds, "'Oh no. There were plenty without me, from Ludlow and all around. Herman Dearman, even, from this neck of the woods and crude as they come—even he aspired to her, knowing no better. She didn't discourage him enough—perhaps didn't know how,' said Judge Moody. 'Perhaps was able to even see something in him'" (304). Thus Julia Mortimer, who was considered beautiful, was far from a wallflower in her younger days—which brings us to the problem of Nathan's murder of Dearman.

According to the voices at the reunion, Nathan killed Mr. Dearman for Sam Dale. No one says why. We assume because Dearman was sleeping with Rachel, but there is no evidence in the text to support that supposition. Neither is there any real evidence that Sam Dale loved Rachel. Nathan could have killed Mr. Dearman for taking his father's store or for destroying the virgin forest, but neither of these motives seems as strong as personal vengeance. Noah Webster calls Nathan Miss Mortimer's "shining light" (235), and we know that he has a habit of paying her morning visits. "Shining light" is very close to "shining knight" and suggests that Nathan was in some way in service to Miss Mortimer. The echo of "knight" also reminds us that the KKK called themselves knights. Nathan kills "Her"man "Dear"-man with a stone to the forehead, reminding us of David and Goliath. Nathan could have killed Mr. Dearman because he felt that he was defiling Julia Mortimer or because on a more sinister level Miss Julia wanted him to slay the giant Dearman who was destroying the forest and threatening to destroy her. If Julia Mortimer were pregnant with Dearman's child, she may have needed to get rid of him in order to keep her job.

Whatever the case, the person who put Gloria in the shoe box and set her in the swing had a strong reason to keep a secret. If Julia had kept Gloria, she would have lost her job; schoolteachers were not allowed to date, let alone marry, let alone have children out of wedlock. Julia Mortimer could not have stood losing her teaching job. She even told her students, "Nothing in this world can measure up to the joy you'll bring me if you allow me to teach you something"(273). And the person who gave away Gloria was very intelligent. She gave her to the woman most likely to respond appropriately, the home-demonstration agent of Boone County, whom she knew would take her directly to the Ludlow orphanage. Moreover, on her deathbed Miss Julia is searching for Gloria. She wants only Gloria. She tells Miss Lexie that Gloria knows it will be for her own good to come to see her. She also tells the judge to come visit and bring his Mississippi law books with him, and he later reads her letter to the reunion guests.

> "There's been one thing I never did take into account," [Judge Moody] continued. "Most likely, neither did you. Watch out for innocence. Could *you* be tempted by it, Oscar—to your own mortification—and conspire with the ignorant and the lawless and the foolish and even the wicked, *to hold your tongue!*" Judge Moody steered the sheet of paper around where a few more lines of writing ran under his eyes along the margin. "Oscar Moody, I want to see you here in Alliance at your earliest convenience. Bring your Mississippi law with you, but you'll have to hear the story. It leads to a child. If I'm finally to reach my undoing, I won't be surprised to meet it in a child. That's what I started with. You'd better get here fast." (300)

Mrs. Moody suggests that Judge Moody was wrong to read the letter because it looked as if it were written on the flyleaf of a Bible page. Earlier, Aunt Beck reminds Uncle Curtis that Gloria can't know who her parents are because she had no parents to write her name down in their Bible (251). Now Miss Mortimer is writing a clue to Gloria's parentage down in her Bible, and she informs the judge that the story she wants to tell him might lead to her undoing. If the story simply had to do with the fact that Gloria was kin to the Beechams this would not lead to Miss Mortimer's undoing; it would have to be something in which she was directly involved. Gloria remembers, "Miss Julia told me there was a dark thread, a dark thread running through my story somewhere. . . . Or my mother wouldn't have made a mystery out of me. And I owed it to myself to find out the worst, and the quicker the better. 'You were found in Medley—that's walking distance of Banner School. Get to work on yourself. And I'll work on you too'" (251). This sounds an awful lot like an assignment to which the teacher already knows the answer. Julia Mortimer would be the most likely person to walk from Banner School to Medley.

Throughout the search for Gloria's parents, the aunts keep saying like mother, like daughter. There are no two people more alike in the book than Gloria and Julia. Gloria is a passionate teacher even if she resists her calling. She is as bright as Miss Mortimer and her match in any battle. Rachel is not bright. She cannot learn arithmetic. Gloria is so good at math, she can calculate how much money to save to get the things she wants. She knows how much fabric to buy to make her wedding dress a maternity/wedding dress. Like mother, like daughter. If Julia did get pregnant she hid it from the world as Gloria would. Gloria was born on April Fool's Day. Her mother, whoever she might have been, fooled everyone. When the judge is listing all the young men who loved Julia, he mentions Gerald Carruthers. "'He trotted off and worked himself to the bone in Pennsylvania Medical School to come home and set up a country practice, you know,' said Judge Moody. 'He had a fond allegiance to her. And he kept coming, didn't he, attending her?'" (304). If Gerald Carruthers attended Julia Mortimer when she was pregnant, which we know he might have done, considering the fact that he helped Beulah give birth to Jack, no one needed to know. She was well protected. Finally, some small but interesting details: All the aunts and Miss Beulah repeatedly assert that Julia Mortimer expected Gloria to fill her shoes. Mrs. Hanks finds Gloria in a clean shoe box. Rachel was poor. The likelihood that she would have a new pair of shoes in a clean shoe box during the Depression is slim; also, new shoes symbolize the start of the school year. Gloria is described as "red as a pomegranate," and Miss Mortimer wears a red sweater. A pomegranate is full of seeds, and Miss Mortimer sends seeds through the mail in boxes. She likes giving her fruits away. If Gloria is her fruit, she gave her away. Finally she wants to pass on the torch, the red fiery torch. Gloria has red fiery hair. She has passed on the torch and Gloria walks in her shoes.

Even if Welty herself chose not to crusade, believing that crusading had little place in true art, she still had great respect for the Julia Mortimers of the world and the kind of work they were trying to do. Julia Mortimer, the social activist, is the heroine of *Losing Battles*, but she is a flawed and difficult heroine. She is a person of passion and inspiration, and such people in Welty's work are always on the edge of sanity. They are capable of great love and great hate, of bringing forth life and murdering. As I have mentioned, Miss Julia's name brings up allusions to Mort, death, and Morrigana, the great sea goddess who lures sailors to their deaths. Morrigana is a triple goddess figure, evoking the maiden, the mother, and the crone. Miss Lexie is Miss Mortimer's shadow. She cannot go to college because she "fell down on Virgil" (276). Unlike Miss Mortimer, Miss Lexie could not love as Dido does, and she would not burn herself to death on a pyre for the loss of a great love. Julia Mortimer would do both, only the difference between herself and Dido is that teaching, not a man, is her great love. Uncle Curtis says about Miss Mortimer, "She was ready to teach herself to death for you, you couldn't get away from that" (240). Miss Mortimer would do all this and more for her love of teaching but not for her love of a man. Dearman, the one man who had tempted her, needed to be out of the picture. Certainly she would not have done this herself, but she could have inadvertently encouraged Nathan. It is easy to put Julia Mortimer on a heroic pedestal, but it is just as important to see her crone/Kali aspect. Like Miss Eckhart, who may have poisoned her mother to keep the old woman from screaming in pain during her piano lessons and who tried to burn herself on "a pyre" when she could no longer play the piano, the great artist is ruthless with everything that gets in the way of her art. Julia Mortimer needs to teach, she needs students, she needs a battle, and while she might lose the battles, ultimately she wins the war against ignorance.

Granny says quite bluntly that Miss Julia could not put two and two together but that she herself could and that if Miss Julia was young once then so was she. With this comment Granny implies that she too has lusted after other men besides Grandpa Vaughn and that she therefore knows what Miss Mortimer was capable of with Mr.

Dearman. Dearman left Banner covered with stumps; he raped a virgin forest and most likely many women. Granny may be putting two and two together by blaming Julia for what happened to Nathan. One could read the text as saying that Nathan killed Dearman for Julia and set out on his quest because of her words, and that Nathan erased any record of Gloria's birth by torching the courthouse in which the records were kept. After all, Miss Julia's advice to Nathan was to begin again. The only way for her to begin all over again was to get rid of Dearman, give Gloria away, and torch the courthouse. At the end of the reunion we watch as, "Presently Uncle Nathan passed close by the porch, going down into the yard carrying upright a hoe with rags draped about the blade in a sort of helmet. There was a cutting smell of coal oil where he walked. After a moment, a red torch shot up fire, moved; then an oval, cottony glow, like utterly soft sound, appeared in the dark—how close, how far, how high up or low down, was not easy for the eye to make sure. Then it went out, and appeared almost at once in a new place" (347–8). The cross-mark in Miss Julia's map symbolizes crossing over into worlds that one might not have experienced, the coming together of two opposite paths, another type of bridge, but it must also in the Mississippi of 1930 or 1960 represent the burning cross ploughed into the front yards of civil rights activists and black citizens. While Nathan is no Ku Klux Klan leader, he is a shining light/knight and he does drive crosses into the ground on a regular basis. He does burn justice in the form of the courthouse. He is in many ways the conscience of the KKK, the one-armed veteran repenting his sins.

We know that at some point Nathan confessed to Miss Julia that he killed Dearman, because she tells him that he can start over with a new life. We assume she did not say anything to the law because he does not go to jail. Julia Mortimer is part of the web of responsibility for the death of the black man who worked at the sawmill. She, like all white southerners, all Americans, is caught in the maze of racism and sexism. Her warning to Judge Moody to beware of innocence is apt. No one is innocent. Everyone is guilty and must begin to find ways to come forward, "to spread out their minds and their hearts to other people, so they could be read like books" (432). Julia wants to tell Judge Moody that she is not innocent, that in order to keep on teaching she let Nathan's crime go unreported, that she was an accomplice to the crime. Like those women who kept secret about sexual liaisons and let African American men die for their honor, she was responsible. As she tells us quite clearly, this may lead to her undoing.

With her final words, "Mourn me you fools," Julia Mortimer makes one last stand in her fight against ignorance. In the climate of 1960s Mississippi, "Mourn me you fools" is a direct call to the citizens of Mississippi to choose desegregation over personal bias: Mourn the judge's unwillingness to cross bridges and enforce the law of the land. Mourn the fact that without busing and desegregation Mississippi faces the death of public education. Miss Julia tells the reunion party to bury her under the cornerstone in front of the schoolhouse, where everyone will use her as a doormat. Judge Moody fears she is humbling herself, but, more precisely, she has learned a lesson he still needs to learn—that one must fall in order to experience communion and only in community is there true freedom and equal education for all. Miss Julia either underestimates the true intelligence of the human beings she has been teaching or knows that faced with this decision they will finally take their education into their own hands and go against her dying wish. The people of Banner know something she has taught them: that the teacher alone does not represent education. They built the schoolhouse. They attended. They keep attending. Even in the midst of the turmoil over the Buick, Gloria and Jack go pick up the children and take them to school. In death they make Julia Mortimer human and bury her with all their kin in the public cemetery. The bridge, which has not wobbled in the cyclone, holds hundreds of cars coming over it for the funeral. Gloria has stepped into her shoes by marrying and having a baby by Jack. If Gloria is indeed Miss Mortimer and Mr. Dearman's child or even their metaphoric child, then in Lady May we have a coupling of New South and Old South mentalities, of progress and tradition, of responsibility and independence, of the communal and the self.

When all the other vehicles have broken down the bus runs easily. Throughout the turmoil the bus and the bridge take the beating of time and neglect and remain intact. A new schoolteacher has come and Vaughn, who is driving the school bus, desires learning; another romance between schoolteacher and student has developed. The school bus leads the caravan of Buick, truck, and mules. The mules may put on the brakes so that the school bus does not move too fast into the future, but with Vaughn at the wheel it speeds down the road. As Noah's Ark, the bus will be driven by Gloria and Jack—the openly sexual, fertile lovers—who have been spared to people the earth, to save us from the flood of ignorance and false innocence. Welty does not ask us, as in a detective story, to discover the "truth" but to entertain a variety of possibilities, possibilities that lead us beyond easy answers, stereotypes, and prejudices. She asks us not to confine individuals into such stultifying categories as old-maid schoolteachers or tired old men, but to allow the possibility that each of us is sexual, each of us is fertile, each of us capable of bearing fruit, each of us capable of murder, each of us capable of being both pupil and teacher. When Judge Moody talks about Miss Julia's learning to drive, he claims she drove backwards with her gaze fixed on a perpendicular cross in front of her. The cross-mark, ploughed into the center. Up until the very end she recognizes the need to transform the cross from the horror of the KKK and the ineffectiveness of organized religion, to make it mean once again a meeting at the crossroads, the fertility of words exchanged between strangers, written letters crisscrossing throughout the world.

*Barbara Ladd*

## "Writing against Death"

### Totalitarianism and the Nonfiction of Eudora Welty at Midcentury

> [A]s the tide of Fascism mounted higher and higher in Europe, and it looked as if Americans had been thrown back on their own resources as never before, the whole emphasis of the early depression literature on national self-scrutiny became a thundering flood of national consciousness and self-celebration. Suddenly, as if it marked a necessary expiation of too rapid and embittered a disillusionment in the past, American writing became a swelling chorus of national affirmation and praise. Suddenly all the debunkers of the past, who had long since been on relief, became the special objects of revulsion and contempt. Suddenly all the despised catchwords of the democratic rhetoric took on a brilliant radiance in a Hitler world; in the emotional discovery of America the country once more became, as Jefferson had long ago foreseen, "this government: the world's best hope."
>
> —Alfred Kazin, *On Native Grounds*

Alfred Kazin—of Eudora Welty's own generation—died in 1998. As I was recently reading the last chapter of his *On Native Grounds*, first published in 1942, I was struck by how relevant his assessment of U.S. literature and culture during the late thirties and early forties is to any attempt to situate Welty in the political context of U.S. literary history.[1] Welty began publishing too late to be associated with the literary radicalism of the thirties—that historical period beginning about 1927 and ending with the Spanish Civil War, which began in July 1936. But the early Welty is evoked, if unnamed, in sentence after sentence of Kazin's chapter dealing with the "New Nationalism" in American literature, which charts the movement from the proliferation of expansive and "definitive" biographies of national heroes beginning in the thirties and continuing through the war years to the documentary ac-

1. See Alfred Kazin, *On Native Grounds: An Interpretation of Modern American Prose Literature* (New York: Harcourt Brace, 1942), 502–3.

tivity of the WPA years of 1935 to 1939 (made possible, Kazin tells us, by the conjunction of the camera and the New Deal) to the appearance in popular culture of peculiarly American kinds of folk heroes (described by Max Eastman as "cockalorum demi-gods") and—it seems to me—illustrated by Welty's own Jamie Lockhart of *The Robber Bridegroom.*

I do not mean to suggest that Welty's work is an acritical part of a "swelling chorus of affirmation and praise," or that she holds the debunkers of the past in "contempt," or that her often-used trope of "radiance" to describe those qualities of vulnerability, love, and daring that she most valued in imaginative prose is merely an evocation of a "democratic rhetoric" (although it is that, as I hope to suggest). Rather, I mean to say that the New Nationalism was part of the political context in which she wrote and within which she was first read and therefore to acknowledge that Welty was immersed in and, as "author" (i.e., in her public persona), created within this discursive context. I also want to suggest that her work is deeply if subtly engaged with some of the most pressing political issues of the twentieth century, most notably with questions of the nature and import of nationalism in the modern world and related questions concerning the impact of the State on private life. For Welty, particularly in the nonfiction she wrote between the late thirties and 1961, the private life—i.e., the subjective consciousness, interiority, intimacy, the experience of place, familiar strangers, and strange familiars—struggles for survival and dignity within the context of totalitarian threats: increasing State intervention in private life and the threat of fascism during the thirties, the development of the atomic bomb and the arms race during the forties and fifties. And for Eudora Welty, ostensibly speaking of Henry Green, whom she admires as much as any writer, but speaking also of herself: "Man's dignity lies . . . in resistance, resourcefulness, devilment, in a bit of consolation." If the "authorial" Welty (like Green) walks through her prose "with a step so light it is like the future's," it may be that she associates such authorial reticence with the private life, with dignity and survival, in an age of totalitarianism devoted to the contemplation of death.[2]

---

2. Eudora Welty, "Henry Green: A Novelist of the Imagination," *Texas Quarterly* 4 (1961): 253, 255.

Outside of her writing, Welty is not so reticent. As Suzanne Marrs observes elsewhere in this collection, Welty has been politically visible. Like many other writers and intellectuals, she was active on behalf of Adlai Stevenson in his campaign for president in 1952, when his positions on the need for liberal reform and internationalism struck many Americans as dangerous. This was, after all, a time when the country was deeply suspicious of the perceived connections between liberal or leftist reformers within the U.S. and Communism, when "internationalism" and "reform" seemed (to Joe McCarthy and members of the House Un-American Activities Committee, among others) more like conduits for Communist infiltration of the United States than a manifestation of traditional American liberalism. Welty was also active on behalf of integration in Mississippi during the civil rights struggles of the 1950s and 1960s; in fact, as Marrs's discussion of the contexts in which Welty agreed to give readings and deliver lectures during those years demonstrates, she was more comfortable acting on behalf of than speaking about civil rights. If her words do not address the civil rights agenda directly or polemically, the integrated contexts in which she insisted on reading and speaking those words speak loudly of her commitment.[3]

Nevertheless, the kind of political activity Welty engaged in would hardly qualify her as political in the sense in which most academics now use the term. For one thing, it was not self-directed. In another essay in this collection, Peggy Prenshaw explores some of the fault lines that divide the realm of the political as contemporary feminist and postfeminist readers understand it from the political as most Americans conceptualized it before the social movements of the 1960s, before the personal became political. Although I do not, in this essay, locate Welty within the same political contexts that Prenshaw does (i.e., within the contexts of southern racism and demagoguery, as relevant as they are) and I do not take Welty's feminism to constitute the political content of her work, I do assume that feminism informs, even fundamentally determines, the political content of her work. My argument is consistent with Prenshaw's in the

3. Suzanne Marrs, "'The Huge Fateful Stage of the Outside World': Eudora Welty's Life in Politics," in this volume, 69–87.

shared premise that our contemporary understanding of the political cannot be inscribed upon an earlier context without the mediations of an active historicizing perspective.[4] In short, the political was as much of a spectacle between the thirties and 1961 as it is today; the personal was not. By that I mean two things: first, that however spectacular politics was, it was not self-directed in the same way that it is today; second, that however dramatic personal or private life was to the participants in the drama, it was not—to the extent it is today—spectacular ("exposed to the public gaze").[5] This is one key to the capacity of the private life to signify as a site of political resistance in the literature of the period in a way that it has not done since the sixties.

If the so-called New Nationalism of the World War II years was "new" in any sense at all—that is, different from the "old" nationalism—it was chiefly in its concurrence with (if not its creation by) the growth of federal investment in the economic, political, and cultural affairs of people all over the United States and, indeed, all over the world as we entered World War II and exited as the most victorious and most prosperous of the Allies. "Nationalism" was of great interest to the State during these years, suggesting not only patriotism in the face of Fascist or Communist forces from abroad but evoking the potential of the relatively new and increasingly well-funded social sciences to manage people and resources. Many writers of Welty's generation were very much concerned about the destructive potential of the State's intervention into private life. There was a good deal of demonstrated resistance throughout the country, including an effort to use "regional-

---

4. Peggy Prenshaw, "Welty's Transformations of the Public, the Private, and the Political," ibid., 19–46. For a discussion of the broad political scope of feminist consciousness, see Marjorie Pryse, "'Distilling Essences': Regionalism and 'Women's Culture,'" *American Literary Realism, 1870–1910* 25 (Winter 1993): 1–15. See also Jim Cheney, "Postmodern Environmental Ethics as Bioregional Narrative," *Environmental Ethics* 11 (1989): 117–34, and Allen Pred, "Place as Historically Contingent Process: Structuration and the Time-Geography of Becoming Places," *Annals of the Association of American Geographers* 74 (1984): 279–97.

5. *American Heritage Dictionary of the English Language,* s.v. "spectacular."

ism" to withstand pressures toward nationalistic homogeneity at the same time that regionalism also celebrated Americanness.[6]

Among the many examples of such resistance is Donald Davidson's 1938 book *The Attack on Leviathan: Regionalism and Nationalism in the United States*, the last chapter of which is titled "The Shape of Things to Come: H. G. Wells and AE on the World State."[7] This book is especially interesting for my argument because of Welty's own reading of AE, her lengthy professional relationship with AE's son Diarmuid Russell, who had come to be a literary agent in the United States (and who wrote at least one celebratory essay on his father for the *Atlantic*, in February 1943), and her philosophical affinities with Russell in her demonstrated resistance to materialism as well as to State intervention in the private domain. In Diarmuid Russell's *Atlantic* essay, he states that his father was, even in 1915, "aware of the growing power of the state" and believed "that in twenty-five years the state would be the single most important influence in people's lives, and that its actions and power would reach into the lives of the most obscure and humble persons."[8] By 1935, the year the WPA was begun,

6. Robert Hewison, *Under Siege: Literary Life in London, 1939–1945* (London: Widenfeld and Nicolson, 1977), 176. The motives of regionalists have always been divided between celebrating the unity that supposedly makes diversity possible and resisting the encroachment of sameness. See David Jordan, "Representing Regionalism," *Canadian Review of American Studies* 23 (1993): 101–14. Regionalism can, of course, be one means by which a more centralizing discourse can make its argument, as in Howard W. Odum and Harry Estill Moore, *American Regionalism: A Cultural-Historical Approach to National Integration* (New York: Henry Holt, 1938) and Merrill Jensen, ed., *Regionalism in America* (Madison: University of Wisconsin Press, 1951). This idea may underlie Welty's characterization of *regional* as a "careless term, as well as a condescending one" in "Place in Fiction," in *The Eye of the Story: Selected Essays and Reviews* (1978; rpr. New York: Vintage, 1990), 132.

7. Donald Davidson, *The Attack on Leviathan: Regionalism and Nationalism in the United States* (Chapel Hill: University of North Carolina Press, 1938). See also Robert Penn Warren, "Some Don'ts for Literary Regionalists," *American Review* 8 (1936): 142–50 and "Not Local Color," *Virginia Quarterly Review* 1 (1932): 153–60.

8. Diarmuid Russell, "AE (George William Russell): An *Atlantic* Portrait," *Atlantic*, February 1943, p. 53.

the State had indeed reached out toward "the most obscure and humble persons" in many ways, not least through the paid documentary activities of writers and artists like Eudora Welty.

But by the early 1940s Welty had come to some conclusions about the cultural impact of the documentary sensibility. One month before the publication of Russell's essay, Welty had written to him regarding his plans to write for the *Atlantic* an article discussing the tendency of professional writers to go "reportorial": "I think too that . . . in a material age readers will fasten onto books that are factual and reportorial just like the flies on over-ripe fruit, and all work together to hasten the decay." Whether she is writing about the essay that became "An *Atlantic* Portrait" of AE a month later or another essay that Russell had in mind, it is clear that Welty shared with him and his father a fear that the facts and reports of "a material age" were contributing to the decay of cultural integrity.[9]

Set over against the reportorial in Welty's eyes was the revelatory or the visionary act of creative and personal understanding that linked the perceiver with the perceived. A couple of years before the above communication, she had written to Russell after having reread *The Candle of Vision* and other books by his father:

> I don't know what I apprehended from them when I read them first—it was not what I understand now or what I may understand later—but I suppose it was what I needed. It was the first crisis of a certain kind in my life, and I was frightened—it was when I was sent to the Middle West to school. I was very timid and shy, younger than the rest and those people up there seemed to me like sticks of flint, that live in the icy world; I am afraid of flintiness—I had to penetrate that, but not through *their* hearts. . . . [I]t was some kind of desire to be shown that the human spirit was not like that shivery winter in Wisconsin, that the opposite to all this existed in full.[10]

In many respects Welty's is a vision very different from AE's. Her imagination is not primarily, like his, a religious or theological one, but it is deeply humanistic. She is more secular and more modern. If

---

9. Michael Kreyling, *Author and Agent: Eudora Welty and Diarmuid Russell* (New York: Farrar, Straus, Giroux, 1991), 6.
10. Ibid., 10.

AE was steeped in the spiritualism of the nineteenth century, for Welty "the spirit world" probably connoted something akin to a post–Theory of Relativity "spirit of place," which encompassed the expression and impression of tradition in the lives of ordinary (or extraordinary) people as well as new conceptualizations of "place" as a function of time and location made possible by conjunctions of astronomy and physics; Welty's allusions to the celestial are everywhere in her criticism and her fiction. But AE's subject in *The Candle of Vision* and throughout his prose work is the threat represented by the State and its materialism to the individual's spiritual sensibility "with its admission of incalculable mystery," and Welty's subject also was becoming human mystery, more particularly a celebration of human mystery in the face of the era's proliferation of facts and reports about humanity.[11]

Welty's own experience with and growing understanding of the impact on private life of the conjunction of the camera and the New Deal may have prompted her growing resistance to the "reportorial." In 1935, while she was working as a junior publicity agent for the WPA, she was also photographing people from all over Mississippi; her photographs were exhibited in New York in 1936 and again in 1937. For the 1937 show, she was specifically asked for photographs of "poor whites." Her first attempt at book publishing was a collection of photographs, with text, titled *Black Saturday*, which was rejected. In 1937 she submitted some photographs to the new magazine *Life*, and one was published there in early 1938. Some of her photographs also appeared in *Mississippi: The Magnolia State*, a 1938 WPA-sponsored guide to the state.[12] She was thus involved in the recovery of the historical, regional, ethnic, and economic underground of American cul-

11. A. E., *Imaginations and Reveries* (Dublin and London: Maunsel and Company, 1915), quoted in Kreyling, *Author and Agent*, 28.
12. Suzanne Marrs, "Photographs," *The Welty Collection: A Guide to the Eudora Welty Manuscripts and Documents at the Mississippi Department of Archives and History* (Jackson and London: University Press of Mississippi, 1988), 78; Hunter Cole and Seetha Srinivasan, "Eudora Welty and Photography: An Interview," *Photographs* (Jackson: University Press of Mississippi, 1989), xix.

ture that was paid for by the New Deal and associated with the New Nationalism of the war years.

Regardless of that fact, most of what Welty has subsequently said about those days suggests that for all her willingness to work for the WPA and her love of traveling the roads of Mississippi, she found herself at odds with those who were motivated by a "cause," who represented those roads as back roads and the people of Mississippi as hapless victims or grateful beneficiaries of a more resourceful elite. Instead, she viewed her travels with the WPA as enabling her to "see the world," and she wrote to her agent Diarmuid Russell in September 1940 that she wished he too "could see Mississippi"

> because I think you might like the things I do about it, the folk quality to the little adventures and stories and the directness and simplicity, really the dignity, in the way they find and hold their beliefs, and the feeling of the legendary and the endurance of something rather wonderful in a way of life, that you get when you see some of the ruins and haunted houses. I don't think it's just in my imagination, I am sure there is a quality and a feeling that is inherent in these places, and I have tried to comprehend it.

Mississippi is less a backwater for Welty than a place of "origin and history and destination," not so unlike the place we return to in Robert Frost's "Directive," a place we can "drink and be whole again beyond confusion."[13]

Welty's objection to the work of WPA documentary photographers has to do with what she perceives as the contempt they exhibit for the privacy and dignity of their subjects. She mentions Walker Evans in several of her conversations about photography, always with some disapproval of the use of photographs for exhortation. She also notes that whereas she would not hesitate to take photographs of the *posters* of freaks displayed at carnivals and fairs as part of a "school of naive folk art," she considers the photographing of the "freaks" themselves by photographers like Diane Arbus to be a violation of privacy.[14]

13. In Kreyling, *Author and Agent,* 43; Eudora Welty, "Ida M'Toy," *Accent* 2 (1942): 214; Robert Frost, "Directive," *The Poetry of Robert Frost,* ed. Edward C. Lathem (London: Cape, 1971), 376.
14. Cole and Srinivasan, "Eudora Welty and Photography," xix.

Welty is consistent in her efforts to distinguish between what a writer or artist does and what a photographer does, and her insistence on distinguishing between photography and imaginative writing always has to do with motivation and use, with the rhetoric more than the aesthetics of photography, and is chiefly determined by the documentary context in which photographs were taken and viewed in the thirties as well as the potential for violation of which subsequent experience with the media has since made us so aware. Once again Alfred Kazin offers a clue to the context of her aversion to documentary photography in his discussion of "what Lincoln Kirstein described as the function of the candid camera in our time, to make up 'in quantitative shock what it lacks in real testimony'":

> It follows from all that has been said of the documentary reporters that the appeal of the camera was not to their superficiality but to their spiritual fatigue, as it were; to their "not knowing . . . society's not knowing." The "keen historic spasm of the shutter," as James Agee called it, served not only "to portray America," but also to answer subtly to the writer's conscious or unconscious unwillingness or inability to go beyond his material. As Agee put it in the documentary book written to end all documentary books, *Let Us Now Praise Famous Men*, with the camera "everything is to be discerned, for him who can discern it, and centrally and simply, without other dissection into science, or digestion into art . . . all of consciousness is shifted from the imagined, the revisive, to the effort to perceive simply the cruel radiance of what is." . . . [T]he camera served to give documentary prose a hard, wry, noncommittal character—a character entirely appropriate to its obsession with the surface drama of the times, its stabbed and stablike consciousness, its professed contempt for "illusion."[15]

But there were uses of the camera that could constitute real testimony—as Agee's book itself makes clear. One wonders, for example, whether Kazin's observations hold true when the person viewing the photograph is the subject herself or a member of her family or community. It is telling, I think, that Welty tried to get prints of her photographs to the subjects, understanding that these were often the only

15. Kazin, *On Native Grounds*, 494–6.

ones they had ever had taken, suggesting that these are the people Welty imagines as viewers as well as subjects. For Welty these "snapshots," as she would later refer to them, were not primarily documentary records "for an agency, or a cause," but intended for the subjects of the photographs and their friends and families, prompts for memory and understanding.[16]

When asked by an interviewer if the technique of the flashback in narrative is comparable to taking a photograph, Welty responds that in a flashback "what is shown is selective. Chosen, specific, pertinent, and thus revelatory," whereas in a photograph one can "compose" or "frame" the subject but cannot, in quite the same way, "choose" or invent the subject. This is true, but as Roland Barthes writes (from a position as implicitly critical of documentary photography as Welty's), photography "induces us, vaguely, to think. . . . [It] is subversive not when it frightens, repels, or even stigmatizes, but when it is pensive." In an important exploration of the intersections between Barthes's aesthetics of photography and Welty's aesthetics of narrative, Harriet Pollack contends that many of Welty's stories demand to be read the way her photographs must be read as if the stories, like the photographs, are composed of "the framing of chance details," "revelation and meaning" produced by "privileging the framed—the random, accidental, signifying detail, and the reverie it evokes." This demand for reverie from the viewer, for the unfolding of meaning only as time passes and we continue to look and to ponder, distinguishes Welty's snapshots as it distinguishes her fiction.[17]

In Welty's own practice, then, if not always in her theory, writing and photography do seem to be related arts, with "vision" being as important to the taking of those photographs and "memory," and "understanding" to the examination of them as "vision," "memory," and "understanding" are central to the writing of her fiction: "in both cases," she says, "writing and photography, you were trying to portray

16. Cole and Srinivasan, "Eudora Welty and Photography," xiii–xv, xix.
17. Ibid., xvi; Roland Barthes, *Camera Lucida: Reflections on Photography*, trans. Richard Howard (New York: Random House, 1981), 38; Harriet Pollack, "Photographic Convention and Story Composition: Eudora Welty's Uses of Detail, Plot, Genre, and Expectation from 'A Worn Path' through *The Bride of the Innisfallen*," *South Central Review* 14 (1997): 17.

what you saw, and truthfully. Portray life, living people, as you saw them. And a camera could catch that fleeting moment, which is what a short story, in all its depth, tries to do." Neither photography nor fiction writing was, in Welty's practice, a reflection of "spiritual fatigue." Both were acts of "knowing"; both constituted "testimony" of the most personal or revelatory kind. Both valued "illusion" and both were signs that consciousness did not have to be violated or fragmented, that prose need not be "hard, wry, noncommittal." I can think of no more politically charged commitment during those days when the United States was moving closer to war against totalitarianism abroad while wrestling at home with the cultural meaning of the growth of the State during the New Deal.[18]

Not surprisingly, it was during the years of America's documentary fervor that Welty began to circulate her stories. They, too, take issue with progressive materialism. If, for Robert Cantwell, "the America revealed in the state guides was a chronicle not of the traditional sobriety and industry and down-to-earth business wit of the American race" but constituted "a grand, melancholy, formless, democratic an-

18. Cole and Srinivasan, "Eudora Welty and Photography," xv. The New Deal and the threat of totalitarianism in the United States are not intended to be synonymous. The liberal reforms of the New Deal could (and did) at times resist governmental intrusion into private life. Nevertheless, the growth of the federal government during the New Deal also suggested for many a potential threat to privacy. It would be impossible to draw a clear distinction between the humanitarianism of the New Deal and the growing power of the State. Adlai Stevenson pointed to the era's ideological questions on this issue in the acceptance speech he gave during the 1952 presidential primary, where he linked "poverty" with "tyranny" as "the great enemies of mankind." The difficulty for that generation of drawing clear lines of demarcation between governmental expansion in Germany under Hitler and governmental expansion in the United States under FDR is also evidenced in Julian Symons's *The Thirties and the Nineties* (Manchester, U.K.: Carcanet Press, 1990), 14ff., in the way he connects (and yet distinguishes) public-works projects in Germany with those in the United States—and in his demonstration that the rejection of proposals for a public-works program by the British Labour Party precipitated the formation of the New Party under the leadership of Sir Oswald Mosley, a man with some admiration of Fascist organization.

thology of frustration and idiosyncrasy, a majestic roll call of national failure, a terrible yet engaging corrective to the success stories that dominate our literature," Welty's writing typically uses the traditional "fanciful, impulsive, childlike, absent-minded, capricious and ingenious" folk character to critique the American ethos of "thrift, sobriety, calculation or commercial acumen," as if to challenge the arrogance of those who saw the folk as cultural or social detritus left behind by the American dream rather than the originators and bearers of the dream. "Death of a Traveling Salesman," published in *Manuscript* in 1936, tells (among other things) of a traveling salesman's misreading of the intimacy between a farm couple in rural Mississippi and looks at the nature of modern alienation; "Flowers for Marjorie" and "Lily Daw and the Three Ladies," published in 1937, are both stories in which haplessness more or less triumphs (in one case tragically, in the other comically). In "A Piece of News," published the same year, Ruby Fisher, an isolated farm woman, reads in an old newspaper a surprising story of another Ruby Fisher who "had the misfortune to be shot in the leg by her husband this week," finding the possibility of such (or, indeed, any) news of herself alternately gratifying then frightening and finally baffling. To the extent that it is focused on rural characters, the simple, the obscure, the feebleminded, the impoverished, and the alienated, this early work is very much a part of the literary mainstream as described by Kazin; its subject, however, is not so much the plight of those characters in a materialistic and progressive world as the plight of the progressive and materialistic sensibility when confronted with these characters. These early stories—and others, including "Keela, the Outcast Indian Maiden" and "The Whistle," collected in 1941's *A Curtain of Green*—are all challenges in one way or another to the condescension of conventional "thrift, sobriety, calculation or commercial acumen" toward fancy, faith, and naïveté.[19]

"A Pageant of Birds," for example, is an assertion of native talent and resourcefulness where many readers of the *New Republic* would least expect to find it, at the Farish Street Baptist Church in Jackson,

19. Robert Cantwell, "America and the Writers' Project," *New Republic,* 26 April 1939, 324, 323; Kazin, *On Native Grounds,* 502; "A Piece of News," *The Collected Stories of Eudora Welty* (New York: Harcourt Brace, 1980), 13.

Mississippi. It is a wonderful critique of condescension and an exploration of the meaning of patriotism to people few would have thought to ask about patriotism. This sketch tells the story of the pageant that Maude Thompson—a woman of imagination and determination—writes, directs, and produces in her church. "I was pleased to learn," Welty writes, "that she had written the pageant herself and had not got it from some Northern YWCA or missionary society, as might be feared." Here, Welty offers us a picture of an obscure woman making a spectacle of her own (but not of herself). That Welty's faith in the imaginative and political resources of Maude Thompson and others like her might not be so widely shared is confirmed by the presence—in the 1943 version of the sketch printed in the *New Republic* but not in the 1978 revision that appears in *Eye of the Story*—of an opening explanation directed to "Northern readers":

> I have been told that this little account needs a generality of some kind made in the first paragraph to Northern readers. I do not think it does, since any generality could only be the commonplace belief I have that magic-making is often the strange compound of humbleness and pride, or in the other direction, out of pride to humbleness, the way the saints, for instance, achieved it. Everywhere, the life in a town that goes mostly unseen, because it does not happen to the spectacular inhabitants, never fails to make its own events out of what it has to work and play with. It has nothing to do with where we live, that we make our own toys and make meaning or bedazzle ourselves out of what is at hand. These colored people I happened to see had got hold of some bright tissue paper.[20]

This preface at once announces the author's awareness that her story might be read as local color with little expected in the way of identification between the northern and presumably white reader and the black southerners who participate in the pageant, and her resistance to the compartmentalizing of southern or African American experience in her assertion that the universality of human imagination

20. "A Pageant of Birds," *New Republic*, 25 October 1943, 566, 565. Hereafter cited in the text as "PB." Also see the revised version in *Eye of the Story*, 315–20.

and illusion "could only be [a] commonplace belief," presumably "common" in the northern reader's "place" as well as Welty's.

"A Pageant of Birds" draws the reader's attention to the capacity of ordinary people full of faith, fancy, and naïveté to become makers and self-makers capable not only of borrowing the conventional symbols of the American dream but also of appropriating them to subversive discourses, in this case aimed at the nation's progressive materialism. The symbols used by Maude Thompson are chiefly patriotic and commercial, although the allegorical content of the drama itself is religious: "On the platform where the pulpit had been was a big easy chair, draped with a red and blue robe embroidered in fleur-de-lys. Above it two American flags were crossed over a drawing of an eagle copied straight off the back of a dollar bill." Images of flags, dollars, and easy chairs are conjoined in this sketch, alluding both to military and economic might. It captures the dream of victory abroad and prosperity at home that in the early 1940s—as the U.S. continued to climb out of the Depression and to abandon the isolationism that had characterized the thirties—would have been as much on the minds of the parishioners of Farish Street Baptist Church as on the citizens of a town hall meeting in Massachusetts. The difference is that these black southerners have a very different experience of American isolationism, which has a definite impact on the way they appropriate the symbols and the rhetoric of nationalism:

> Maude Thompson made an announcement to the audience that everybody had better be patient. "Friends, the reason we are late starting is that several of the birds have to work late and haven't arrived yet. If there are any birds in the audience now, will they *kindly get on back here?*" ... The audience fanned, patted feet dreamily, and waited.
>
> Then came the entrance of the Eagle Bird. Her wings and tail were of gold and silver tin-foil, and her dress was a black and purple kimono. She began a slow pace down the aisle with that truly majestic dignity which only a vast, firmly matured physique, wholly unselfconscious, can achieve. She had obviously got to be the Eagle because she was the most important. Her hypnotic majesty was almost prostrating to the audience, as she moved, as slowly as possible, down the aisle and finally turned and stood beneath the eagle's picture on the wall, in the exact center of the platform.[21]

21. "A Pageant of Birds," *New Republic*, 25 October 1943, 566.

The seating of the eagle is accompanied by flag waving and the singing of "The Star-Spangled Banner" by the audience, which is "almost prostrat[ed]" (whether prostrated by laughter or awe is unclear) and is followed by the "procession of the lesser birds" who bow to the Eagle Bird and to the audience before "taking their positions." Among the birds were bluebirds, four redbirds, a couple of robins, two peacocks, some goldfinches, a purple finch, canaries ("announced as 'the beautiful canaries, for pleasure as well as profit'"), parrots (man and wife), a couple of "pink birds," and "only one beautiful blackbird, alone but not lonesome." The procession ends with "the white dove of peace": "There came two doves, very sanctimonious indeed, with long sleeves, nurse's shoes, and white cotton gloves. They flew with restraint, almost sadly." When the doves have taken their places, the entire flock of birds begins to sing:

And I want TWO wings
To veil my face
And I want TWO wings
To fly away,

And I want TWO wings
To veil my face,
And the world can't do me no harm.

In the weeks that followed, "Every time [Welty] would be getting on a train, [she] would see [Maude Thompson] in the station . . . putting on a coffin, or receiving one, in a church capacity. She would always tell me how the pageant was doing. They were on the point of taking it to Forrest or Mount Olive or some other town. . . . 'This is going to be one of those things going to grow,' said Maude Thompson."[22]

Here Welty tells a story of the appropriation and transformation of national symbols by people who are not spectacular, who are largely unseen, who are in that respect more like angels than national heroes or "cockalorum demi-gods." But the narrative is complex. Although the patriotic and economic allusions in Maude Thompson's pageant are foregrounded, the allegory draws a good deal of its significance from the religious and political traditions of the African American church, linking political and commercial symbols subversively with

22. Ibid., 566–7

religious discourse and community (rather than State) activism. The drama is both a satire of nationalistic rhetoric and a celebration of communal life: the one blackbird "alone but not lonesome"—and alone without parodying antics—stands out in this assembly of strutting majesty, the "assurance that came from complete absorption in . . . roles," and "head-wagging."[23] The procession itself is, of course, a variation on the cakewalk, a parody of pretentious (often white) dress and behavior, and possesses much of the satiric power of the traditional cakewalk. Undercutting the worldliness and pride of the birds during the processional is the concluding song's emphasis on hiding and flight from a threatening world to another, presumably spiritual, one of peace—which is associated by the Farish Street Baptist Church with community caregiving during illness and death.

The way World War II ended, with the bombing of Hiroshima, would impress upon everyone (not only the members of the Farish Street Baptist Church, who are somewhat ahead of their time) the power of the State in the nuclear age to deal out death on an unprecedented scale regardless of the nation's political traditions. It is within this context that Welty begins to articulate her own aesthetic. By the 1940s, Welty was an active and increasingly confident writer; she would later call the forties her most productive decade.[24] In contrast with the thirties, when so many Americans (writers and intellectuals among them) hoped to stay out of the war in Europe and felt that Hitler represented no real threat to the United States, and the fifties, when Americans were anxious about Communist infiltration, the forties were unusually cosmopolitan for many American writers. This limited cosmopolitanism (admittedly limited to the political and more broadly cultural traditions of Britain and Western Europe and centered in the United States) had been developing since the mid-1930s—for obvious reasons having to do with what was happening at the time in the Soviet

23. Ibid.
24. Hewison, *Under Siege*, 176; John Griffin Jones, "Eudora Welty," in *Conversations with Eudora Welty*, ed. Peggy Prenshaw (Jackson: University Press of Mississippi, 1984), 326. See also Michael Kreyling's *Author and Agent*, a study of Welty's development as reflected in her correspondence with Russell.

Union, Italy, and Germany—and coexisted with the New Nationalism in the United States. World War II, unlike World War I, was not so much a war fought in trenches but a war that sent men and women all over the world. Welty herself traveled relatively widely in the forties. A number of British and Continental writers came to the United States to wait out the war, among them W. H. Auden, who became an American citizen in 1939. Also in 1939, Ford Madox Ford, traveling in the U.S., offered to help Welty find a British publisher (and this was before she had found an American publisher). He wasn't successful, but following the purchase of *A Curtain of Green* by Doubleday Doran in 1940, it was not long before that collection appeared in England, where it went into three printings by the time her second collection, *The Wide Net*, was published there in 1945. In Kazin's words, the United States emerged during the war years as "the repository of Western culture in a world overrun by Fascism."[25] What "Western culture" was supposed to stand for during the war years—for U.S. writers as well as those in Britain and France—was political and personal freedom.

"Individualism" is a concept that is so differently problematized in the late twentieth century that we are likely to overlook the fact that it bore a very specific meaning during the years of World War II. During that period, individualism was, for the most part, defined by contrast to "totalitarianism" as represented by Mussolini, Hitler, and Stalin, and it evoked the human factor as potential and potentially subversive of system. Additionally there had been for some time fears among U.S. citizens that totalitarianism was making its way to the U.S. via the New Deal, which increased the size of the federal government and its power over people's lives (a fear utilized by some Republicans in the 1952 presidential campaign and which helped to keep the fires of McCarthyism burning), but despite that fact, by the time of the Spanish Civil War, for most people in Britain, France, and the United States—artists and intellectuals included—native traditions of government

25. Hewison, *Under Siege*, 121; Kazin, *On Native Grounds*, 488. See also Horst Frenz's "Nationalism and Cosmopolitanism in American Letters: A Backward Glance," *Proceedings of the IVth Congress of the International Comparative Literature Association* (Paris, The Hague: Mouton, 1966), 459–60.

stood for an alternative to totalitarianism and the U.S., if not perfect, was at least, as Kazin points out, "the world's best hope."[26]

It was during the 1940s that Welty's literary criticism first appeared, beginning with the reviews she wrote for the *New York Times Book Review* in the early years of the decade. Her *Atlantic* essay "The Reading and Writing of Short Stories," published in 1949, is her first sustained attempt at literary criticism outside of those book reviews. She would continue to write criticism throughout her long career, but the criticism she wrote between the forties and 1961, when she published "Henry Green: A Novelist of the Imagination" in the *Texas Quarterly*, is clearly distinguishable as part of that era's conversation about the destructive potential of modern State-sponsored warfare and the means of survival in a post-Hiroshima world. One might, in fact, compare the remarks Welty makes about Ernest Hemingway in the 1949 essay to those she makes about Henry Green in 1961 in order to get some sense of the importance of modern war to Welty across more than a decade as well as of the vast difference between World War I and World War II in terms of their impact on the way survival, and dignity, were conceptualized.

Hemingway and Green are both writers of the early to mid–twentieth century whose work is a response to war—Hemingway's largely to World War I and the Spanish Civil War and Green's largely to the Second World War, to its advent as well as its aftermath.[27] For Welty, Green's is the more compelling vision. "Our belligerent planet Mars has an unknown and unrevealed heart," she says of Hemingway in "The Reading and Writing of Short Stories." "Hemingway's world is again and again a world of fear. Of physical cruelty, pain, the giving of pain, and for a counter the inability to receive it except in propriety—one way. In Hemingway there is only one way, you know. It is a fear-

26. Kazin, *On Native Grounds*, 502.
27. Michael North argues that Green (and other writers of his generation in Britain) were shaped by a perception of belatedness in the sense that they were too young to fight in the Great War yet close enough in age to those who were fighting to look at World War I as a missed opportunity. This may well be true, but North underestimates the shaping impact of World War II on artists of Green's generation. See his *Henry Green and the Writing of His Generation* (Charlottesville: University Press of Virginia, 1984).

ridden world, in which the only exorcisement is ritual—the bullfight-
er's code, the rules of sport, of warfare. This story is over and over
again told with a kind of appetite, gusto; and this paradox of essence
and effect is one of the hypnotic and incomparable things about Hemingway—his value and his mystery." There is no doubt that Welty admires Hemingway, but for her the "atmosphere" of his stories is
opaque; they are "moralizing stories" and "to be moralizing is to be
flat-surfaced, to take up your stand behind a shield."[28] It is no coincidence that Welty wrote these words during the first years of the cold
war, when Americans were struggling with questions about the kind
of relationship the U.S. would have with the Soviet Union and its sat-
ellites behind the Iron Curtain. Liberals like Adlai Stevenson advo-
cated opening channels of communication with Communist bloc
countries—and during the 1952 presidential campaign he made a famous speech to a tough audience, American Legionnaires, in which he
defined patriotism as the "love" and not the "fear" of something; men
like Joe McCarthy pursued an agenda of defensiveness. Artists and intellectuals were very much engaged in the debate. Faulkner, for example, traveled on behalf of the State Department as a kind of emissary of
postwar Americanism and participated in public conversations about
ways to expose people from behind the Iron Curtain to the "American
way of life" (albeit with a good deal of the typical Faulknerian cyni-
cism about what exactly the "American way of life" signified after
World War II). Even though Welty never traveled as an official representative of the United States, she did, as I mention above, travel during the late forties and early fifties. More importantly, her books (like
those of many American authors) were during these years translated
into Danish, Swedish, Japanese, Italian, French, German, and Bur-
mese. (It would be a bit later—the 1970s—before her work would be
translated into Czech and Polish.) It is easy to underestimate the importance of this postwar U.S. internationalism for a writer like Welty

28. Eudora Welty, "The Reading and Writing of Short Stories," in *The Complete
Works of Eudora Welty*, vol. 8: *Uncollected Pieces*, ed. Isuzu Tanebe (Kyoto:
Rinsen Book Co., 1988): 138, 139. This essay was originally published in two
installments in the *Atlantic* in February and March 1949, pp. 54–8 and 46–9,
respectively.

who held no official political position and whose writing seldom took up political issues in any overt way. Nevertheless, to read her out of this context, out of this history, is to ignore a vast arena of meaning and significance.

Welty must have missed in Hemingway what she missed in Colette when, in 1951, she wrote that Colette's work, full of the "undismayed," is characterized by the *absence* of love, vulnerability, and daring—perhaps the three defining qualities of Welty's own work.[29] It is in Welty's commitment to love, vulnerability, and daring in the post–World War II and cold war contexts that we find at least one reason for her great admiration of Henry Green, as well as additional evidence that the commitment was indeed a means of resistance to the impact of State power upon private life as it was felt during this era. Green wrote a number of novels dealing with the war and postwar years, often focusing on the intensity and claustrophobia of private life in a totalitarian age. In 1960, he published an essay on his World War II experiences in the *Texas Quarterly*. Titled "Firefighting," it is a retrospective commentary on Green's work with the Auxiliary Fire Service from the early days of what the British referred to as "the phoney war" through the Blitz. Welty's essay "Henry Green: A Novelist of the Imagination" was published in the same journal a year later and does not refer directly to "Firefighting." It does, however, bear some relationship to the experiences Green describes in his essay, experiences of World War II in London just before and during the Blitz. Reading the two essays together as expressions of two novelists with a great deal in common—a comic turn of the imagination, an interest in obscure or ordinary characters, and a fierce devotion to privacy and the personal life—underscores the political content of Welty's commitment in what readers of a later generation (largely my own generation of Baby Boomers) have mistakenly seen as apolitical. For Welty and Green also share a vision of private life made more intense for its setting in a world where vision itself ("illusion" Welty calls it in her essay) has

29. Eudora Welty, "Short Novels of Colette" (review of *A Collection of Colette: Six Novels in One Volume,* by Colette), *New York Post,* 30 Dec.1951, 12M; reprinted in Pearl McHaney's *A Writer's Eye: Collected Book Reviews* (Jackson: University Press of Mississippi, 1994), 101–2.

been threatened by World War II, the postwar development of the cold war, and the proliferation of nuclear weapons as each side tries to outdo the other in destructive capacity.

"Signs, omens," Welty writes of Green's work, "charms and works, hopes, confidences, deceptions and self-deceptions, truth and lies, loving and harmdoing, everything sweet or formidable that we go provided with, all in the end will tell what we tried to provide against. All, down to the most frittering talk and the most antic behavior of daily living, are eloquent of the complicated, almost oriental threats that are constantly being made against our living at all. Death by inches is waiting just beyond the door, and someday the dead pigeon, or the fire bomb, will come tumbling down from the sky straight for somebody's head." This in 1961, during the cold war, which followed the development of the atom bomb—about a writer whose work announces on every page its inception in violence and alienation and the vulnerability of its characters to the threat of State power. "He is writing against death," Welty tells us. For her, Green "reflects on the fate of individual man set down very much alive in a dying society," and the fact that she wrote this essay (and that several other writers wrote books about Green, a couple of which Welty reviewed) in the early sixties indicates that he may have been especially relevant for readers in the nuclear age, i.e., readers confronted with the life-destroying consolidation of State power in the form of the bomb.[30]

The word "radiance" has been used several times in the present essay. For Kazin, "democratic rhetoric took on a brilliant radiance in a Hitler world"; for James Agee the camera is devoted "to the effort to perceive simply the cruel radiance of what is." The bomb, too, is remembered for its terrible radiance. And again and again in her literary criticism, Welty returns to the imagery of "radiance." When she praises, she praises in terms of radiance, but for Welty it is a very different kind of radiance—neither rhetorically "brilliant" nor "cruel." Instead, her tropes are drawn from cosmography and astronomy (constellations, meteors, comets) in order to talk about what the imagination does. Intriguingly, she refers to Sir Arthur Eddington's definition of entropy as "becoming" in "The Reading and Writing of Short Sto-

30. Welty, "Henry Green," 247, 255.

ries," suggesting that she may have read some of the work of this articulate scientist who wrote for laypersons.[31] For Welty, radiance suggests
a kind of vulnerability associated with visibility and transparency.
This is a powerful expropriation of the political vocabulary of her
time, a master stroke on behalf of the human factor.

Perhaps Welty's final reservation about Hemingway's stories is that
they are "not radiant, but spotlighted," the "beam of light" coming
from "without the story, from a moral source." In contrast, Henry
Green is "original," "pure and changing," "vital." Each novel, she
writes, "has been made to stand as clear as possible out in space." But
for all this purity, light, and motion, Green is always "in the world
with us," a writer "in our time." His characters "are people who are
ordinary inside their world and might have stepped into being as part
of their year of origin." He is "richly aware" not only "of the comic"
but "also of the outrageous, the bizarre, the awful, the inhuman." In
an attempt to distinguish him from Jane Austen (of whom he reminds
Welty in some ways), she tells us that he is in no sense a child of Austen's earlier time of order, but a modern writer and descendant of Ro-
manticism: "[H]is seems a lyric voice that first and last praises the
phenomenon of life, and the effect of his fiction is that we have been
charged in various and astonishing ways with seeing the phenomenon
and in time, before its radiance is spent." When Welty comments on
"the power of the personal" in his work, "all but incredible," what she
suggests is the encroaching power of the impersonal that must be resisted. For her, Green's "one theme" is "the extreme, almost triumphant vulnerability of man." For both of them, the "personal" in its
triumphant vulnerability is at the center of vision as a kind of radiance
very different from and subversive of the brilliant or cruel radiance of
what a documentary photographer can reveal or the terrible radiance
of the bomb. As such it is placed in a dialectic with the totalitarian,
the "statist," and is nothing if not political. What Welty values in
Green is what she herself aspires to (and attains): "There is no need to
say whether such writing is of the exterior or the interior world."
Green's "deepest feeling . . . abide[s] in indelibility in the face of
chaos"; "a shape for indelibility is what he has made." This is not apo-

31. Welty, "The Reading and Writing of Short Stories," 134.

litical. Within the context of totalitarianism and world war—as within the context of the nuclear threat that Welty, like everyone else, felt in the fifties and sixties—indelibility in the face of chaos is the most pressing goal of all politics.[32]

"Now that each passing day makes some threat or other not only against continuing reality on earth but against our illusion of it," she concludes her essay on Green, "it is in the reading of novels by one of ourselves that we live on as never before, and this is not absurd, for in novels, if they are good, life on earth is intensified in its personal meaning, and so restored to human terms."[33] Her use of "absurd" in this context to signify the alienation of human beings from the systems by which we are governed (be they conceptual, economic, or political), as well as her faith in "the reading of novels by one of ourselves" to ensure the continuance of reality and our illusion of reality, illustrates her political and ideological connections to the age of war, both hot and cold, and the centrality of the private life to political resistance during that age. Welty's concern with singularity, with consciousness, with private and even obscure characters, and with small-town or domestic settings places her firmly within a mid-twentieth-century political discourse—that discourse taking as its subject the relationship of the person to the State and the State's impact upon private lives. In refusing (as she would later refuse) to "crusade," to speak to people en masse as political spokeswoman, and yet to insist on the situatedness and potential of voice, as she does in her many discussions of "place," Welty's work has both a political context and a political content.

32. Ibid., 138–40; Welty, "Henry Green," 246–8, 253–4.
33. Welty, "Henry Green," 256.

*Sharon Deykin Baris*

## Judgments of *The Ponder Heart*

Welty's Trials of the 1950s

Responding to critics whose questions during the turbulent 1960s posed doubts concerning the political and social stance she had taken toward racial tensions in the South, Eudora Welty showed a rare flash of anger. "I felt like saying I didn't need their pointers to know that there was injustice among human beings," she asserted, adding that she had declared her views by "letting my characters show" just such injustice or "trouble." Essential to her forceful response was another fact she decisively expressed: she believed, as she described her feelings in the early 1960s, that she had been "writing about that *steadily right along.*"[1]

Welty has consistently taken an interest in social and political events and has continued to follow human "trouble" within the national press—not only the southern press—throughout her life. She stepped into politics briefly in the 1950s, promoting Adlai Stevenson in his presidential campaign against Dwight Eisenhower in the fall of 1952. She wrote a brief essay for a special issue of the *New Republic* honoring Stevenson soon after Eisenhower's victory.[2] But her most powerful social and political statements, I would argue, were indeed presented steadily and right along in her fiction from the outset of her career.

Never blatantly addressing one cause or another, Welty's work

1. Jean Todd Freeman, "An Interview with Eudora Welty," in *Conversations with Eudora Welty*, ed. Peggy Whitman Prenshaw (Jackson: University Press of Mississippi, 1984), 182 (emphasis added).
2. For a discussion of Welty's interest in the 1952 campaign see Michael Kreyling, *Author and Agent: Eudora Welty and Diarmuid Russell* (New York: Farrar, Straus, Giroux, 1991), 161–2. Kreyling includes an excerpt from Welty's Ste-

characteristically carries the "intimation of a community" noted by her literary agent in 1942; her own description, later in the 1940s, of the "passion" that so often has sparked her interest—both consciously and unconsciously (as she herself acknowledged)—lends significant support to a sense of her keen and abiding social consciousness. The very fact of such intensely felt pressures, and the way they work in a resultant process "nearly impossible to recover," are further indicative of the many and timely concerns she has faced.[3] I take Welty's slender novel of the decade before the 1960s to be a brilliant case in point. A powerful expression of her sense of political injustice, it is fiction rooted in the conditions of its time.

*The Ponder Heart*, completed in the summer of 1953, has typically been seen as a colorful depiction of the delightful habits and folkways of a sleepy southern town. My response to just such an evocation of prevailing habits of thought and action, however, diverges sharply from insouciant readings of this work or of Welty's vision as an author. The novel's purposive dynamics and its mood are darker than has been imagined, for it speaks to the social and political tensions of its era— the period of the McCarthy hearings, the Rosenberg trials, and other tests of American loyalty that then prevailed.

It is true that the courtroom scenes toward the end of *The Ponder Heart* stage Daniel Ponder's trial for murder, following the bizarre death of his young wife Bonnie Dee, in a lively and preposterous manner. But the fiction itself, in its more encompassing implications, presents its own test of American attitudes in the 1950s. At once blithely and provocatively expressive of the dangerous, even deadly, hidden forms that repression can take and did take during certain truly grip-

---

venson essay, some of which went unused in the *New Republic* version of January 5, 1953.

3. Welty's agent Diarmuid Russell noted an important sense of community in an early story, in a letter to her of December 1942; Welty acknowledged her work's subconscious underpinnings in a letter to him concerning another story, earlier that same year. The comments on the untraceable but important impressions behind her writing process were made by Welty in a 1946 speech (Kreyling, *Author and Agent*, 96, 90, 162). The speech was revised as an essay in 1955,"Writing and Analyzing a Story," in Eudora Welty, *The Eye of the Story: Selected Essays and Reviews* (London: Virago Press, 1979), 108–9.

ping political trials, *The Ponder Heart* brings Uncle Daniel's and the other citizens' favorite stories—told in Clay and spread over "a wide, wide territory"—to judgment.[4] Contemplating such an apparently comic fiction in which one young woman might, as the saying goes, "die laughing" while under the presumably warm-hearted care of a widely accepted and lovable protector, Welty's readers in turn are challenged. They sense ways in which certain foundational narratives and idealistic notions they have been granted—in the name of their great land or of loyalty to its causes—might lead them as well to laugh themselves to death, on second thought. Their rueful laughter in such an event is directed less at the comic style of Welty's fiction than at the implications of the familiar stories ("Oh, the stories!") that public spokesmen such as Uncle Daniel and others love to proffer. *The Ponder Heart* as Welty's fictional case study of American beliefs about truth, evidence, and justice thus makes consensus itself a major talking point—or laughing question—for serious discussion.

Without naming names, the novel calls to mind certain famous or infamous political and legal cases of the 1950s. It mentions specific dates, describes lawyers' characteristics, and suggests tactics of silence. It even shows the possibility of electrocution to be central to the deliberations it presents. With seeming irrelevance, the narrator's comments include references to well-known events, social and commercial developments, and elements of common usage in conversations and newspapers of the period. Welty thus definitively locates her novel's action in the culture of its time. Doing so, she not only dramatizes the mood of one small southern town but also draws attention to stories circulating at home and in more widespread versions that serve as declarations of American selfhood. For it is these assertions that her fiction places under reexamination. Beyond the mere recognition of such hegemonies, the novel obliquely, mockingly and hilariously lays bare the painful consequences of their enforcement, in ways that need be understood. Welty's strategies of dissent from widespread conformist attitudes, when read in light of the terrifying atmosphere of accusations and reprisals in the early 1950s, may have been daring. Her judgment, then as now, is wise and trenchant.

4. Eudora Welty, *The Ponder Heart* (New York: Harcourt Brace, 1954), 17. Hereafter cited parenthetically by page number in the text.

Crucial to such a reading of *The Ponder Heart* is the timeliness it conveys. Edna Earle Ponder's narration as she addresses a passing wayfarer at her hotel seems mindlessly ahistorical. By indirect means, however, Welty has cannily set both the period and the actual dates during which the fictional trial of the novel's central figure occurs in the southern town of Clay. Uncle Daniel is accused of the murder of his wife Bonnie Dee after "five years and six months" of marriage, and we learn that that wedding was sometime after Daniel's two-month marriage to Teacake Magee toward the end of 1944. This brings the action to the early fifties, probably to 1952–53—after elections and peach-canning time (47, 59, 93). And then we are told that Bonnie Dee's strange death happened on the sixteenth of June, a date that is mentioned four times in the course of the ensuing trial: "On Monday, the sixteenth of June, Mr. Ponder, would you say she loved you?" (133; cf. 95, 101, 134).

To represent Daniel in his trial, his niece Edna Earle has chosen a man of seventy-five, a "splendid lawyer and our best friend" (63; cf. 84). But before the case begins, this elderly, convivial lawyer yields his client's defense to his grandson, who then surprisingly and emphatically urges Daniel not to open his mouth at the trial: "not at all, not a word" (84). The final courtroom scene in *The Ponder Heart* nevertheless is unduly uproarious, breaking all bounds of decorum, so that near the trial's end Judge Waite remarks from the bench, "I have never, in all my jurisprudence, seen more disrespectful behavior and greater commotion and goings-on at a trial" (150). These assorted allusions to lawyers' ages and trial tactics, to dates, settings, and even sudden courtroom outbursts, if noticed at all amid the excessive detail of Edna Earle's narrative, might seem adventitious. When considered within the historical context of Welty's writing, such scenes could be seen as the merely natural expression of the author's awareness of many hearings widely aired on radio and television in that era, especially in the years just prior to 1953. Such details bear a remarkable similarity, however, to a very specific series of legal proceedings that then gripped the minds and hearts of Americans.

The Ethel and Julius Rosenberg case history began on June 16, 1950, when Julius was first brought in for questioning as a suspected participant in a scheme for betraying American atomic secrets to the Russians. That same date of June 16 was again emphasized three years later, when both Rosenbergs, having battled their 1951 conviction for espionage, sought to bring their appeals to the highest court. Their lawyers' appeals drew to a frenzied climax during the third week of June 1953, leading to the nineteenth, when the execution of the Rosenbergs took place. It was on June 16, 1953, that Ethel Rosenberg wrote her famous personal appeal to President Eisenhower, and on that day the lawyers' desperate pleas on new legal grounds were brought to Supreme Court justices in Washington. That was the day an unforgettable photograph appeared in print, showing the Rosenberg sons' last visit with their parents in prison. These were public facts seized upon by the major newspapers of the time.[5]

More personal background information was also widely discussed. The Rosenbergs' two defense lawyers throughout their trials and appeals were a father and son, Alexander and Manny Bloch. Ethel Rosenberg's attorney, the elderly Alexander Bloch, was a convivial and kindly figure whom Ethel fondly called "Pop." Like Welty's fictional lawyer, he was an experienced jurist in his seventies. From the beginning, however, he deferred to his son Manny, who represented Julius. It was Manny's insistence upon the Rosenbergs' silence, on Fifth Amendment grounds—like Welty's younger lawyer's demand for "not a word"—that prevailed during most of the proceedings.[6]

The March 1951 Rosenberg trial more or less followed legal precedent; but a sense of the many unusual stages of the ensuing hearings

5. Under the heading "Chronology of Spy Case" in the *New York Times*, June 20, 1953, the "high points of the Legal Chronology in the Case of Julius and Ethel Rosenberg" begin: "June 16, 1950—arrest of David Greenglass; June 17, 1950—arrest of Julius Rosenberg." Ethel Rosenberg's letter with its June 16 date was published in full on June 19, 1953, in the *Washington Post*, page 2; see Walter Schneir and Miriam Schneir, *Invitation to an Inquest* (New York: Pantheon Books, 1983), 238, 458.

6. Ethel Rosenberg's fondness for the elder lawyer she called "Pop" is noted by Ilene Philipson, *Ethel Rosenberg: Beyond the Myths* (New Brunswick: Rutgers University Press, 1993), 307–8. Other details of lawyers, dates, and proceedings are provided by Ronald Radosh and Joyce Milton, *The Rosenberg File: A Search for the Truth* (New York: Holt, Rinehart, and Winston, 1983), 236–7.

and appeals, and especially the last-ditch pleas for stay of judgment in June 1953, is conveyed with startling similarity by the emotional pitch and confusion of Welty's trial. The Ponder courtroom might be described in terms used by one Rosenberg legal historian, who writes of the "touches of both tragedy and high comedy" in the appeals heard during the "last session of the Supreme Court of the United States [that opened] on Monday, June 15, 1953."[7] The novel, with all its details of intense heat, outspoken comments from the courtroom audience, and a hasty disbanding, seems to enlarge colorfully upon certain vagaries of the Rosenberg hearings, especially the growing confusion and intensity of those five hot and historic days in June.

But *The Ponder Heart* does not drive unrelentingly toward electrocution as the punishment meted out at the close of protracted proceedings. Welty is not restaging the Rosenberg trial. Although Daniel Ponder is hinted at as playing the role of a Rosenberg defendant, precluded as he is by his attorney from testifying, Julius Rosenberg was never tried for the death of his own wife. In obverse perspective, it is not the serious, dark, intellectually driven mother Ethel Rosenberg, but Bonnie Dee, a thoughtless, weightless, blonde youngster, who dies unexpectedly and for no reason at all. Granted, the question whether Bonnie Dee was electrocuted by the shock of lightning's "ball of fire" is foregrounded by Welty's plot and courtroom proceedings. Yet I would argue that, oddly enough, it is these and other strangely heightened disparities—between the death of a truly comic fictional waif and that of an actual, bold, intellectual figure—that become our greater cause for wonder. We feel moved, that is, to measure the *differences* between the nation's courtroom scenes and those of the novel as well as to wonder at the similarities.

Most surprising are the variant effects of the trials' similar outcomes. After the fictional trial, the answer remains unclear to everyone, readers and characters alike, whether Daniel's young wife was killed by electricity or instead suffocated by his efforts to protect her. But in nearly all the public trials and hearings of that day, and most egregiously in the Rosenberg case history, a vastly different sense of a

---

7. Joseph H. Sharlitt, *Fatal Error: The Miscarriage of Justice That Sealed the Rosenbergs' Fate* (New York: Charles Scribner's Sons, 1989), 46ff.

need for overwhelming certainty seemed insistently to prevail. Hence a strange inversion in Welty's rendition should be noted. Uncle Daniel, as the one accused of causing a pale young woman to die, lives on at trial's end, and in the reader's mind, with an aura of uncertain evidence or even unstated terms of guilt remaining in the air. But in the Rosenberg case, the very momentum of the proceedings seemed to require total resolution or closure, thus dooming a real and deeply impassioned woman, Ethel Rosenberg, to her immediate fate.

What Welty's novel brings out, then—as it brilliantly plays upon an actual trial similar to the fictional one in dates, odd personal and procedural details, and even the electrocution of a woman—is less a sense of resemblance between these stories' external features than of the vast gap between the basic logic operating within each of them. In the fictional instance, a woman's death (that of Bonnie Dee) is tangentially associated with written threats, forgotten lightning rods, fireballs, protective gestures, and uncontrolled laughter. All are juxtaposed in the novel's pages as if they were hinted bits of mounting evidence for a case to be formed against Uncle Daniel in the mind of Welty's reader, if not of the town's attorney. But the novel's conclusion posits absolutely no overriding cause for combining these factors or forming a basis for condemnation. Indeed, one key exhibit, a note declaring "I'm going to kill you dead" (91), serves instead as a thoroughly personal speech act of love that all the listeners including the judge can understand in their own ways.

In the highly publicized historical instance, quite the contrary, a woman's death (that of Ethel Rosenberg) results from the government prosecutors' insistent tactics, along with the president's compliance (Eisenhower swiftly refused Ethel Rosenberg's plea for clemency) and an entire community's silent consensus. All are conjoined in taking one view, framing massive support for a decision that itself had been based upon the linking of a series of exhibits into a monolithic proof.[8] (The crime of forcible linkages during the Rosenberg trials became a governing image in E. L. Doctorow's 1971 novel *The Book of Daniel*,

8. For a postmodern, feminist view of such framing as the frame-up of a woman, see Virginia Carmichael, *Framing History: The Rosenberg Story and the Cold War* (Minneapolis: University of Minnesota Press, 1993), 104ff.

which retrospectively considers this same era; in that work it is a young man named Daniel who resists such logic.)

Thus a fundamental paradox in *The Ponder Heart* becomes apparent. While the many associations that can be made between the novel and the contemporaneous representations of a famous trial seem striking enough as to call out for some line of reasoning to tie one with the other, another sense of the inner contradictions in doing so must also be maintained. Might not a literary work such as Welty's (or a theorizing paper such as this one) in shaping some suggestive relationship between *The Ponder Heart* and the Rosenberg case—itself built, according to one 1953 newspaper report, as if joining "link after link" in a "chain"[9]—seem to be using an all too similar form of literary linkage? Such a troubling problematic would make it essential for this reading of the novel not only to note some random distinctions between the two cases, but also to emphasize a more fundamental basis for maintaining such differences. That is to say, Welty's project *must* playfully resist the logic of the actual trial and its demands for absolute proof, especially while these events were drawing the eyes of persons both in America and abroad. The novel's logic would thus hold the very definition of history at stake—for the nation and for its role within the world.

Deploring the means that government lawyers used in insisting upon litanies of loyalty, Welty may have noted an odd suitability in prosecutors' tactics: their strategies enacted a dynamic that the very logic of national identity and world role would seem to require. In amassing harsh lines of evidence, those prosecutors were arguing for an even more basic premise or underlying theory of linkage. They saw themselves to be furthering a national cause that itself had been conceived in terms of relentless successions. The New World nation, according to earlier forebears, had been founded as destined by a principle of *translation,* or universal course of westward progress. If scriptural prophecies and their early exegetical interpretations had predicted that a new nation would be the final realm in a series of the whole world's kingdoms that had risen and fallen, then America

9. Terms of links and chains were emphatically used in the report of the *Washington Post,* June 20, 1953.

would be the culmination of that destiny made manifest. Its national identity, one could say, was proven by a veritable universal logic of linkages.

In support of such determinedly unswerving historic progress, many citizens during the first two centuries of American history, and especially in the mid-twentieth-century moment of asserting a national world role following World War II, formed an equally insistent line of argument for an American destiny—and for loyalty to its cause. Such premises would go far to explain their fervor for maintaining a singular and singly conceived historic chain of events: its logic simply must not countenance wayward views, one could even say. But Welty and other American citizens might want to challenge both such monolithic concepts and their univocal expressions as forms of loyalty. These Americans might well be moved to do so in the name of different views of citizenship or of national history, especially during this same widely felt crisis of national and personal self-definition.

The wildly disruptive proceedings of *The Ponder Heart* would then do their work. With another kind of insistence, they would deflect such abstract and impersonal, yet at that time seemingly attractive, Americanist presumptions—whether promoted in Uncle Daniel's confident stories told in one small town or iterated as statements of loyalty in the courtrooms of New York and Washington. Welty's sense of selfhood would be declared in ways both variant and eccentric. Her novel's courtroom logic—or comic illogic—would indeed be her passionate response to these times. Like her concept of history itself, her text would be only "frailly held together," as she herself would like to put it.[10] History for Welty does evolve from wayward acts and takes shape through many discrete moments of human understanding by real or fictional judges, by legal historians, by Edna Earle's lone listener ever-present in the outer frame of the novel's narration, and even by Welty's own readers. Such understandings need be no less powerful than those framed by famous spokesmen in shaping the terms and staking the claims for loyalty, truth, or national identity.

If a sense of discontinuity between the social contexts of the early

10. Welty favors a logic of frail connections in her 1974 essay "The House of Willa Cather," in *Eye of the Story*, 46.

1950s and Welty's comic trial thus haunts the margins of her novel, a sense of doubt moves to the center of *The Ponder Heart*. An atmosphere of crisis, indeed, hovers over its narration from the outset, hanging above it—somewhat like Uncle Daniel's large hat—as if to convey both the nature of his thinking and the questionable influence of his stories throughout the midcentury novel. For Daniel speaks not merely as any patriarchal figure who insists on being heard, nor is he some vaguely American persona like Uncle Sam (Sam is the name of his father) whose significance may be noted only incidentally. Uncle Daniel has been brilliantly crafted, at once as the man on trial whose guilt cannot be proven and as the very model of a spokesman for the mood of the 1950s. His style and manner, drawn from the original declarer of the national dream, are suggestive of another Daniel's views: the prophet-dreamer of the Bible who spoke of rising and falling realms. For the biblical Daniel's words had told great stories of the advancing progress of a New World destiny, with all its manifest power and great foundational promise.[11]

Edna Earle's monologue makes repeated reference to towns with proud names commemorating a trajectory of American success. The city named Jackson, in recalling the role of Jackson as the president who promoted western expansion, would be one fine example; places named Polk and Clay honor great national leaders as well. But other place names chosen by Welty suggest a less promising future for the nation. Often Edna Earle speaks of other southern cities including Memphis, Delhi, and Jericho.[12] Their names trace a path not of power but of the ruination that occurs in any inexorable swath of conquest. (We may recall the kingdoms in the Book of Daniel that are "broken in pieces . . . and the wind carried them away" [Dan. 2:35].) These place names, along with other components of Edna Earle's colorful lingo, seem to hint at just such a fateful course. Then, too, she mentions as if

11. Albert Devlin shows that Turner's Frontier Thesis, seen as an outgrowth of the doctrine of Manifest Destiny, was a subject of interest at the University of Wisconsin, where Welty studied. Albert Devlin, *Eudora Welty's Chronicle: A Story of Mississippi Life* (Jackson: University Press of Mississippi, 1983), 35–6.
12. Welty comments on American towns named Rome and Troy as expressive of "ideals and aspirations" in "Names on the Land," in *Eye of the Story*, 187–8.

for no reason at all the Fatimas that Daniel smokes (53) and names the film *Quo Vadis* showing nearby (123). She says Daniel is "rich as Croesus" (132) and describes him and Big John as speaking like a pair of "Moguls" (92).

Many of these place names had become factual and ordinary, and other terms can be heard as buzzwords of the time—yet taken all together such language carries a certain cultural sense and weight. Fatima cigarettes, however large they were deemed to be (their "King Size" is promoted in a double column advertisement in the *Washington Post* of June 16, 1953), recall the old Fatimite dynasty that once ruled Egypt and Northern Africa but all too quickly vanished. *Quo Vadis* (like another film about Nero reviewed in the *New York Times* of June 20, 1953), plays spectacularly upon great kingdoms' ruinations. Moguls evoke Far Eastern potentates now forgotten, and Croesus, remembered as the wealthiest ruler of ancient Lydia, ironically became the very cause of his empire's demise.[13]

Mulling over the mood of her times, the import of ordinary usage, and even the implicit relevance of familiar advertisements, verbal expressions, and movie reviews appearing during June 1953, Welty may well have found support therein for the strategic patterns operating within her text. For her novel both uses and mocks the very terms prevailing in the current pages of the press that she, like so many others, then avidly surveyed. The linguistic devices of her text can be seen to trace a pattern of a far more dismal westward movement, as if to cast doubt on any exceptional premise for American history, to lend more particular comment concerning the Rosenberg trials, and—most especially—to undercut the logic of the overbearing prosecutors' relentlessly single-minded tactics. *The Ponder Heart* thus hints that national and personal betrayal can arise not, or not only, from alien or external sources working in subversive plots as the televised reports of the hearings of those days would have it. More devastatingly, as Welty's complex strategies seem to suggest, some of our deepest betrayals may dwell within our storied presumptions.

13. References to Fatimites, Moguls, and Croesus are found in *Brewer's Dictionary of Phrase and Fable*. Louise Westling reports that *Brewer's* has always been on or near Welty's desk. Louise Westling, *Eudora Welty* (London: Macmillan, 1989), 43.

A demonstration of such national self-deceptions is the implicit politics "shown" (as Welty would say) by the novel's settings. An old flag and a drooping tree are propped in a corner of Clay's courtroom (105); its central fountain is noticeably cemented over (88). What these scenic details suggest is less a fallen Eden (or even a Daniel's sealed dreams) than an America whose great promise has been lost or abandoned. Such abandonments everywhere had been glimpsed in the town of Clay. When a passenger train was no longer scheduled to stop there, that may have been somewhat of a local social nuisance. But when Edna Earle counted the seventy-nine cars in a freight train that bypassed the neighboring town of Polk, she went a long way to register a sense of far deeper worries now impressed upon her mind (79). What Edna Earle must acknowledge in Polk might be a premonition of trends soon to become still more apparent. Wayside stops, along with individual needs, are increasingly ignored. If the people of nearby Polk were cloning themselves in swift profusion, so too might one foresee a similar proliferation of indifferent and undifferentiated look-alikes in Clay—somewhat like the string of Woolworth's stores such people so loved to frequent.

When Bonnie Dee learns to "make change" in such a store (41), however, the changes she makes seem to make no individual difference at all. The success of her achievement can be measured only as one act among many others, in repetitive succession. So if, in a scene of increasingly impersonal proliferations, Bonnie Dee's look-alike sister with a sound-alike name had been spotted one day in another look-alike Woolworth's in Memphis, one could sense the humor of that moment to be Welty's prescient understanding of problems of urban sprawl. As the quintessential example of succession itself, such replications were the endangerment not only of local economies, but of any sense of individual worth.[14] This couple's marriage (appropriately begun in a ten-cent store) had, like the whole town and country one could say, been moving "past redemption."

Woolworth's replications, so boldly foregrounded in *The Ponder*

14. A survey of burgeoning business chains and discount stores of the 1950s would include Korvette's, McDonald's, and of course Woolworth's; see David Halberstam, *The Fifties* (New York: Random House, 1993).

*Heart*'s brilliantly expressive illustrations, were indicated by their familiar signs. But the book's illustrations also included many other kinds of actual signs and suggestive signals. (Welty worked closely with her illustrator Joe Krush in planning their subjects and arrangement.)[15] Used as witty chapter headnotes, the illustrations included trains, feathers, Ferris wheels, and cash registers, as if to serve as evocative reminders, however charmingly broad and stylized, of the incessant longings and desires driving current trends toward successive successes. What these drawings might also imply—very much like the fallen sign on the Beulah Hotel—was the falling away of traditional recognitions and satisfactions, as evidenced in the text.

Driving such suggestions home in an almost literal way, Edna Earle seems perpetually alert to Daniel's desires and his felt depletions. She reminds us of his gnawing hungers. For what this hero requires is constant replenishment—much like the supplies implicit in Mr. Springer's name and career. Endlessly desirous of repeated stories, more food, and new shows with further rounds of old excitements (evoked by the feathers, wheels, and churning machinery of the illustrations), and all the while longing for Bonnie Dee (or at least her sisters' near-replications), Daniel yet fails to find a personal or individual means of fulfillment. His supplies serve only to replace one another in turning out replicative parts—only parts—in an overarching process. A principle of incessant demand and nearly indistinguishable replacements becomes a fetishistic means of fulfilling Daniel Ponder's life or love, and on a larger scale, of achieving a national sense of history. Indicative of the principle of succession itself, with an ever unattainable end in sight, such views carry a terrible burden as well. A concomitant sense of nagging human insufficiency lies in the heart of this spokesman of Clay; it may also have lurked at the very core of the presumptions ruling the trials of the 1950s.

This is why Edna Earle, after describing Daniel's habit of eating her "out of house and home," so wisely goes on to add that he did so "not so much to be eating as to be consoling himself and us" (52). Aware of his unappeasable need to meet his own expectations, she whispers,

15. Suzanne Marrs, *The Welty Collection* (Jackson: University Press of Mississippi, 1988), 79–80, 180.

"Uncle Daniel! F.H.B.!" at the dinner table. Her whisper might have sounded like some harmless in-joke of the 1950s, when someone might hint F.H.B.—or "*Family Hold Back*" on the food intake—when unexpected guests arrived (52). But Welty's keen ear for speech acts seems to have heard that message as a signal for the whole nation. Its citizens, too, might well be warned, with more serious reason, to Hold Back on their insatiable, fetishistic demands to see the nation's destiny as ideal.[16]

The novel thus works toward making its similar plea for delimiting Americans' insatiable demands. Yet Welty herself, at a certain point in the writing, may have felt the need to hold back her work's progress, too. There seemed cause for hesitation as the events of June 1953 moved forward. While a drive toward clear condemnation of the Rosenbergs needed to be based upon a series of facts forcibly linked throughout their many hearings and trials, Welty's own textual dramatization must work—humorously or earnestly—toward *failing* such a test of clear or insistent linkages. In yet another turn of fate, then, coincidence itself might play its important part. With just such a turn of fate—or chance—in mind, I would like to examine once again the parallels between the Rosenberg trials and various details of *The Ponder Heart*.

The date of Bonnie Dee Peacock's death is reiterated by Clay's assertive prosecutor: "On Monday the sixteenth of June, Mr. Ponder," he intones (133). In fact, the sixteenth of June—the day Ethel Rosenberg wrote the president—was a Tuesday that last week of the Rosenbergs' appeal. But on the next Monday, June 22, it was the Rosenberg funeral that was reported on the front page of the *New York Times*. As it turns out, that report appeared at the bottom of the page beneath and, in the newspaper's columns of print, adjacent to another story that unfolded

16. Among the many renditions of Freud and his studies of narcissism circulating at this time, Erich Fromm's popular study of the loss of individuality in modern America and a concomitant loss of self-worth was perhaps the most familiar. Fromm ties this loss to a sense that "there is never any real satisfaction . . . [only] an endless effort to satisfy [some] need," with no personal "satiation." Erich Fromm, *Escape from Freedom* (1941; rpr. New York: Avon Books, 1969), 136–7.

under far bolder headlines. The biggest news items that Monday were reports of sudden electrical storms that had occurred the day before and generated balls of lightening resembling Welty's fictional one. So it was that the Rosenberg funeral account, startlingly enough, appeared alongside the full description of a woman's freak electrocution—by a ball of lightning. Her name was Estelle Siegal, and at thirty-six years old she was one year younger than Ethel Esther Rosenberg was at her electrocution and burial, which was taking place not far away, at nearly the same moment. As if to round out these front-page stories' seeming parallels artfully, one might note that the electrocuted Estelle, like Ethel, was from the Bronx.

Welty has repeatedly declared in interviews and essays that facts, as she stated in 1965, "can be used to show anything, absolutely anything."[17] So, too, any parallels found between events, characters, and dates in *The Ponder Heart* and those of real life, especially of the Rosenberg trial, or between two tragic stories told on one front page the Monday after the deaths by electrocution of two women with similar names who came from the Bronx, however factual, should bear little value for use in the traditional sense of historic evidence.[18] Or rather, what such imagined linkages themselves might prove is, merely, that anything these seemingly connected events could show, to rephrase Welty, would be absolutely nothing beyond sheer suggestion itself. It could not even show, one must add, that the author had or had not adapted the dates of her manuscript while following the Rosenberg trial. (That the manuscripts' dates were altered in variant editions is

17. Welty, "Must the Novelist Crusade?" in *Eye of the Story,* 149.
18. Some readers of earlier drafts of this paper have offered other "odd" facts that might be thought relevant to these dates, including the correct days of the week in June of the prior year, 1952, or similar dates during the Medgar Evers trial a decade later. Their point, like mine, would be that parallel dates or disparate elements of circumstantial evidence make sense only when placed (or "used" in Welty's term), whether imaginatively or forcibly, in particular contexts. It is our recognition (or creation) of connections that allows us to view occurrences as history. Interesting to note is that June 16 is also a focal date in Alfred Hitchcock's 1950s spy film *North by Northwest,* as James Mason accusingly addresses Cary Grant: "On June 16th you . . ."

evident from versions on file in the Mississippi Department of Archives and History; the numbers indicating 16 were last added in pencil.)[19]

We do not know the extent to which Welty perused the extensive press reports of the Rosenberg trials in the *New York Times* and in the *Memphis Commercial Appeal* (which is mentioned in the novel's pages), with their emphasis upon the trial's strangely repeated dates. Had she pored over photographs concerning the Rosenberg hearings and mused about their relevant details? Looking over the novel's pages with hindsight, one does find indications that the author took serious note of peripheral cultural events and terms in these newspapers' accompanying features and reviews, even as she continued to follow the unfolding hearings in the news.[20] So if Edna Earle speaks of her penchant for newspaper clippings, stating that she "just cut out" ads and information to put "away in a drawer—I forget where" (44), might not Welty have considered doing the same? In light of the strategies of her novel, might she, unlike Edna Earle, *not* forget the ads for Fatimas, or reviews of Nero and their hints of kingdoms, and moguls—all relevant during the shaping of her text, and especially in its final stages that June.

We can never, of course, be certain as to the nature or the details of the items to which Welty would be attracted, in her habitual and thoughtful newspaper perusals.[21] What we can tell concerning her atti-

19. Marrs provides descriptions of the holdings in the Mississippi Department of Archives and History, Jackson. See Marrs, *Welty Collection*, 35–6. The *New Yorker* manuscript page proofs dated July 20, 1953, are at the Humanities Research Center of the University of Texas. See Noel Polk, "Appendix B: A Handlist of Eudora Welty Manuscripts in Other Collections," in Marrs, 229. See also, however, note 31 below.

20. My review of the daily *Memphis Commercial Appeal* of the week of the final appeals shows that several advertisements, references, and photographs relevant to the terms used in this novel appeared in those editions. See also a featured pictorial essay, "Grim Final Chapter in the Rosenberg Atom Spy Case," Saturday, June 20; other reports Welty might have read were in the *New York Times*, the *Washington Post*, and syndicated papers.

21. In recent conversations with two of her friends and critics, Sally Wolff and Michael Kreyling, Welty acknowledged that she read the *New York Times* daily during the 1950s, as always. In response to questions that Kreyling and

tudes during those difficult times may be drawn from Michael Kreyling's recounting of Welty's final stages of work on her unfinished
novel at just about these same moments. Although *The Ponder Heart*
had been well on its way in January when Welty read portions of it
aloud to William Maxwell, the fiction editor of the *New Yorker*, her
literary agent Diarmuid Russell "waited until July" to begin what
Kreyling (rephrasing Welty) calls the implementation of the agent's
"masterpiece of selling" this novel. "Welty needed that much time to
complete the revision and retyping of the final version," Kreyling observes. She was troubled by the *"flawed ending,"* as she herself put it
(emphasis added).[22] Indeed, an account of the particular period of late
May through early July in the summer of 1953 may be summed up by
Kreyling's comment, "She was having misgivings about Uncle Daniel
finishing Bonnie Dee off at the end." Such thoughts might be understood as aesthetic, cultural, and political problems Welty would face.

She may have been disturbed by certain unanticipated parallels between life and art in her nearly finished novel. If she later would state
how keenly aware she was of the "menace of neatness" when political
arguments are carried into fiction, she may have had this particular
moment of impasse in mind.[23] As her work sought to undo, or hold
back, the drive toward monolithic principles of linkage implicit in
American stories, or within the contemporary litanies demanded as
proof of American (or un-American) activities, she may have reconsid-
ered her story's different stance. Her trial's dynamics, in their richly
associative (corresponding), distinctive (avoiding neatness), and variant (hence questioning) way, would have to be consistent in *dis*proving
any single and singularly given design. As she paused to ponder her
own novel's implications during the last days of the Rosenberg case,
therefore, Welty may well have hoped (as so many others in crowd
scenes depicted in the current press were also shown to be hoping) that
the factual and fictional patterns before her—on the pages of her

---

Wolff each raised in separate discussions with Welty (after they heard a short
version of this paper delivered in Jackson, April 11, 1997), Welty twice confirmed her keen interest in the Rosenberg trial and hearings in the 1950s.

22. Kreyling, *Author and Agent*, 167; cf. 161–9.
23. Welty, "Must the Novelist Crusade?" 149.

manuscript and in pages of news—would significantly and mercifully diverge, and that there would in fact be no electrocution.

The author's hesitation in completing the novel might also be understood on cultural grounds. If the exponent of national consensus in *The Ponder Heart*—Uncle Daniel is dressed "fit to kill" in "sparkling white" with touches of red, to suit his eyes of blue (11; cf. 12, 52)— were to be judged as an American spokesman, the author need not be alone in making such estimations. Until now, Welty's sternest trial of Uncle Daniel had consisted of dramatizations of his misplaced enthusiasm for well-worn tales insistently told to Clay's willing elders and spread by salesmen like Mr. Springer. But when her glance was leveled against the powerful consensus these men conveyed over "wide, wide territories," with no room in their versions' contexts for Edna Earle's tales of her own to tell, Welty depicted Edna Earle's growing tide of resentment. Daniel's stories—like Mr. Springer's very strange drugs or even like Daniel's purportedly pleasing but even stranger hugs and protective tickles—were far more widely troubling than may have been surmised. If Edna Earle once commented, upon listening to their stories, "I was getting numb!" so too would their terms of consensus be unacceptably stifling to many others upon whom they were foisted. Such others might include Bonnie Dee Ponder and Teacake Magee (a famously full-throated singer who can only hoot a word or two of denial before fainting into total silence during her scene in the trial) and the enigmatic yet powerful black woman Narciss, whose silence at the novel's end speaks volumes. A recognition of cultural dissent in *The Ponder Heart* should not be minimized. Could intimations of disaffection and mounting ire felt between the lines of its narration and beyond its pages have pulled the author up short, hindering her from bringing the work to completion and publication in such a mood of crisis?[24]

24. In a discussion of this work's unheard stories and laughter, I allude to Welty's anthology, *Friendship,* and suggest that the novel's outer frame of conversation between two women allows for the suggestive prospect of true friendship—which might now stand opposed to the declarations of loyalty so harshly demanded by the trials of the 1950s. Sharon Deykin Baris, "Welty's Philosophy of Friendship: Meanings Treasured in *The Ponder Heart*," *Southern Literary Journal* 27 (1995): 43–61.

\*   \*   \*

It is on political grounds, finally, that Welty may have found greatest cause for alarm as she moved toward completion of the manuscript during mid-June 1953. When, on the sixteenth of June, Ethel Rosenberg sent her personal plea for clemency to the president, attention in America and abroad turned toward the appeal, in hopes that this renowned leader would find grounds or precedent within the law or mercy in his heart to grant this mother of two young children a reprieve from imminent death. Perhaps only a public statement of personal clemency could satisfy the hungers of a nation and the concerns of the author at such a moment, as all awaited the outcome of Ethel Rosenberg's plea. When President Eisenhower responded, Welty may have felt a thrill, or shiver, of recognition.

Here indeed was an American spokesman, if not dressed fit to kill in red, white, and blue, then as much as draped in an American flag—bold commander in the recent world war, victorious politician in the elections just past, now beloved leader of his country. Depicting her own colorful hero in a work that her agent called a "funny story" and her editors termed a "masterpiece," but that she privately called her "Daniel story,"[25] Welty had drawn deeply upon traditions of American thought. Perhaps now the actual public hero might, in a bolder version of scriptural precedent, have "Dared to be a Daniel," as was said of the president (Truman) before him, and "Dared to stand alone."[26] Or would he fail, in this historic moment, to play that daring role?

Early in the writing of the novel Welty had presented Daniel in all his impersonal failings. Gradually her critique had acknowledged even harsher forms of endangerment that such abstract visions promoted. Now, in the crisis, she perhaps harbored far worse suspicions. Was there yet some more terrible kind of violence to be accounted for in a leader whose widely spread stories only *seemed* to offer civic trust or genuine individual protections? As the nation's intense focus on pub-

25. Kreyling, *Author and Agent*, 162, 167.
26. The *Boston Post* editorial of October 27, 1948, praising President Harry S. Truman, carried the heading, "Captain Courageous," and cited the "words of an old song" showing that he "Dared to be a Daniel, / Dared to stand alone." See David McCullough, *Truman* (New York: Simon and Schuster, 1992), 698.

lic declarations and testimonies became more and more newsworthy that month, Welty herself may at first have paused to sigh. Then she may have felt the increasing stress of her own position in the face of such hegemonies. Was she not simultaneously tracing, in her manuscript and in the press, the strange cases of women stifled—even muffled to death— for even the mere thought of such widely held, yet benumbing views and stories? Wanting to "hold back" the dangerous and even deadly presumptions of a nationally beloved spokesman, Welty might have found cause for concern at the prospect of going further, in bringing such a person to judgment.

One could say that if *The Ponder Heart* portrayed its hero as a blue-eyed, fair-haired wonder, that was but the literalization of definitions in Webster's dictionary or *Brewer's Dictionary of Phrase and Fable*, of a communal "favorite"—with all the prejudicial levels of racial, gender, and political consensus that such an image implied. The text conveys a deep resistance, however, to the very thought of accepting any such blithe definitions, a resistance with clear implications for the national political scene. More daringly, its pages portray the insidious moral and mortal harassments such a favorite imposed, seemingly in the name of public good will. Perceiving as much, Welty saw the most imposing figure of her times as but a "fair-haired" leader, one she well understood.

It was after the election of November 1952, during which Welty entered the actual arena of politics in favor of Adlai Stevenson and against Dwight Eisenhower, that she contributed her essay honoring Stevenson to the *New Republic*. But she wrote the essay in the form of a personal letter to Stevenson, as if declaring her deepest political passion. That would be a continuing "moving fact" for her far beyond the "finish of any race," for Welty's interest in "what was said" by Stevenson would surely continue.[27] So too, one must feel, would her attention toward his opponent be intensified, as she and many others waited for him to speak out the next June.[28] When Eisenhower voiced

27. See Kreyling, *Author and Agent*, 162.
28. "According to the *Washington Post*, the White House received . . . 21,500 telegrams . . . between June 16 and 21," Schneir and Schneir, *Invitation to an Inquest*, 241.

his views, then, he spoke not only to Ethel Rosenberg, or to the whole nation and indeed much of the world; he spoke in effect to Welty at this moment. When he declared himself in support of the court rulings, sealing the dire outcome for the Rosenbergs, Welty could well have noted how consensus was being spread over wide, wide territories.

The president began his public statement by acknowledging a deep interest in the personal aspects of this case that were "aside from the considerations of law." Immediately thereafter, however, he turned his attention solely to national and international threats of atomic war. In raising such universal concerns, he demonstrated an attitude that was neither personal nor strictly national. Yet as Eisenhower earlier in the week had explained himself in a letter to his son, his rationale was based upon one particular American concern: the need, as he put it, to "protect" American women. He must deny clemency, he explained, lest the Soviets later "simply recruit their spies from among women."[29]

The letter's revealingly abstract, patriarchal, and even prejudicial language was privately addressed, it is true. But in Eisenhower's public speech of June 19 (reported on radio and in the press the following day), the president was only slightly more circumspect in taking a similarly generalized view, insisting that the Rosenbergs after all had had "every safeguard which American justice can provide." Although he went on to note the matter of "the execution of two human beings" to be very grave, he yet weighed that imminent reality as less troubling to him than a theoretical concept: "the thought" of an outcome made possible by their espionage. Announcing that he thus could not "intervene in this matter," Eisenhower denied executive clemency within a half hour of the Supreme Court's refusal of any further stay of judgment.[30]

Almost simultaneously, Welty completed her novel, in which Daniel's very strange protections "finish off" Bonnie Dee. Having written with a knowledge of her times that was even more perceptive than she

29. This letter, written on June 16, 1953, is cited by several Rosenberg historians. See Schneir and Schneir, *Invitation to an Inquest*, 242.
30. Carmichael, *Framing History*, 117–8; see also Schneir and Schneir, *Invitation to an Inquest*, 248–9.

herself may have imagined, Welty at last deemed her work ready for publication. It was soon thereafter submitted to the *New Yorker* by her agent, and the completed page proofs on file are dated July 20, 1953.[31] The work appeared as a long story in the December issue, and was published in book form early the next year by Harcourt Brace. If a likeness between Welty's fictional figure and the nation's spokesman did give the author pause for contemplation and worry, we can only estimate the extent and the nature of the profound hesitations that preceded its final publication. So, too, the role played by the strangely adjacent front-page headlines of the June 22, 1953, *New York Times* will remain cause for wonder.

On the one hand, such reports might show some readers, if only in hindsight, how coincidence itself can be a factor in history, especially when personal details are heeded. Such an insight would give weight to a correlative sense of how *unreliable* "clear" facts or parallels between even real events can be in understanding our own and others' fates. On the other hand, it might be—to rephrase Edna Earle herself— that "what's hard to believe" about truth itself is not the clarity of its outline, but how dependent its significance must be upon some understanding of "who it happens to"(143).

From Welty's point of view, what the juxtapositions on a single front page of the *Times* could have shown, by the very fact of her noting their existence (if ever she did), was that these two women's stories might be related to those of many others ("Oh, the stories!"), including her own in completing this novel. By the logic—or illogic—of their appearance, the juxtapositions would have demonstrated that coincidence *could* play its part in maintaining her position. Links alone show nothing! Hence her work could continue. For in a prospective light even that newspaper page might one day be used if ever the need arose—then in the era's trials, or today in a reading of her novel—as

31. Documentation of this date can be confusing for a close reader of Welty bibliographical materials because of conflicting reports. Polk's reference to the date of galley proofs for the *New Yorker* appears in his appendix included in Marrs, *Welty Collection* (229) as July 20, 1953, which agrees with the records of the Texas collection. Polk's later notation of that date as "20 June 1953" is probably a typographical error. See Noel Polk, *Eudora Welty: A Bibliography of Her Work* (Jackson: University Press of Mississippi, 1994), 80, 458.

disproof that Welty had been parodying the country's highest court or questioning the basic values of its foremost national spokesman.

Eudora Welty never wanted to point her finger in judgment at an individual or even a whole society, and certainly not at an American president. But it was her "wish, indeed . . . continuing passion" (as she described her aim in creating books of both photography and fiction), to part the curtain or "veil of indifference"—however widespread its national or international dimensions might be—to particular and personal human feelings.[32] Such indifference inherent in America's sense of some exceptional prophesied history, expounded by a local hero's colorful and insistent stories, promoted in oaths of loyalty, and voiced by the president in the name of overwhelming protection, was what Welty most passionately sought to render and thereby disrupt. *The Ponder Heart* served as her stay of judgment, her personal act of clemency, its case offered to her readers as testimony to *their* greatest humanity.

32. Welty, "One Time, One Place," in *Eye of the Story*, 355.

*Danièle Pitavy-Souques*

# Private and Political Thought in *One Writer's Beginnings*

> She communicates vastly more than she writes.
>
> —Willa Cather about Katherine Mansfield

> I glimpse our whole family life as if it were freed of that clock time which spaces us apart so inhibitingly, divides young and old, keeps our living through the same experiences at separate distances.
>
> —Eudora Welty, *One Writer's Beginnings*

Though seldom overtly assertive or militant, southern women writers have been committed to the political since the end of the nineteenth century. They have long known that writing fiction is never a neutral activity, that all great texts are revolutionary because they change attitudes—mental, social, and political. Though southern women writers have generally had their parts cut out for them, they have redefined those parts in the course of their work. Moreover, they have played their redefined roles with the utmost commitment, all the more since they knew they were composing from a region where the violence of History doubled their responsibilities as writers and artists.[1]

Because their art touches their deepest convictions so intimately, and because it gives rise to sharp criticism for either excess or deficiency of engagement in political causes, many southern women writers have felt the need to publish autobiographies, usually for the pur-

---

1. The epigraphs are from Willa Cather, *Stories, Poems, and Other Writings* (New York: Library of America, 1992), vol. 3, 878, and Eudora Welty, *One Writer's Beginnings* (Cambridge: Harvard University Press, 1984), 102. Future references to *One Writer's Beginnings* will be made parenthetically in the text.

pose of justifying themselves and their fiction, which they feel has been misread. Thus, any evaluation of the political in these women's work must necessarily include an evaluation of their autobiographies, a task that requires insight as well as discrimination on the part of the critic. Despite the recent reappraisal of feminine fiction and the considerable achievement of feminist criticism in this field, there still lingers the suspicion that feminine writing is not on a par with masculine writing. Harold Bloom's recent book on the American canon, with its blatantly unfair omissions, is proof of this ongoing battle that women writers must continue to fight in order to see their works fully acknowledged. Critically at least, and politically as well when they belong to ethnic groups outside the dominant white majority, they are treated as members of a minority, and more or less consciously they adopt the strategies of minority people of both sexes when writing their autobiographies: paradoxically, they portray themselves as both victimized and guilty. Yet some are strong enough to write in defiance of such commonly accepted strategies and produce proud affirmative texts.

Eudora Welty's autobiography must be read in such a light, especially since the event that led her to pen *One Writer's Beginnings*—the William E. Massey lecture series on American civilization at Harvard in April 1983—attests to how politically oriented her talks were, a preoccupation further corroborated by Welty's first declining the invitation, then accepting it at Daniel Aaron's suggestion that she speak about what made her into a writer. The aging writer was glad to pick up the challenge and trace those informing patterns that had fashioned her imagination, technique, and political attitudes. Moreover, implicit in her tracing of these patterns is a rejection of the mutilating label of regionalist writer—a southerner writing in the wake of William Faulkner. The lectures turned out to be immensely successful, and *One Writer's Beginnings* (their published form) was on the bestseller list for over ten weeks. Some deep chord in the American heart and imagination must have been struck. The book proved truly meaningful to Welty's newly gained audience, which read it as a reflection of the nation's destiny.

*One Writer's Beginnings*'s implicit call for a reorientation of critical approaches was not so successful. While perceptive readers were confirmed in their critical guesses, the narrow-minded and politically biased continued to be prejudiced against a work to which they applied ill-fitted critical tools. Misunderstanding is not over yet. Along with the popularity of cultural studies and multiculturalism on the current American critical scene, the old academic activity of comparing authors and their works is still going full speed, making for all sorts of pairings. The validity of such activity rests on respect for authors in the form of an honest attempt to understand their intentions, to compare what is comparable, and to locate new cross-cultural insights when seemingly divergent texts are read together. That this technique is not always appropriate, respectful, or fair is evidenced by two recent essays (among others) that compare Welty's autobiography with, respectively, that of a black male writer, putting the emphasis on racial issues only, and that of a white woman writer of the preceding generation, concentrating on the painting of the self alone.

Richard Brodhead's "Two Writers' Beginnings" is an indictment of Welty's blindness to segregation in Jackson at the time she grew up, an indictment that would be appropriate if Welty's purpose had been to draw a picture of Jackson in her childhood and youth. But it wasn't. Similarly, in a sensitive collection of essays titled *Feminine Sense in Southern Memoir*, Will Brantley compares Glasgow's *The Woman Within* with Welty's *One Writer's Beginnings*. In his insistence on emphasizing the sheltered life, he reduces the scope of Welty's project and achievement. As is evidenced by the origin of Welty's text and by the very title she chose for the publication of her three lectures delivered to an audience that included Harvard historians, she clearly meant to depart from Richard Wright's racial plea, or from Glasgow's plea for a true self. Indeed, before they have opened her book, Welty's readers are warned that this is not an ordinary autobiography, but what Michel Beaujour defines as a self-portrait, which he differentiates from the autobiography: "Self-portrait," he explains, "differs from autobiography by the absence of a continuous narrative, and by the subordination of the narration to a logical development, made up of elements brought or joined together, that provisionally we shall call thematic elements."[2]

2. Richard Brodhead, "Two Writers' Beginnings," *Yale Review* (April 1996): 1–21; Will Brantley, *Feminine Sense in Southern Memoir* (Jackson: University Press of Mississippi, 1993), 86–132; Michel Beaujour, *Miroirs d'encre: Rhétorique de l'autoportrait*, trans. Françoise Lionnet (Paris: Seuil, 1980), 8.

In this disruptive light that negates continuity and supposes a reorganization of the facts, a more judicious comparison would bring together Zora Neale Hurston's *Dust Tracks on a Road* and *One Writer's Beginnings*. Both books share comparable techniques and intents: a desire to control rather than privilege the writing of the self and to transcend the burden of history. Above all, as each rewrites a history of the development of the American imagination, with all its cultural components, she takes her turn addressing the issue of the political at its highest level, emphasizing a positive assertion of multiculturalism rather than concentrating on victimization. In her superb study of *Dust Tracts on a Road*, Françoise Lionnet calls Hurston's book an autoethnography: "that is, the defining of one's subjective ethnicity as mediated through language, history, and ethnographical analysis; in short, the book amounts to a kind of 'figural anthropology' of the self."[3] While I will not compare Hurston's and Welty's autobiographies here, I will make occasional use of *Dust Tracks on a Road* to clarify various points I make about Welty. Hurston's highly criticized stand on racial issues stems from a political attitude not unlike Welty's, and she also is a victim of hasty judgments. Great women writers of the South have shown more daring and broader views than their male counterparts, although this has been little acknowledged as yet.

This essay will focus on the quintessential relationship Eudora Welty entertains with the political in *One Writer's Beginnings*, a book that, paradoxically, defines American mythologies rather than Welty's private ones. Briefly defined, the political indicates a concern with the general, with public and social ethics, including the issues of race, class, gender, and history. Though adamantly refusing to write fiction polemically, Welty has always been a progressive *engagé*, an active supporter of Adlai Stevenson and a courageous lecturer at the worst time of the civil rights movement, as Suzanne Marrs argues in "'The Huge Fateful Stage of the Outside World': Eudora Welty's Life in Politics," elsewhere in the present volume. Moreover, Welty produced two of the finest stories on the sixties' conflicts, the first one written out of

3. Françoise Lionnet, *Autobiographical Voices: Race, Gender, Self-Portraiture* (Ithaca: Cornell University Press, 1989), 99.

her personal anger at the racist mentality that had resulted in the murder of Medgar Evers. More generally, she has shared the democratic values of the Founding Fathers of the American Republic from the first, taking pride, as she recently told me, in being born on the same day as Thomas Jefferson, the thirteenth of April: "Jefferson is my hero, and as my mother would say 'at least that was something I could do for you.'"[4] Educated in a family from which racism was absent, Welty's stand on racial issues led her to write stories about African Americans, which have won her the respect of the black community.

With regard to *One Writer's Beginnings*, the question is not really Welty's particular brand of liberalism, using Brantley's definition of liberalism as "a belief in human rationality and accountability, and if not a belief in human perfectability (as O'Connor would have it), at least a desire to make life better for the entire diversity of the nation's citizens."[5] Instead, Welty shows a genuine concern for the general and the abstract, and above all for the representativity of her own biography. Therefore, I propose to examine *One Writer's Beginnings* from an American point of view rather than from a strictly southern point of view in order to show how Welty's Americanness inscribes her production solidly within the canon of American literature.

The technique of the self-portrait—as exemplified by Augustine or Michel de Montaigne, for example—gives writers great freedom to play with light and shade, to privilege that side of themselves they want to reveal to the public eye. And Eudora Welty had a double purpose in composing her self-portrait: to meet the requirements of the Massey lectures on the history of American civilization, she chose to emphasize the Americanness of her family background and education, and to place her canon in a true perspective, she chose to dismiss the image of the southern regionalist by emphasizing what had been there all along—the general and the universal.[6] These gestures of the writer will be restored with each new reading, as Welty's slim volume feeds

---

4. Eudora Welty, personal conversation with author, April 13, 1997.
5. Brantley, *Feminine Sense*, 7.
6. Welty failed to convince Frank Lentricchia, at least, who called her "the Cumean Sibyl of the new regionalism," as late as 1989 (cited by Brantley, *Feminine Sense*, 120). For a discussion of Ruth Vande Kieft's defense of Welty, also see Brantley, *Feminine Sense*, ibid.

the meditation of future generations in the tradition of great self-portraits.

Eudora Welty achieves her ultimate triumph of style and composition in this text, written with as much passion as courage. The style she chose explains the misreadings as well as the praise. The superbly crafted language is designed to achieve a delicate balance between the specificity of the self with its private world and the representative portrait of a continent fostering dreams and illusions. Throughout her career, Welty has polished and perfected her style, adapting it to the genre of the work: the fiction is written in an elaborate, elliptical, resisting manner, verging at times on the overwrought. In the essays the language is simpler, yet still dense and terse, with a fine sense of formula. Finally, the ongoing simplifying process reaches its climax in the autobiography. Here Welty refines her style to its utmost simplicity, yet without compromising its elegance and precision; more importantly, she plays with the multilayered possibilities of language, which itself then becomes motif and theme. Language functions as motif when its naked spontaneity echoes the pragmatic language of the pioneers Welty celebrates, especially that of Benjamin Franklin—a language meant to arouse the reader's reflection rather than his emotion as fiction does. Language becomes theme when it serves Welty's purpose to present a general picture of America rather than the private picture of her own life, when she scrapes off the surface of her narrative the too salient telling of intense anecdotes and minimizes personal emotion. This meticulous work on the texture of her style creates the very tension of the autobiography, which achieves a balance between the specificity of the self and the representative depiction of a life. The work's dramatic strength, like its originality, rests on this paradox, which feeds it, polishes it, and fashions the strategies Welty adopts. Yet, for all the book's guardedness, Welty's violence is there all the same—lucid, angry, and militant.[7]

The technique she uses to paint her panorama of an American

---

7. In *One Writer's Beginnings*, Eudora Welty disclaims that she ever wrote out of anger except just once, after the murder of Medgar Evers: "There was one story that anger certainly lit the fuse of" (38). Nevertheless, controlled indignation before injustice and prejudice has always been present in her work.

childhood stems partly, I suggest, from her experience as a photographer, especially from the pictures she took of Union Square in New York during the Depression and later from views of back streets and social events in Jackson, New Orleans, and France. Those photographs exemplify political attitudes that would feed her fiction later; they also taught her about narrative technique, as Harriet Pollack has shown in two essays on the relationship between Welty's photographs and the techniques of her story composition. The camera eye takes in everything, so that the photographs of large cities are crowded with details: publicity, posters, people. They give no sense of depth, instead flattening their subjects, and this is true also of the photographs with reflections in shop windows. I will argue that this flattening creates an effect similar to that achieved by modern painters when they discard perspective and emphasize the value of the ground (what Pollack calls "details, circumstances, life around the figure"). For this pictorial technique, Rosalind Krauss describes how Piet Mondrian covered his canvas with a grid to eliminate successiveness, and figured forth simultaneity "in this brilliant obsessional hatching. It would be his first truly systematic reinvention of the ground as figure."[8] The disconcerting effect Welty achieves in *One Writer's Beginnings*, which critics like Brantley find difficult to sum up, comes from a similar technique. Since Welty builds her narrative upon an accumulation of small details, she multiplies information about her home life and family background, schools and libraries in Jackson, summer travels through the country, and life in the early days of the pioneers, always insisting on mirror effects through endless echoes and multiple repetitions that work like so many small touches of paint on a canvas, or like Mondrian's grid, to convey the intellectual perception of what life was like in America at a certain time. At the end of our reading, we feel the simul-

8. Harriet Pollack, "Photographic Convention and Story Composition: Eudora Welty's Use of Detail, Plot, Genre, and Expectation from 'A Worn Path' through *The Bride of the Innisfallen*," *South Central Review* 14 (1997): 15–34, and "Eudora Welty's 'Too Far to Walk It': Out Farther Still? A Correction," *South Central Review* 14 (1997): 114–6; Rosalind E. Krauss, *The Optical Unconscious* (Cambridge: MIT Press, 1983), 16. I am indebted to Françoise Palleau for drawing my attention to Krauss's excellent study of Cather (unpub. diss., Paris III Sorbonne Nouvelle, 1995).

taneity of hundreds of perceptions and thoughts, rather than the sequentially organized sensory experience of impressionism. The background has become exactly coincident with the foreground.

The possibilities offered by this technique of the ground as figure help Welty define her attitude toward the South and make her point on such controversial issues as racism or history. She treats racist bigotry in an exemplary way, showing its absence rather than its presence, and, more subtly, she implies that black voices and black talents for storytelling were part of her education as a fiction writer. Race relations is the oblique reference when throughout *One Writer's Beginnings,* and specifically in the first section, "Listening," Welty shows how Jackson taught her the sounds of life and the voices of southern storytellers, and how early she became aware of the creative power of those voices. Not least among them is Fannie, the African American seamstress, whom Welty places side by side with her mother's white friends in the acknowledgment of her debt as a writer. She writes eloquently and lovingly and wryly of Fannie's teaching regarding the dramatic possibilities of a good telling of family gossip.[9] Welty's point is that her early education gave her no sense of racial difference or inferiority. Quite the opposite, for Fannie is given the title of author: "The gist of her tale would be lost on me, but Fannie didn't bother about the ear she was telling it to; she just liked telling. She was like an author. In fact, for a good deal of what she said, I daresay she *was* the author" (14). In this example, Welty shows the background exactly coinciding with the foreground: in the South black culture and white culture work together to yield the unique southern culture.

The same attitude of open acceptance and admiration colors Welty's treatment of African Americans in her fiction. She shares Hurston's political project to place the emphasis on celebration rather than on victimization. And just as Zora Neale Hurston fully integrates black culture into the American experience and celebrates her ethnic heritage, Eudora Welty claims her own American heritage in the story

9. With more emotion and at greater length, Ellen Glasgow acknowledges a similar debt. Yet her moving portrayal turns her black mammy into a fictional character as opposed to a real person, thus intimating the faintest touch of condescension (*The Woman Within* [New York: Harcourt Brace, 1954], 18).

"Powerhouse." With it, she boldly asserts that jazz music represents the most outstanding American artistic contribution to the arts in this century. Thus, by placing "Powerhouse" directly before "A Worn Path" at the end of her first collection of short stories, with both texts celebrating the greatness of the black community and its deep interaction with the white community that sees it as other, Welty builds up an aesthetic and emotional climax that is also strongly political: she proudly claims her black heritage as an American citizen, at the same time undermining the white southern prejudice present in both stories. What Françoise Lionnet writes of Hurston applies at least to some extent to Welty's political attitude:

> I would thus argue that her unstated aim is identical to Fanon's later formulation: to destroy the white stereotype of black *inculture* not by privileging "blackness" as an oppositional category to "whiteness" in culture but by unequivocally showing the vitality and diversity of nonwhite cultures around the Caribbean and the coastal areas of the South, thereby dispensing completely with "white" as a concept and a point of reference.[10]

This ground-as-figure technique inspires Welty's treatment of her family's political background in reference to historical events. She may have borne in mind Willa Cather's own research, and the technique that author used in *Death Comes for the Archbishop*, about which Cather explains: "The essence of such writing is not to hold the note, not to use an incident for all there is in it—but to touch and pass on."[11] Similarly, Welty uses short genealogical sketches to draw a po-

---

10. Lionnet, *Autobiographical Voices*,105.
11. Willa Cather in a letter to *Commonweal*, November 23, 1927, as quoted by Sharon O'Brien, ed., *Later Novels* (New York: Library of America, 1990), 973. Deep affinities between the two writers rather than Cather's influence on Welty seem a more appropriate explanation for *One Writer's Beginnings*. From what she said to John Jones, Welty did not realize Cather's possible influence upon her work before she reread Cather's work for an essay she contributed to the Cather centennial celebration in 1974. Welty later included this essay under the title "The House of Willa Cather" in *The Eye of the Story: Selected Essays and Reviews* (New York: Random House, 1978), 41–60. See the Jones interview in *Conversations with Eudora Welty*, ed. Peggy W. Prenshaw (Jackson: University Press of Mississippi, 1984), 324.

litical map of the United States, establishing, for instance, West Virginia as a place where slavery was refused and the lofty ideals of the Republic fulfilled, without dwelling too long on the point. With the same lightness of touch, she asserts the origins of her family's devotion to independence and its rejection of racism:

> The Cardens had been in West Virginia for a while—I believe were there before West Virginia was a state. Eudora Carden's own mother had been Eudora Ayres, of an Orange County, Virginia, family, the daughter of a Huguenot mother and an English father. He was a planter, fairly well-to-do. Eudora Ayres married another young Virginian, William Carden, who was poor and called a "dreamer"; and when these two innocents went to start life in the wild mountainous country, in the unknown part that had separated itself from Virginia, among his possessions he brought his leather-covered Latin dictionary and grammar, and she brought her father's wedding present of five slaves. The dictionary was forever kept in the tiny farmhouse and the slaves were let go. One of the stark facts of their lives in Enon is that during the Civil War Great-Grandfather Carden was taken prisoner and incarcerated in Ohio on suspicion of being, as a Virginian, a Confederate sympathizer, and lost his eyesight in confinement. (58)

Beyond facts and history, this incident picks up again the debate about private and public guilt, alluded to earlier in the autobiography, and as it completes the picture, it clearly states Welty's project, for in *One Writer's Beginnings*, Welty shows how her sense of guilt was displaced from the traditional public southern guilt over slavery, racism, and the Civil War to a more generally American sense of guilt of an ontological nature: the Puritans' or Hawthorne's. This deeply political gesture has liberated not only Welty herself but younger southern writers after her.

The guilt in *One Writer's Beginnings* touches on the origin of writing. "Listening" literally "stages" language, with this first chapter generating dislocation and estrangement through a journey *into* language, a strictly lexical adventure. The intimation of mortality present on the very first page is a poetical strategy, an exploration by language of that hinterland prowled by death, the supreme form of otherness, which will be at the heart of Welty's fiction as both metaphor and theme from "Death of a Traveling Salesman" to "The Demonstrators." The method reflects Welty's political options, in the displacement resulting from the strategy of metonymy, i.e., contiguity, which Welty uses to link together incidents ranging from the particular to the general. As a supreme manifestation of the carnivalesque, verbal games assert that any act of language is linked with death through its transgressive nature of exceeding boundaries. The first incident, based on the revelation of the secret of life and death, is the mother's admission of the birth and dramatic death of an eldest brother, which starts for young Eudora a network of guilty feelings associated with the principle of pleasure.[12] The metonymic construction of the page invites the reader to speculate upon that universal link that relates the functioning of the mind by associations of ideas to the pleasure/guilt polarity, right to the ontological guilt of survival. In the telling, Welty insists on dramatization, which once more leads to serious thinking on guilt and expiatory modes; in addition to the guilt of the survivor, there is the guilt connected with sexuality, with the parent-child relationship, with excess of tenderness or with a wish for happiness, and above all with a desire to transgress the laws of piety, filial or religious—a supreme transgression that will become the source and the theme of all Welty's writing. Thus the political intrudes where a reflection on writing is a reflection on life or vice versa, and where the lexical and mental structures are altered as is shown by the next two increasingly complex incidents, which are built upon the principle of theatricality and the reader/audience response.

The first plays upon lexical alteration (for the rhyme) and upon the passage from biological necessity to poetical necessity to assuage the fear of death:

> In the Spanish influenza epidemic, when Edward had high fever in one room and I high fever in another, I shot him off a jingle about the

12. Welty closely associates artistic pleasure, such as going to the theater or writing, with guilt. When her mother sent her along with her father to see *Blossom Time*, young Eudora experienced guilt in spite of all the excitement and wonder: "I could hardly bear my pleasure for my guilt" (15). Likewise, when as a twenty-something woman Welty left her mother at home and journeyed to New York in an effort to sell her stories, she felt guilt at "being the loved one gone" even as she experienced the "joy connected with writing" (94). Both experiences imply the guilt of severing ties with the mother; this theme recurs not only in *One Writer's Beginnings* but also in many Welty stories.

little boy down our street who was in bed with the same thing: "There was a little boy and his name was Lindsey. He went to Heaven with the influenzy." My mother, horrified, told me to be ashamed of myself and refused to deliver it. (36)

The second piece of writing plays upon literalness. Welty takes to the letter a phrase commonly used in the South ("by an act of God") and, by a turn the young student had not anticipated, her public in the person of H. L. Mencken read the joke literally in his turn:

> After great floods struck the state and Columbus had been over-flowed by the Tombigbee River, I contributed an editorial to *The Spectator* for its April Fool issue. This lamented that five of our freshman class got drowned when the waters rose, but by this Act of God, it went on, there was that much more room now for the rest of us. Years later, a Columbus newspaperman, on whose press our paper was printed, told me that H. L. Mencken had picked up this chirp out of me for *The American Mercury* as sample thinking from the Bible Belt. (79)

Welty thus makes her point wittily: all misreadings come from political prejudice and an excess of literality. By doing so she gives her audience something to consider when passing judgment upon her as a woman writer from the South, or more generally when the North and South appraise each other (a sly echo of the past with the fate of her great-grandfather, and of the present with the North's self-satisfaction during the civil rights movement).

The echoing effects of these sketches link together transgression, guilt, and writing—or, to put it differently, Welty invites her reader to read them as a political statement: all serious writing aims at disrupting known forms of authority, as it does in the description of Welty's mother's attachment to the Bible: "Then from time to time her lips would twitch in the stern books of the Bible, such as Romans, providing her as they did with memories of her Grandfather Carden who had been a Baptist preacher in the days when she grew up in West Virginia. She liked to try in retrospect to correct Grandpa too" (33). Furthermore, all serious writing, in Welty's case at least, aims at fully accepting the guilt, the better to transcend it; this is the meaning of her central metaphor for the artist—Perseus slaying the Medusa. Pure exhilaration comes from this liberating gesture of the artist and her characters.

Moreover, what makes *One Writer's Beginnings* such an exemplary American piece is recasting of the American myths of the frontier. The project to write about the American imagination itself is emphatically and modestly stated on the first page. The theme is deceptively simple: time and space. The manner is emphatic: Welty's favorite narrative strategy of dramatization/theatricality, which means displacement or transgression when applied to a genre other than drama. To dramatize a scene or moment is an eminently political gesture because it shifts the respective positions of reader and writer from intimate exchange to public performance: it transforms the world (of the work) into a stage, on which everyone ceases to be an individual and becomes character *and* audience in a formal dialectical relationship. Thus, like drama originally, the autobiographical text does not aim at transmitting information about the self, but at reiterating that word that founds all societies. The intimate confidence becomes the public reiteration of the origin. By a mirror effect, the writer establishes herself as stage director, and in the distance she has just introduced, she places a reflection on fear and death, while at the same time celebrating her art. *One Writer's Beginnings* opens onto a cosmogony, a staging of the origins of the world in which the writer was born, thus establishing her within a community. Conversely, Richard Wright in *Black Boy* chose to stress his personal family configuration (the opening scene is the pitiable image of a four-year-old child scolded by his mother on the day his grandmother died) and then proceeded to present bleaker and bleaker variations on this theme, as Richard Brodhead's study of the revisions of the manuscript shows. If we go back to the beginning of Hurston's *Dust Tracks*, however, we find another cosmogony, splendid, militant, and highly political:

> Like the dead-seeming, cold rocks, I have memories within that came out of the material that went to make me. Time and place have had their say. . . .
>
> I was born in a Negro town. I do not mean by that the back-side of an average town. Eatonville, Florida, is, and was at the time of my

birth, a pure Negro town—charter, mayor, council, town marshal and all. It was not the first Negro community in America, but it was the first to be incorporated, the first attempt at organized self-government on the part of Negroes in America.[13]

Welty's cosmogony is just as present on the page as Hurston's but is deconstructed, represented by elements that seem disparate yet function together as in a Paul Klee painting. By choosing to stage sound effects Welty puts time, the emblem of the living world, at the origin of her text. The striking and chiming of clocks in the Weltys' house places her within the genealogy of her family (Swiss ancestors), as well as within the American tradition of mixed ancestry. When Welty goes on to discuss the scientific use of the instruments her father loved, she opens the family house and the child's imagination onto the cosmos and its temporality, and also asserts the full cosmic dimension of the American frontier. Under the appearance of the familiar and the anecdotal, Welty reveals what characterizes the universal writer for her: an obsession with the flight of time toward inexorable death. In the essay "Some Notes on Time in Fiction," she observes, "We are mortal: this is time's deepest meaning in the novel as it is to us alive."[14]

"My father loved all instruments that would instruct and fascinate" (3). The word "fascinate" asserts that science is the daughter of imagination and feeds it. Beyond the narcissistic quest of the self, Welty stresses the general and indicates an opening. Hurston places her infancy on the historical and political American scene. Likewise, on the first page of her autobiography, Welty draws the great axis of the American (and feminine) imagination—the vertical axis of the cosmic vision. That she should relate in similar terms her epiphany at the top of the mountain in West Virginia, where she has the revelation of both her independence and her vocation as a writer, shows her will to acclaim herself fully an American writer. As we know from similar experiences by other women writers, this insistence on the vertical axis and its reversibility (Welty sees stars in the well), the depth of the earth and the clouds in the sky all contribute to suggest some gigantic

13. Zora Neale Hurston, "My Birthplace," *Folklore, Memoirs, and Other Writings*, ed. Cheryl A. Wall (New York: Library of America, 1995), 561.

14. Eudora Welty, "Some Notes on Time in Fiction," in *Eye of the Story*, 168.

volcanic eruption emblematic of the creative experience of a feminine "venue à l'écriture," in Hélène Cixous's phrase. No doubt Miss Eckhart should undergo such transfiguration when she becomes at last the great artist she is before two ignorant little girls. Welty's experience is in no way comparable to Ellen Glasgow's, although Will Brantley writes that she "describes a naturalistic experience on a West Virginia mountain top that helped to crystallize her love of independence (a moment that bears comparison to Glasgow's experience in the Alps)."[15] Glasgow clearly writes of a pantheistic moment, which followed the death of the man she loved. After despair over the haunting persistence of death in her life, she experiences "union," "peace" that comes from integration into the great natural cycle of decay and renewal. Welty experiences an opposite pull, not into but out of, something she will fictionalize in "A Memory," with its images of a volcanic eruption at the moment the girl has an intimation of creativity and of the forces of death—the artist's great theme.

As the narrative of *One Writer's Beginnings* unfolds, Welty establishes through the figures of her mother and father the paradoxical quality of the American myths. In so doing, she is not defining her own self as would be expected in an autobiography: rather, she is defining the American identity as simultaneously a reaffirmation of the Puritan past and a reshaping of it in the name of the future. With her mother's ancestors—preachers and lawyers, schoolteachers and scholars—she establishes the link with the drafters of the American Constitution and beyond that with the Puritans and their intense preoccupation with New Beginnings.

It is worth noting that Welty reorganizes the mythical geography of America. As she recaptures her heritage in order to see how much of it went into her writing, she identifies West Virginia, her mother's country, as both Eden and the Promised Land—an Eden for her mother, but the wild promised land where she will have to fight ceaselessly to ensure her independence. Recoiling from the encroachment of the pigeons is the negative counterpart of her epiphany at the well. Both

15. Brantley, *Feminine Sense*, 112. On Miss Eckhart in "June Recital" as an example of the experience of creativity, see my "Watchers and Watching," *Southern Review* 19 (1983): 483–509.

events lead to freedom and independence, which is what her whole production as an artist has aimed at. Ohio, on the other hand, her father's country, becomes the place where, for her, the myths of American pragmatism and simplicity and efficiency begin. Welty soon discards the negative aspect related to a sad private past in order to recreate the pristine simplicity of the frontier through sensations and sparse telling: a simpler frontier, closer to most of her readers' experience, yet full of promises since it produced that typical American—her father, a man who loved scientific instruments and was always ready to experiment with new technologies, as his final achievement, the Lamar Life Insurance Building, Jackson's first skyscraper, amply proves. She further presents him as filled with the pioneer's love of change and movement, ready to seize new opportunities in places far away from home (such as his prospective trip to Niagara Falls) and eager to reenact with the same spirit of adventure the exploration of the width and depth of the North American continent. Welty's insistence on the role played upon her creative imagination by railroad journeys with her father defines, it seems, wandering as the quintessential American dream and shows how deeply ingrained the wanderer is in the heart of a writer some have called a "southern recluse," as it is deeply ingrained in the nation's imagination. Indeed, traveling for Welty has always meant a journey toward freedom, exploration, and creativity under the auspicious ministering of angels such as the African American woman who provided coffee to night travelers in Welty's student days and who figures in "The Key," one of her best stories about fiction writing.

When she chooses to quote her maternal grandfather Ned Andrews's dedicatory address for the opening of a new courthouse, the eighteenth-century rhetoric (one can even hear the accents of Chateaubriand's celebration of the New World in *Attala* or *Les Natchez*) exemplifies the nature of the American West (this is West Virginia, for a Virginian) as both invitation and end, origin and destiny. Here the landscape is haunted by the ruins of former democracies and former empires, and the assertion of America's Manifest Destiny. We find some of the rhetoric of the Puritans celebrating the founding of the New Jerusalem and the unwavering belief in Progress. As a true revolutionary "son," if we follow Bancroft's theories, Ned Andrews is obeying his Puritan fathers. He is also a true man of the New West in the nineteenth century and sees the West not as wilderness but as empire-building country: "The student turns with a sigh of relief from the crumbling pillars and columns of Athens and Alexandria to the symmetrical and colossal temples of the New World. As time eats from the tombstones of the past the epitaphs of primeval greatness, and covers the pyramids with the moss of forgetfulness, [the architecture of the building] directs the eye to the new temples of art and progress that make America the monumental beacon-light of the world" (47).

Thus as Welty finally perceives the pattern that organized her heritage, the gap between her parents' families does not seem as wide as she had first imagined. One line of ancestors, the mother's side, represents the side of the myth that is the fulfillment of a promise. In her important essay "'Pockets of Life': Rediscovering America in Paul Auster's *Moon Palace*," Kathie Birat uses Sacvan Bercovitch's analysis of American cultural history to show how "the projection of a scriptural consecration into a certain future prepared the way for other fruitful paradoxes of openness and enclosure," and how Auster "consolidated the myth of a new set of fathers," thereby setting in motion the process by which America would "prove its promise from one frontier to another" through "rhetorical invention."[16] On the other hand, Welty's father in the autobiography embodies a man turned to the future, always seeing America as the Promised Land, a land of technological invention, progress, and unlimited hope. So the strategy established in the book rests on the dialectics of the literal, achieved by the mother's many speeches and comments, and the metaphorical, the silent text, represented by the father's optimistic belief in the future of America.

By introducing distance between the personal and the general, the private and the public, Welty liberated the self from the danger of exposure. This gesture corresponds to that deep strain visible in every form of her production as an artist—photography included—which is a

---

16. Kathie Birat, "'Pockets of Life': Rediscovering America in Paul Auster's *Moon Palace*," in *Moon Palace*, ed. François Gallix (Paris: Editions du Temps, 1996), 131–45.

continual movement toward abstraction. In this respect, Welty thinks along the lines of Willa Cather. She simplifies, erases, and leaves only a rarefied substance that her readers or viewers must interpret. Such a technique is responsible for the intemporal beauty of her work, which will make it endure time and repeatedly fascinate readers and viewers. I further argue, in the light of *One Writer's Beginnings*, that Welty writes not so much *about* the South than as *with* the South.

Just as Rembrandt's magnificent last self-portrait teaches much about an artist's enterprise and risk through the veins, scars, and marks of life on a face, the very texture of *One Writer's Beginnings*, presenting as it does the eroded yet forever alive and animated face of Welty's world, teaches us much about America and the risk of writing about her. This book is Eudora Welty's most secret piece of work, filled with holes in its texture, blanks in the writing, and silences in the voice. In its secret[17] there lies an excess of meaning and brooding guilt—the guilt of a writer's venture. For there is forever the lucidity inherent in the secret that doubts and battles against the unsayable, and yet tries to the last to say it. It is no wonder then that the autobiography should end like *The Golden Apples*, the work "closest to [her] heart," with a magnificent rewriting of the American Dream. Virgie's portrait is Welty's feminine counterpart of Fitzgerald's vision of the Dutch sailors. By a daring *effet de superposition*, Welty represents Virgie as both America and the Quintessential American, since the two parts of a long sentence about Virgie in *One Writer's Beginnings* apply equally to the woman and to the land. America seen as battered (not waste) land and Promised Land, while, sitting on the stile in silent companionship with Minerva, the old African American woman who functions as her double in a mysterious and mythical way, Virgie is shown as the buffeted yet undefeated American adamantly sustained by his/her sharing of the Promise—which has always been Welty's subject:

> Passionate, recalcitrant, stubbornly undefeated by failure or hurt or disgrace or bereavement, all the while heedlessly wasting of her gifts,

---

17. From the Greek *kritein*, to discern, come *secret* and *citic*, and also *crime, certitude*, and *crisis*—a whole semantic network that binds together the strange avenues of this unique book.

she knows to the last that there is a world that remains out there, a world living and mysterious, and that she is part of it. (102)

With this forceful reiteration of her acceptance of the full American heritage, Welty also celebrates the undaunted spirit that creates this mysterious world. America as the Pilgrim/Pioneer's dream and challenge, America as the writer's secret territory: the political gesture of the writer will be restored again and again with each new reading, as Welty's slim volume feeds the meditation of future generations in the tradition of great self-portraits.

*Harriet Pollack and Suzanne Marrs*

## Seeing Welty's Political Vision in Her Photographs

The essays of this collection suggest that Eudora Welty's fiction is any-thing but "apolitical." Her photographs provide additional evidence that, though she did not set out to make polemical statements with her camera, Welty has from the start been politically engaged. These framings reveal what Eudora Welty was choosing to look at in the 1930s and, concurrently, what she was able to see. Many of these pho-tographs reveal a political vision that penetrates her times and antici-pates issues to come. The selection that follows, published here with the permission of the Mississippi Department of Archives and History, is a first effort to bring her framing and exposing political vision into focus for her readership.

The daughter of an inveterate amateur photographer, Welty made photographs for twenty years, perhaps beginning sometime between her 1929 graduation from the University of Wisconsin and her subse-quent enrollment in the Columbia University School of Business. At first she used a Kodak camera with a bellows, and she continued to use that camera until 1935, when she purchased a more sophisticated Re-comar. Late in 1936, she changed cameras once again, buying the Rolleiflex that she used until 1950, when she accidentally left it on a Paris Metro bench; she has told the story of how, annoyed with her own carelessness, she refused for many years to replace it.

Welty's early photos were the subject of not one, as was long as-sumed, but two New York City shows. The first was sponsored by Lu-gene Opticians at the Photographic Galleries, the second by the Cam-era House. The first show, held March 31–April 15, 1936, consisted of forty-five photographs, many of African Americans. Three photo-graphs from this show are included here: "Making a Date," "Washwoman," and "Dolls." Samuel Robbins, who had worked on Welty's first show, contacted her when he moved from the Lugene Gallery to the Camera House and proposed a second show of her photographs, March 6–31, 1937. He requested photos of "poor whites," and while it seems impossible to determine precisely which photographs were exhibited, a number of mounted original prints held at the Mississippi Department of Archives and History seem likely candidates; among them is "Political Rally on the Courthouse Grounds," another print that we have chosen to discuss. Not only galleries but also publishers in the 1930s were interested in the images Welty submitted to them; at that time, however, publishers were reluctant to incur the high cost of reproducing the prints, and Welty for many years turned her attention to fiction alone. It was not until 1971 that her photographs were published in book form, in *One Time, One Place*. Since then, two new books of Welty photographs have been issued, *In Black and White* and *Photographs*, and two exhibition catalogs edited by Patti Carr Black, *Welty* and *Other Places*, have been published.[1]

The representative photographs we reprint here—undoubtedly readers will know and think of others—all frame details of the world at which Welty was looking closely in the 1930s. Some of the images offer quiet, straightforward statements; more offer, as Patti Carr Black has observed, ironic commentary, using irony as Welty uses it in her conversation and fiction—to bring into focus perspectives that should not go unseen, to expose myths and misconceptions, smugness and self-deception.[2] But whatever the approach they take, these photographs are invitations to speculate on meanings that, more often than not, would today be called political.[3]

1. This information about Eudora Welty's career as a photographer appeared in slightly different form in Suzanne Marrs, *The Welty Collection* (Jackson: University Press of Mississippi, 1988), 77–8.
2. In a letter to the authors of this essay, Patti Carr Black noted the prevalence of irony in Welty's photographs as in her conversation and writing, and Black added that Welty's "weapon in politics *was* irony."
3. As more and more study is devoted to the Welty photographs, it becomes important to establish as definitively as possible where and when they were taken and, more important, to correct any errors that have been made in reprinting them. Building upon the meticulous work of Patti Carr Black and the staff of

the Mississippi Department of Archives and History, the *Welty Collection* and *Photographs* have provided valuable clarification, but many ambiguities remain. The photographs of political rallies long identified as Tupelo and Pontotoc, for instance, seem most likely to have been taken solely in Pontotoc. Certainly one of this series (*Photographs* 62) has definitely been misidentified as Tupelo. In addition, although the photograph titled "Hello and Good-bye" has typically been printed with the beauty queens waving their left hands, we now know (thanks to Forrest Galey at the Mississippi Department of Archives and History) that the negative was flopped when such prints were made. The queens were waving their right hands and facing to their right just as they do in Welty's story "Hello and Good-bye." We have printed the photograph correctly in our essay.

## Political Rally on the Courthouse Grounds

Pontotoc, 1930s

This is one of a series of photographs Welty took at a political rally or two in northeast Mississippi. The series, as Peggy Prenshaw notes in her essay for this collection, exposes

> the ineffectuality of "official" public speech to communicate much of anything trustworthy or meaningful to the public. In an image enti-tled "Political Speaking" in *One Time, One Place,* the speaker is en-tirely absent from the scene and the audience is revealed as inatten-tive, even bored. Centering the photograph is a parked car, site of the only animated conversation seeming to take place. . . . In an adjacent photograph, "Political Speech," the viewer's eye is directed to the sleeping figure of a young girl, whose whole body is turned away from the speaker.

In the image we include here, Welty has photographed a telling gather-ing of three men and two women who are engaged in rapt conversa-tion. The five seem to have come from the country to town for the rally; the women are in simple dresses and two of the men are in over-alls. All five are especially neat and clean in attire; the occasion seems to have commanded this degree of respect. Their conversation is in-tense. Private conversation occupies them fully as the rhetoric and posturing of candidates could not. And in this informal group, women participate actively. Although one woman seems to be serving water-melon to the others, her attention is riveted on the discussion, and the second woman in the photograph is hunkered down and leaning for-ward as if to contribute to the debate. If public avenues of political power were typically unavailable to women, informal avenues of in-fluence and negotiation were open. This photograph offers further evi-dence for Prenshaw's assertion that, suspicious of Mississippi politics in her time, Welty relocates or displaces "the public and political spheres to private . . . ones."

All photographs appear courtesy of the Eudora Welty Collection, Mississippi Department of Archives and History, Jackson

## Delegate
Jackson, 1937

Late in the 1930s Welty photographed this delegate, who wears a banner of the United Daughters of the Confederacy. Her impassive stare and her sagging body seem expressions of an exhaustion not shared by the figures around her. The delegate seems self-possessed with a sense of her power, a power due to class and lineage perhaps, and she certainly represents a group that ties social hierarchy to reverence for and position in the past. That importance seems irrelevant to those about her: one man and a barely perceptible woman seem curious about the photographer, but the delegate herself, despite badges and banners, commands only Welty's attention. Welty, in turn, commands us to see this woman as comically imperious, just as she later will bring us to see, for example, Mrs. Comus Stark. Other and quite different Mississippi women held a more vital kind of political power, the kind that comes with election to office or with political appointment, but they were few in number.[1] The political roles played by women typically were more conventional and confined and led women to the Governor's Mansion, which lies in the photograph's background, only in the role of delegate or of first spouse.

1. See Joanne V. Hawks, M. Carolyn Ellis, and J. Byron Morris, "Women in the Mississippi Legislature (1924–1981)," *Journal of Mississippi History* 43.4 (1981): 266–93.

**Colored Entrance**

Jackson, 1930s

This image provides a striking example of Welty's attitude toward institutionalized segregation in the South. A young African American man is compelled to use the black entrance to a movie theater as two white women, seen mostly as a blurred image at the edge of the photograph, rush by. The women are seemingly oblivious to the young man's situation, to the inequity at the heart of the social order. Welty herself, however, was not oblivious. During her graduate school days in New York City, Welty had often been part of integrated audiences and had loved the opportunity to listen to music at the Cotton Club or Small's Paradise. When she returned home, she frequented music stores in the black business district and was among the few whites who attended black concerts. She knew the connection that music, theater, and film could bring to members of an audience, no matter how diverse the cultures from which they came. And she knew that music and story could successfully create bonds across diverse cultures. Her photograph conveys the irony of a system that inhibits such connection by insisting on separateness.

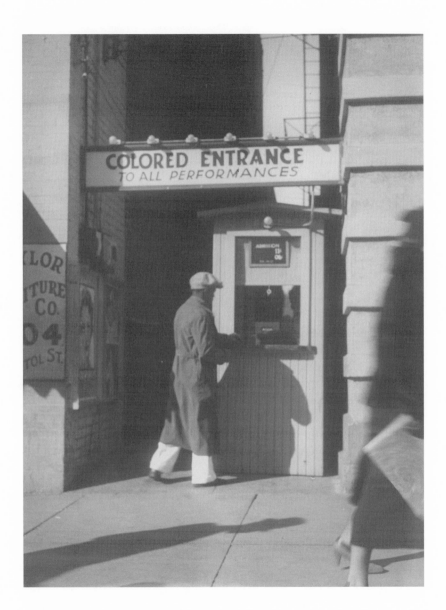

## Dolls

Jackson, 1930s

This photo frames a racial predicament that Welty, with a political vision ahead of her time, could see in the 1930s. It is what Toni Morrison helped all the rest of us see in 1970 when in her novel *The Bluest Eye* she wrote:

> The big, the special, the loving gift was always a big, blue-eyed Baby Doll. From the clucking sounds of adults I knew that the doll represented what they thought of as my fondest wish. . . . [A]ll the world had agreed that a blue-eyed, yellow-haired, pink-skinned doll was what every girl treasured. "Here," they said, "this is beautiful, and if you are on this day 'worthy' you may have it." . . . I could not love it. But I could examine it to see what it was that all the world said was loveable.[1]

Provocatively, Morrison was the rare early reader to speak of Welty's work as political. She called Welty "fearless" on the topic of apartheid culture in a 1977 interview which she gave to Mel Watkins. "Nadine Gordimer and Eudora Welty," Morrison said in the interview, "write about black people in a way that few white men have ever been able to write. It's not patronizing, not romanticizing—it's the way they should be written about."[2]

In Welty's photo, the faces of two African American children are not as clearly visible as the faces of the white dolls that they have been given to love. Coincidentally, a chain hangs on the fence behind them.

1. Toni Morrison, *The Bluest Eye* (New York: Penguin, 1994), 20–1.
2. *New York Times Book Review* 11 September 1977: 48–50.

## Hello and Good-bye
Jackson, 1939

Welty took this photograph when she was working for the Mississippi Advertising Commission, and eight years later she wrote a story based upon her experience doing so. Published in the 1947 *Atlantic* but never collected in any of her books of fiction, "Hello and Good-bye" is narrated by a woman assigned to photograph two young beauty contestants, one innocent, the other modeling recently gained experience. Standing on the steps of Mississippi's New Capitol building, the young women strike their poses, and the older and wiser signals their readiness with the word "Give." Welty recalls that with this word the beauty queens raised their bosoms and their hands. Neither of the contestants saw any humor in the command or the pose. Eudora Welty did. Her picture and her story show good-natured amusement, but also show Welty's sense that she, like the narrator of the story, was photographing an absolutely absurd event, one that represented the way women sought power in a world of sexual politics. These young women, caught in their artificial, almost identical poses, wave their hands in a queenly (as in the Queen of England) fashion, but they are dwarfed by the capitol building looming over them. The realm of the beauty queen is a small one indeed.

**Courthouse Steps**

Fayette, 1930s

Here the steps of another official political building are seen from yet another angle. The photographic composition leads our eyes to the backs of three guarding gargoyles—white male figures form a class coalition of overalls, white shirt, and suit jacket. The three hats, which top vigilant, surveying faces, form an arresting triangle, and its direction brings our eyes to the comfortably clasped, powerful hands of the jacketed man, dressed-for-success in spite of the heat, positioned as if the power just behind the other figures. What might have been felt by an African American man, or a young woman, seeking a hearing and walking past a congress of sentries, up the courthouse steps?

**Making a Date**

Grenada, 1935

The lines of this photo bring our eyes down two tattered figures to two pairs of shoes that are the emblems of working poverty in the African American community of depression-hit Grenada, Mississippi. The title of the photo, and the man's earnest, cap-in-pocket approach to the woman he is courting, reveal life and hope prevailing even in this extreme, almost obscene, poverty. The challenging glance of the woman, meeting the eye of the camera and now our observing eye, is full of provocation and a considering judgment that assesses how she is being seen and by whom. These figures in their worn clothes are framed and hemmed in by the merchandise-filled store windows on the left and the high-priced cars on the right.

## Washwoman

Jackson, 1930s

The figure of the laundress is a portrait of work paused briefly. The downward gaze of the woman seems to be focused inward. Her tired body is peaceful now; her facial expression is poised midway between depression and relaxation. The woman has the look of someone slipping into fantasy. But her head-rag and apron are stretched to a tension that matches the tension in the shirts pulled to dry on the line. Empty washtubs suggest both a job done and one that will again have to be done. The dog behind her weary back is a more at-ease figure: the cat nearer her—also washing—is more agile and energetic. The dappled light of the photograph is beautiful; the setting itself is not. The woman's gaze directs our eyes down toward pronounced shadows cast by the sun. While the freshly washed shirts absorb the sun's heat, the laundress—more comfortable than when laboring in that heat—stretches into stillness in partial shade. The figure is personal; the figure is political.

**Washwomen Carrying the Clothes**

Yalobusha County, 1930s

This lyric photograph about work communicates a mixing of cultures visible in Yalobusha County, Mississippi. The two women carrying laundry on their heads center a Mississippi landscape so that it can seem to image a scene on a West African savannah. The likeness evokes the cultural merging that began when Africans were compelled to bring their cultures to America. Here, perhaps without consciously knowing their African heritage, these two Mississippi women demonstrate generations of African women's experience balancing loads. These confident, capable figures—decoratively dressed, adorned with headcloths that help cushion against and steady the weight they bear—stand against a softly cloudy and yet shimmering southern sky. Their faces, however, are somewhat obscured beneath the bundles they carry.

## Pageant of Birds

Jackson, 1930s

This photo is one of several with which Welty documented a pageant written and staged by Maude Thompson at Farish Street Baptist Church. The spectacle was also the subject of Welty's essay "A Pageant of Birds," first published in the *New Republic* (25 October 1943) and then in an altered version in *The Eye of the Story: Selected Essays and Reviews* (1978). Welty wrote about it as a demonstration of magic-making, of our tendency to "bedazzle ourselves out of what is at hand. These colored people I happened to see had got hold of some bright tissue paper." Barbara Ladd, earlier in this collection, discusses the political symbolism of the pageant. According to Ladd, the pageant is about patriotism; it borrows "the conventional symbols of the American Dream . . . appropriating them"—perhaps in the satiric tradition of subversively signifying. Ladd quotes Welty's description as it appeared in the *New Republic:*

> Then came the entrance of the Eagle Bird. Her wings and tail were of gold and silver tin-foil, and her dress was a black and purple kimono. She began a slow pace down the aisle with that truly majestic dignity which only a vast, firmly matured physique, wholly unself-conscious, can achieve. She had obviously got to be the Eagle because she was the most important. Her hypnotic majesty was almost prostrating to the audience, as she moved, as slowly as possible, down the aisle and finally turned and stood beneath the eagle's picture on the wall, in the exact center of the platform.

Of this passage Ladd writes: "The seating of the eagle is accompanied by flag-waving and the singing of 'The Star-Spangled Banner' by this audience which is 'almost prostrat[ed]' . . . and is followed by the 'procession of the lesser birds' who would bow to the Eagle Bird and to the audience before 'taking their positions.' Among the birds [was] . . . 'only one beautiful blackbird, alone but not lonesome.'"

## Tomato-Packer's Recess

Copiah County, 1930s

Zora Neale Hurston, in *Their Eyes Were Watching God* (1937), wrote about a Florida migrant labor camp. There, after "chugging on to the muck" and "all day, all night, hurrying in to pick beans," workers took ease when they found their way to jook joints: in those recesses, Hurston pictured "blues made and used right on the spot" for a "hopeful humanity."[1] In this photo Welty too is emphasizing the community that can be harvested from hard work. Her camera frames not the men's arduous work as packers, but their joyful discovery of community, expressed in music.

1. Zora Neale Hurston, *Their Eyes Were Watching God* (Urbana: University of Illinois, 1978), 196–7.

## The Unemployed in Union Square

New York, 1930s

Welty's New York City photographs depict ordinary-looking people who during conventional business hours are sitting on Union Square park benches or gathering for protests because they have no jobs to occupy their days and provide them with purpose and sustenance. Belief in official insensitivity to their plight prompted the unemployed to demonstrate in New York and elsewhere; in 1935, for instance, seventy-five demonstrators, "demanding more free clothing," and five thousand "spectators and sympathizers" gathered at one Home Relief station in New York City; it took fifty policemen with tear gas to disperse them. A smaller demonstration at City Hall resulted in the Workers Unemployed Union being summarily rebuffed by Mayor LaGuardia.[1]

In this picture Welty captures still another protest waged in the city against tremendous odds. The demonstrators are confined between triangular lines on the pavement and are overshadowed by commercial establishments, by a substantial truck with trailer, and by a large traffic sign commanding them to "KEEP RIGHT."

1. "Angry Crowd Locks Itself in Relief Office; Defies 50 Policemen till Routed by Tear Gas," *New York Times* 19 July 1935: 1; "Mayor Rebuffs Idle at City Hall," ibid., 3 August 1935: 28.

## Union Square

New York, 1930s

In this photograph we see a number of suggestive images: one clock on the left below the center of the photograph and another at the upper right, the NRA Code sign in the upper center, the Union Square Savings Bank in the center, and men and women in the park across the foreground. The bracketing clocks show the time to be 3:35, but these people of the 1930s sit in the park nevertheless. Perhaps, like Howard in Welty's story "Flowers for Marjorie," they have no jobs to command their awareness of time or to provide them with a livelihood. The movement of time stands in contrast to the stagnation experienced by victims of unemployment.

The NRA Code sign high above the unemployed is another crucial image. By May 1935, when it was declared unconstitutional, the National Recovery Administration had, despite the declared intentions behind it, seriously compromised the position of workers in America. Though industries under NRA protection from anti-trust prosecution improved the economic situation of some workers, they cut the hours and income of others, laid off many more, and increased the prices of products.[1] The NRA Code sign thus ironically represents not recovery so much as economic suffering. A similar irony is implicit in the image of the Union Square Savings Bank looming over the unemployed. The government, in resolving the nation's banking crisis of 1932–1933, had not solved the difficulties of those whose money had been lost in bank failures or those who simply had no money to deposit.

This photograph and the various images it encompasses establish Welty's very political concern with the Great Depression. As Welty told interviewers Hunter Cole and Seetha Srinivasan in 1989, "These people of the Great Depression kept alive on the determination to get back to work and to make a living again. I photographed them in Union Square and in subways and sleeping in subway stations and huddling together to keep warm, and I felt, then, sort of placed in the editorial position as I took their pictures. Recording the mass of them did constitute a plea on their behalf to the public, their existing plight being so evident in the mass."[2]

1. William J. Cooper and Thomas E. Terrill, *The American South* (New York: Mc-Graw Hill, 1991), 677–8.
2. Hunter Cole and Seetha Srinivasan, "Eudora Welty and Photography: An Interview," in *More Conversations with Eudora Welty*, ed. Peggy Whitman Prenshaw (Jackson: University Press of Mississippi, 1996), 194–5.

## Blue Heaven

Jackson, 1930s

In her work for the WPA in 1935 and 1936, Welty had seen plenty of poverty in Mississippi. Her Mississippi photographs show people in patched and tattered clothes, people looking longingly in store windows, people living in unpainted shacks with rotting porches. But the temperate climate of Mississippi and the possibility that one might be able to plant a garden, own chickens, maybe have a cow even in town—these factors meliorated to some extent the effects of poverty in an essentially rural southern state. So too did the smallness of Mississippi's population. As Welty writes in the introduction to *One Time, One Place:*

> In New York there had been the faceless breadlines; on Farish Street in my home town of Jackson, the proprietor of the My Blue Heaven Café had written on the glass of the front door with his own finger dipped in window polish: "AT 4:30 AM WE OPEN OUR DOORS. WE HAVE NO CERTAIN TIME TO CLOSE. THE COOK WILL BE GLAD TO SERVE U. WITH A 5 AND 10C STEW." The message was personal and particular. More than what is phenomenal, that strikes home. It happened to me everywhere I went, and I took these pictures. (3–4)

The BLUE
HEAVEN
LUNCH
STAND
AT 4 30 AM
WE OPEN OUR DOORS.
WE HAVE NO CERTAIN
TIME TO CLOSE.
The COOK WILL BE
GLAD To SERVE U.
WITH A 5 And 10¢
STEW.

# Contributors

SHARON DEYKIN BARIS teaches in the English department at Bar-Ilan University, where she is senior lecturer in English and American literature. She has published articles on—among others—Nathaniel Hawthorne, Henry James, George Eliot, Wallace Stevens, and Eudora Welty, and her book in progress is a study of the influence of the biblical Book of Daniel on American thought and writing.

SUZAN HARRISON is associate professor of rhetoric and chair of the humanities division at Eckerd College in St. Petersburg, Florida. She is the author of *Eudora Welty and Virginia Woolf: Gender, Genre, and Influence*. In addition to her work on Welty, she has published articles on several other southern writers and is currently working on a study of southern fiction and the civil rights movement.

BARBARA LADD is associate professor of English at Emory University. Her articles have appeared in *American Literature*, the *Bucknell Review*, the *Mississippi Quarterly*, and elsewhere. Her book *Nationalism and the Color Line in George W. Cable, Mark Twain, and William Faulkner* was published by LSU Press in 1996.

REBECCA MARK is associate professor of English at Tulane University. Her books include *The Dragon's Blood: Feminist Intertextuality in Eudora Welty's "The Golden Apples"* and an edition of Gertrude Stein's *Lifting Belly*, and she has published articles on Welty, feminist literary theory, and pedagogy. She is presently working on an examination of the connection between homophobic and racist discourse in the violent rhetoric of the post-Reconstruction South.

SUZANNE MARRS, professor of English at Millsaps College in Welty's hometown of Jackson, Mississippi, has served as Welty Scholar at the

Mississippi Department of Archives and History. She is the author of *The Welty Collection* and has published articles about Welty in a variety of journals, including the *Southern Review*, the *Mississippi Quarterly*, and the *Southern Literary Journal*.

DANIÈLE PITAVY-SOUQUES is professor of North American literature at the University of Burgundy, France. Her essays on Eudora Welty were among the first to shift Welty criticism toward narrative technique and writing strategies. She has published extensively on Welty and other American women writers, both in France and in the United States. Among her books are *La Mort de Méduse: l'Art de la nouvelle chez Eudora Welty* (Lyon: Presses universitaires de Lyon, 1991) and *Eudora Welty: Sortilèges du conteur* (Paris: Belin, 1999).

NOEL POLK is professor of English at the University of Southern Mississippi. He is the author of numerous articles and books on Faulkner and Welty, including *Eudora Welty: A Bibliography of Her Work* (1994), *Children of the Dark House* (1996), and a memoir, *Outside the Southern Myth* (1997). He has lectured widely in this country, Europe, Japan, and the former Soviet Union.

HARRIET POLLACK, associate professor of English at Bucknell University, is the editor of *Having Our Way: Women Rewriting Tradition in Twentieth-Century America*. Her articles on Welty have appeared in such journals as the *Mississippi Quarterly*, the *Southern Quarterly*, the *Southern Literary Journal*, and the *South Central Review*. She and Suzanne Marrs codirected the 1997 Eudora Welty Society conference "Home Ties" (Jackson, Miss., April 1997), which in turn led to this book.

PEGGY WHITMAN PRENSHAW is Fred C. Frey Professor of Southern Studies in the English department at Louisiana State University. She has edited collections of interviews with Welty and Elizabeth Spencer, as well as several volumes of essays on Welty and other southern women writers. She serves as the general editor of the University Press of Mississippi's *Literary Conversations* series.

ANN ROMINES is director of graduate studies and professor of English at George Washington University. She is author of *The Home Plot: Women, Writing, and Domestic Ritual* (1992) and of *Constructing the Little House: Gender, Culture, and Laura Ingalls Wilder* (1997), which won the annual Children's Literature Association Award for the best scholarly book on children's literature. She has also published numerous essays on American women writers, including Eudora Welty. She is editor of *Willa Cather's Southern Connections: New Essays on Cather and the South* (University Press of Virginia, 2000) and of the forthcoming University of Nebraska Press scholarly edition of Cather's *Sapphira and the Slave Girl.*

# Index

Aaron, Daniel, 204
AAUP, 77
Adams, John Quincy (Millsaps professor), 75
AE, 13, 159–61
*Aeneid* (Virgil), 95
African Americans. *See* Civil rights movement; Integration of education; Lynchings; Race and racism
Agee, James, 163, 175
Agrarians, 52, 53
*Alice in Wonderland* (Carroll), 57
American Legion, 73, 173
American Red Cross, 71
Americanness of Welty, 15, 207–21
Andrews, Ned, 218–9
Anti-Communism. *See* McCarthyism; Rosenberg case
Anti-Semitism, 70, 71, 93. *See also* Nazism
Arbus, Diane, 162
Arendt, Hannah, 6, 24–5
Aristophanes, 22
Artist, metaphor for, 215
Aswell, Mary Lou, 81, 83, 85*n*21
Atomic bomb, 13–4, 156, 170, 175, 176
*Attack on Leviathan* (Davidson), 159
*Attala* (Chateaubriand), 218
Auden, W. H., 171
Augustine, 207
Austen, Jane, 176
Auster, Paul, 219
*Author and Agent* (Kreyling), 35

Autobiographies, 203–4, 205. *See also* *One Writer's Beginnings* (Welty); Self-portraits

Baker, Jean H., 73–4
Bakhtin, Mikhail, 119*n*13
Bancroft, George, 218–9
Baptist Church, 166–70, 242–3
Baris, Sharon Deykin, 11, 14–5, 17, 124, 131–2
Barthes, Roland, 54, 164
Beaujour, Michel, 205
Beauvoir, Simone de, 54
Beckwith, Byron de la, 47–8, 92–3
Bentley, Joseph, 105
Bercovitch, Sacvan, 219
Bible, 30, 214
Bilbo, Theodore, 20, 69–71
Biographical information about authors, 56–7
Birat, Kathie, 219
Black, Patti Carr, 84*n*21, 224, 224–5*nn*2–3
Black as Other, 93–101, 106
*Black Boy* (Wright), 53, 60, 215
"Black Monday" (Brady), 129–30
*Black Saturday* (Welty), 161
Bloch, Alexander, 183
Bloch, Manny, 183
"Blue Heaven" (Welty photograph), 250–1
"Bluest Eye" (Morrison), 232
Boatwright, James, 39

*Book of Daniel* (Doctorow), 185–6
Borinski, Ernst, 75
*Born of Conviction* statement, 76–7
Boyd, George, 77
Bradley, Mamie, 130
Brady, Tom, 129–30, 133
Brantley, Will, 205, 207, 209, 217
*Bride of Innisfallen* (Welty), 58–9, 61–2
British Labour Party, 165n18
Brodhead, Richard, 205, 215
Brooker, Jewel Spears, 105
Brooks, Cleanth, 52
*Brown v. Board of Education*, 11, 17, 124, 129–30
Bryant, Roy, 130, 132, 134
Bryant, Mrs. Roy, 130, 133, 134
Bunting, Charles, 11–2, 123, 128
"Burning" (Welty), 3

Camera House, 223, 224
*Candle of Vision* (AE), 13, 160–1
Cantwell, Robert, 165–6
Carnival and carnivalesque, 119, 119n13, 213
Carroll, Lewis, 57
Carter, Hodding, 136
Cather Willa, 203, 211, 211n11, 220
*Chamber*, 7, 47–50
Chaney, James, 93, 124
Chappell, David, 86
Chateaubriand, François, 218
Chekhov, Anton, 42
Chivalric myth, 133–4, 136–7
Circe, 61–2, 65–6
"Circe" (Welty), 61–2
Citizens' Council, 48, 82, 125, 144
Civil rights movement: violent resistance to, 2, 10, 38, 47, 80–2, 84–5n21, 85, 92–3, 110, 112, 124, 129, 130–1, 152; and Welty, 2, 8, 38, 74–87, 110, 124, 157, 179, 206–7, 230; and Medgar Evers's murder, 10, 47,

80, 92–3, 110, 112, 129, 207, 208n7; and *Losing Battles*, 11–2, 17, 123–54; and legislation on civil rights, 20; and Methodist church, 76–7; white southerners in, 86; in Little Rock, Arkansas, 125; and Till's lynching, 130–6; North's self-satisfaction during, 214. *See also* Integration of education; Race and racism
Cixous, Hélène, 217
*Clansman* (Dixon), 55
Clinton, Bill, 37, 87
Cobb, James C., 28
Coetzee, J. M., 45
Cold war, 13–4, 52, 55, 173–5, 199. *See also* McCarthyism; Rosenberg case
Cole, Hunter, 248
Colette, 174
*Collected Stories of Eudora Welty* (Welty), 24
"Colored Entrance" (Welty photograph), 230–1
Columbia University, 75, 223
Communism, 157, 158, 170, 173
Concentration camps, 33–4
Cooley, John R., 90
Corruption. *See* Political corruption
"Courthouse Steps" (Welty photograph), 236–7
Cowley, Malcolm, 18
Creekmore, Hubert, 69–70
*Criticism and Social Change* (Lentricchia), 106
Crone, 146, 151
Cultural studies, 205
*Curtain of Green* (Welty), 5–6, 24–6, 32, 166, 171

Daniel, Book of, 188
Davidson, Donald, 159
De Man, Paul, 56
Death as metaphor and theme, 212–4, 217

*Death Comes to the Archbishop* (Cather), 211

*Death in the Delta* (Whitfield), 130, 135–6

"Death of a Traveling Salesman" (Welty), 6, 26, 27, 39, 166, 212–3

"Delegate" (Welty photograph), 228–9

*Delta Wedding* (Welty): Trilling's review of, 3–4, 22, 90; private versus public spheres in, 6, 35–6; as response to World War II, 34–5; ring symbolism in, 133

Democratic Party, 69–70, 109, 124. *See also* Politics

"Demonstrators" (Welty): public versus private spheres in, 6; race and racism depicted in, 9–10, 21–2n4, 43–4, 84, 92–108; filial piety in, 11, 111–2, 115–20; Welty on, 120n15; death as theme and metaphor in, 212–3

Desegregation. *See* Integration

Devlin, Albert, 4–5, 19–20, 35, 96, 188n11

Dewey, Thomas, 70

"Directive" (Frost), 162

Dixiecrats, 70

Dixon, Thomas, 55

Doctorow, E. L., 66, 185–6

Documentary photography. *See* Photography

"Dolls" (Welty photograph), 223–4, 232–3

Dolson, Hildegarde, 81n16

Donaldson, Susan, 5, 35–6, 39, 60–1, 91, 102

*Dragon's Blood* (Mark), 103–4

"Dry September" (Faulkner), 57

Dukakis, Michael, 37

DuPlessis, Rachel Blau, 105

*Dust Tracks on a Road* (Hurston), 15, 206, 215–6

Eastman, Max, 156

Eddington, Sir Arthur, 175–6

Eisenhower, Dwight, 179, 183, 185, 197, 198–9

Eliot, T. S., 10, 56, 102–5

Ellison, Ralph, 75, 80, 81, 81n16, 84

Evangelicalism, 29–30

Evans, Sara M., 37–8

Evans, Walker, 162

Evers, Medgar, 10, 47, 48, 80, 93, 110, 112, 129, 193n18, 207, 208n7

*Eye of the Story* (Welty), 98, 167, 242

*Facing the Extreme* (Todorov), 33–4

Fascism, 12–4, 56, 155, 156, 158, 165n18. *See also* Totalitarianism

Faulkner, William: compared with Welty, 5, 59, 92, 204; race and racism depicted in works of, 50n1, 52, 57, 106; and New Criticism, 52, 53, 55; politics of, 56–7, 62; Polk on teaching of, 59–62, 64; Welty on, 85–6; as State Department emissary of postwar Americanism, 173. *See also* specific writings

*Feminine Sense in Southern Memoir* (Brantley), 205

Feminism: and personal as political, 19, 54, 109, 157–8; and Welty, 19, 23, 58, 91–2, 109, 157; women's suffrage movement, 31

Feminist criticism, 33, 55, 89, 91–2, 109, 204. *See also* specific feminist critics

Ferguson, Suzanne, 103

Ferris, Bill, 42

Fertility myths, 104, 146–7

Fetterly, Judith, 1–2

Fiction. *See* Politics of literature; and specific works of fiction by Welty

Filial piety: and Welty, 10, 80–2, 110–2, 120–1, 213n12; in Welty's fiction, 10, 11, 111–22; definition of filiality, 112

Films, 7, 47–51, 189, 193n18
"Firefighting" (Green), 174
"First Love" (Welty), 3
Fitzgerald, F. Scott, 56, 220
Flashback in narrative, 164
"Flowers for Marjorie" (Welty), 25, 166, 248
Ford, Ford Madox, 171
*Forrest Gump*, 51
Forster, E. M., 44
Foucault, Michel, 54, 66
Franklin, Benjamin, 15, 208
Frazer, James, 146–7
Freud, Sigmund, 192n16
*From Ritual to Romance* (Weston), 104
Fromm, Erich, 192n16
Frontier, 188n11, 215, 216, 218
Frost, Robert, 162
Fugitives, 52, 53

Galey, Forrest, 225n3
Gendering and gender relations, 19, 33–5, 40–1, 58–9, 89, 91–101, 140–1
*Ghosts of Mississippi*, 7, 47, 48
*Giving Offense: Essays on Censorship* (Coetzee), 45
Glasgow, Ellen, 205, 210n9, 217
*Go Down, Moses* (Faulkner), 5, 53, 60, 92
*Golden Apples* (Welty), 5, 17, 58–9, 61, 92, 104, 112, 220
*Golden Bough* (Frazer), 146–7
Goodman, Andy, 93, 124
Goodman, Walter, 70
Gore, Al, 37, 87
Graff, Gerald, 57
Grant, Cary, 193n18
Great Depression. *See* New Deal; Poverty
Greek polis, 24–5
Green, Henry, 12, 13–4, 156, 172, 172n27, 174–7

Greer, Germaine, 54
Gretlund, Jan, 42
Grisham, John, 47–9, 66, 67
Ground-as-figure technique, 209–12
Guilt, 212–5, 213n12, 220

Hackman, Gene, 48
Hains, Frank, 84–5n21, 123
Halberstam, David, 73
Hamblin, Robert, 85
*Hamlet* (Shakespeare), 75
Harlem, 75
Harrison, Suzan, 5, 9–10, 41
Harvard University, 15, 204, 207
Hawthorne, Nathaniel, 212
Heilbrun, Carolyn, 59, 90
"Hello and Good-bye" (Welty photograph), 225n3, 234–5
"Hello and Good-bye" (Welty short story), 234
Hemingway, Ernest, 12, 56, 172–3, 174, 176
"Henry Green: A Novelist of the Imagination" (Welty), 172, 174–5
Hill, Samuel S., 29–30
Hiroshima bombing, 13–4, 170
History: Welty and, 3, 5, 155–77; and Welty's ancestry in *One Writer's Beginnings*, 16, 211–2, 216–9; and Manifest Destiny, 186–9, 188n11, 218–9; Welty on, 187; and frontier, 188n11, 215, 216, 218
Hitchcock, Alfred, 193n18
"Hitch-Hikers" (Welty), 25
Hitler, Adolf, 12, 56, 70, 165n18, 170, 171. *See also* Nazism
"Hollow Men" (Eliot), 103
Home mission movement, 30–2
"House of Willa Cather" (Welty), 211n11
House Un-American Activities Committee, 71, 157. *See also* McCarthyism

*Huckleberry Finn* (Twain), 66
Huie, William Bradford, 134
*Human Condition* (Arendt), 24–5
Hurston, Zora Neale, 13, 15, 206, 210, 211, 215–6, 244

*Imaginations and Reveries* (AE), 13
*In Black and White* (Welty), 224
Individualism, 12, 171–2
*Inside Agitators* (Chappell), 86
Integration of education: Welty on, 2, 8; in Mississippi higher education, 8, 11, 74–80, 124; and *Brown v. Board of Education*, 11, 17, 124, 129–30; and school busing, 11, 124, 142, 144
Integration of theaters, 84–5n21, 230
Intertextuality. *See* Textuality and intertextuality
*Intruder in the Dust* (film), 50n1
Irony in Welty's photographs, 224, 224n2

Jackson, Jesse, 84, 85n21
*Jackson Cookbook* (Welty's foreword to), 122
Jackson State College, 84–5n21
Jefferson, Thomas, 207
Jones, John, 211n11

Kazin, Alfred, 155–6, 163, 166, 172, 175
Keats, John, 1
"Keela, the Outcast Indian Maiden" (Welty), 6, 8–9, 28–29, 82–3, 166
Kennedy, John F., 20
"Key" (Welty), 25, 218
King, Edwin, 79, 80
King, Martin Luther, 130
King, Richard H., 4, 22, 90
Kirstein, Lincoln, 163
Korean War, 73–4
Krauss, Rosalind, 209

Kreyling, Michael, 35, 39, 89, 121n17, 130, 179–80n2, 194–5n21, 195
Krush, Joe, 191
Ku Klux Klan, 81, 93, 129, 147, 152, 154

Ladd, Barbara, 5, 12–4, 92, 242
Lentricchia, Frank, 106, 207n6
*Let Us Now Praise Famous Men* (Agee), 163
Liberalism, definition of, 207
*Light in August* (Faulkner), 53, 57, 59–60
"Lily Daw and the Three Ladies" (Welty), 26, 166
Lionnet, Françoise, 206, 211
Literature. *See* Politics of literature; and specific literary works
Little, John, 22n4, 93, 120n15
Long, Huey, 70
"Looking at Short Stories" (Welty), 98
*Losing Battles* (Welty): public versus private spheres in, 6, 27, 38–41, 44, 60; and civil rights, 11–2, 17, 123–54; reviews and critical canon on, 11–2, 123–4; compared with "Death of a Traveling Salesman," 27, 39; political views in, 27, 38–41, 60; gender role reversal in, 40–1; and filial piety, 111, 121; Nathan's murder of Dearman in, 123, 148, 152; school bus image in, 124, 139, 141–2, 144, 153–4; reading strategy for, 126–8; map in, 127–8, 144–5, 147, 152; maze or web in, 128, 145–6; and lynchings, 129–30; and Till's lynching, 130–6; coded commentary in, 131; drafts of, 131, 135, 141; ring story in, 132–7; women's sexuality in, 134, 146–53; legal system in, 137–40; mothers in, 139–41, 145;

gender roles in, 140–1; education and teachers in, 143–5, 148–9, 151, 153–4; Gloria's parentage in, 145–51; Miss Julia as fertility goddess in, 146–7

"Love Song of J. Alfred Prufrock" (Eliot), 103

Lugene Gallery, 224

Lugene Opticians, 223

Lynchings, 11, 12, 17, 57, 124, 129–37, 144. *See also* Race and racism

"Making a Date" (Welty photograph), 223, 238–9

Manifest Destiny, 186–9, 188*n*11, 218–9

Mansfield, Katherine, 203

Mark, Rebecca, 5, 11–2, 17, 34, 91–2, 103–4

Marrs, Suzanne, 7–9, 17, 124, 141, 157, 194*n*19, 206

Mason, James, 193*n*18

Maxwell, William, 195

McCarthyism, 2, 7, 17, 38, 70, 73, 157, 171, 180

McDowell, John Patrick, 30–1

McMillen, Neil, 51

"Memory" (Welty), 217

Mencken, H. L., 214

Menendez brothers, 47–8

Meredith, James, 11, 76, 124

Methodist church, 30–2, 76–7

Milam, J. W., 132, 134

Millsaps College, 8, 74–80, 82–3, 84, 86–7, 111*n*3

*Mississippi: The Magnolia State*, 161

*Mississippi Burning*, 50

Mississippi Department of Archives and History, 16, 17, 81, 82, 83, 85, 86, 223, 224, 245*n*3

Mondrian, Piet, 209

Montaigne, Michel de, 207

Moody, Anne, 79–80

Moore, G. E., 35

Moore, Ross, 75

Morrigana, 151

Morrison, Ann, 85*n*21

Morrison, Toni, 9, 94, 232

Mortimer, Gail, 34

Mosley, Sir Oswald, 165*n*18

Multiculturalism, 205

Mussolini, Benito, 12, 171

"Must the Novelist Crusade?" (Welty), 1, 2, 4, 6, 8, 9, 12, 23, 44, 46, 57, 82, 90–1, 125–6

NAACP, 80

"Names on the Land" (Welty), 188*n*12

Narcissism, 192*n*16

Narrative strategies: as "political," 4–5; obstruction as, 98–100, 105; in *One Writer's Beginnings*, 208–15; of Welty generally, 208; ground-as-figure technique, 209–12. *See also* specific titles of works by Welty

*Natchez* (Chateaubriand), 218

National Recovery Administration (NRA), 248

Nationalism: New Nationalism, 155–6, 158, 171; and "Pageant of Birds," 166–70, 242; and Manifest Destiny, 186–9, 188*n*11, 218–29; in *Ponder Heart*, 188–90

*Native Son* (Wright), 53, 60

Nazism, 33–4, 47, 56, 70, 71, 165*n*18

Neault, D. James, 89

New Criticism, 1, 2, 52–6

New Deal, 27–8, 31, 156, 161–2, 165, 165*n*18, 171, 248

New Nationalism, 155–6, 158, 171

New Stage Theatre, 84, 84–5*n*21

Nielsen, Aldon L., 94, 99, 106–7

North, Michael, 172*n*27

*North by Northwest*, 193*n*18

Norton Anthology, 54–5
*Norton Book of Friendship,* 122,
　196n24
Novels. *See* Politics of literature; and
　specific novels by Welty
NRA, 248
Nuclear weapons, 13–4, 156, 170, 175,
　176

Obstruction, 98–100, 105
O'Connor, Flannery, 207
Odysseus, 61, 64, 65
*On Native Grounds* (Kazin), 155
"On the Politics of Literature" (Fet-
　terly), 1–2
*One Time, One Place* (Welty), 17, 36,
　122, 224, 226, 250
*One Writer's Beginnings* (Welty): and
　Americanness of Welty, 15, 207–21;
　compared with other writers, 15,
　205–6; first draft of, as Harvard
　speech, 15, 204, 207; as self-portrait,
　15–6, 205, 207–8, 220–1; family's po-
　litical background and ancestry in,
　16, 211–2, 216–9; evangelicalism in,
　29; parents in, 58, 216, 217–8; Heil-
　brun on latent and implicit anger in,
　59, 90; Welty's imagination in, 72;
　filial piety in, 121–2; as best seller,
　204; writing style of, 208–15; ground-
　as-figure technique in, 209–12; race
　and racism in, 210; death as meta-
　phor and theme in, 212–4; guilt in,
　212–5, 213n12, 220; cosmogony in,
　215, 216–7; ending of, 220–1
*Optimist's Daughter* (Welty): public
　versus private spheres in, 6, 36; com-
　pared with *Losing Battles,* 41; filial
　piety in, 111, 121; writing and publi-
　cation of, 121, 121n17; and coming
　to terms with death, 122
Orr, Linda, 91, 105, 107–8

Other as black, 93–101, 106
*Other Places* (Black), 224

"Pageant of Birds" (Welty essay), 12,
　13, 166–70, 242–3
"Pageant of Birds" (Welty photograph),
　242–3
"Pantaloon in Black" (Faulkner), 106
Parks, Rosa, 130
Personal as political, 19, 54, 109,
　157–8. *See also* Private versus public
　spheres
"Petrified Man" (Welty), 26
Petty, Jane Reid, 76, 84n21
Photographic Galleries, 223
*Photographs* (Welty), 36, 224
Photography: by Welty, 12, 13, 16–7,
　36, 122, 161, 163–4, 209, 220,
　223–51; by WPA documentary pho-
　tographers, 162; and violation of pri-
　vacy, 162; compared with imagina-
　tive writing, 163–5, 209; Welty's
　aversion to documentary photogra-
　phy, 163; Barthes on, 164; compared
　with flashback in narrative, 164;
　cameras used by Welty, 223; photo-
　graphic shows for Welty, 223–4; er-
　rors in reprinting of Welty's photo-
　graphs, 224–5n3; identification of
　date and place of Welty's photo-
　graphs, 224–5n3; irony in Welty's
　photographs, 224, 224n2; Welty's
　books of photographs, 224
"Piece of News" (Welty), 26, 96, 166
Pierpont, Claudia Roth, 17–8
Pitavy-Souques, Danièle, 15–6, 102
Poetry, Keats on, 1
Polis. *See* Greek polis
Political corruption, 2
"Political Rally on the Courthouse
　Grounds" (Welty photograph), 224,
　226–7

"Political Speaking" (Welty photograph), 36

"Political Speech" (Welty photograph), 36

Politics: of Welty, 7–9, 37, 42, 69–87, 109–10, 124, 157, 198–9, 206–7; definitions of, 19, 54, 206; personal as political, 19, 54, 109, 157–8; Welty on, 20–1, 41–6, 62; and Welty's photographs, 36, 209, 223–51; in "Demonstrators," 43–4, 92–108; of Faulkner, 56–7, 62; and "Pageant of Birds," 166–70, 242. *See also* Civil rights movement; McCarthyism; Race and racism; Rosenberg case

Politics of literature: Fetterly on, 1–2; and Welty generally, 1–18, 21–27, 91–2, 179–80; Welty's aversion to politicizing of fiction, 1, 2, 4, 6, 8, 9, 12, 21–3, 37, 42–5, 57–8, 62, 82, 89–91, 125–6; and story patterns, 4–5; and definitions of politics, 19, 54, 206; and New Criticism, 52–6; and Nortonized literary canon, 54–5; and teaching of literature, 54–7, 62–5; and biographical information about authors, 56–7; by southern women writers, 203–4. *See also* specific issues, such as Civil rights movement

Polk, Noel, 6–7, 124, 200*n*31

Pollack, Harriet, 17, 36, 98–100, 105, 124, 164, 209

*Ponder Heart* (Welty): and Rosenberg case, 11, 14–5, 17, 132, 180–6, 192–6, 200–1; Welty's writing process for, 15, 195–7; as play, 84–5*n*21; courtroom scenes in, 180–2, 184–5, 195; comic elements of, 181; Bonnie Dee's death in, 182–6; place names in, 188–9; Uncle Daniel's significance in, 188, 191–2, 196–8; national self-deception and, 189–90; illustrations in, 191; ending of, 195, 196; publication of, 200

Porter, Katherine Anne, 60–1, 62, 65

Pound, Ezra, 56

Poverty, 27–8, 128, 161, 165*n*18, 224, 250

"Powerhouse" (Welty), 8, 78–9, 211

Prenshaw, Peggy Whitman, 2, 5–6, 11, 57–8, 60, 89, 124, 157–8, 226

Price, Reynolds, 81

Private versus public spheres, 6, 23–5, 32, 35–8, 40, 41–2, 156, 157–8. *See also* Personal as political

Public versus private spheres. *See* Private versus public spheres

Puritans, 212, 218–9

*Quo Vadis*, 189

Race and racism: in Mississippi generally, 2, 27, 80–2, 125; in films, 7, 47–51; in narratives about the South, 7, 53–4; and "Powerhouse," 8, 78–9; and "Demonstrators," 9–10, 22*n*4, 43–4, 84, 92–108; Morrison on, 9; and *Losing Battles*, 11–2, 17, 123–54; and Welty generally, 16, 70–1, 74–87, 90, 179, 207, 210–2, 230; depicted in "Where Is the Voice Coming From?" 17, 21–2*n*4, 80, 128–9, 131, 132; and private relationships between blacks and whites, 20–1; and "Keela, the Outcast Indian Maiden," 28–9, 82–3; and Faulkner, 56, 57, 106; and Bilbo, 71; and Rankin, 71; and Welty's photographs, 122, 223–4, 230–3, 238–43; in Little Rock, Arkansas, 125. *See also* Civil rights movement; Lynchings

Rankin, John, 70–1

Rape, 133–4, 144, 152

"Reading and Writing of Short Stories" (Welty), 98, 172, 175–6

*Reading "The Waste Land"* (Brooker and Bentley), 105

Regionalism, 3–4, 15, 158–9, 159n6, 204, 207, 207n6

Religion: Baptist Church pageant in Jackson, Miss., 12, 13, 166–70, 242–3; and evangelicalism, 29–30; and Bible, 30, 214; Methodist church and women's home mission movement, 30–2; Methodist church and civil rights movement, 76–7

Rembrandt, 220

Republican Party, 171

*Resisting Reader* (Fetterly), 1

Rich, Adrienne, 109

Roach, Florence, 84–5n21

*Robber Bridegroom* (Welty), 156

Robbins, Samuel, 224

Robinson, John, 70

Romines, Ann, 10–1, 34

Roosevelt, Franklin Delano, 27–8, 31, 69, 165n18. *See also* New Deal

Rosenberg case: and *Ponder Heart,* 2, 11, 14–5, 17, 132, 180–6, 192–6, 200–1; and execution of Rosenbergs, 15, 183, 185; charges against Rosenbergs, 182–3; defense lawyers for Rosenbergs, 183; Ethel Rosenberg's appeal to Eisenhower, 183, 185, 192, 197, 198–9; trial and appeals, 183–4, 185, 189; and Doctorow's *Book of Daniel,* 185–6; newspaper reports of, 192–4, 194–5nn20–1, 200; Rosenberg funeral, 192–3; and newspaper report of Estelle Siegal's electrocution by lightning, 193, 200

Royals, Tom, 22n4, 93, 120n15

Ruas, Charles, 33

Rubin, Louis, 126–7

Russell, Diarmuid: and totalitarianism, 12–3, 159–60; AE as father of, 13, 159, 160; letters of Welty to, 35, 125, 180n3; and concern for Welty's safety, 80; on Welty's writing versus her filial piety, 111, 117; and Welty on racial conflict in Little Rock, Arkansas, 125; and Welty's love of Mississippi, 162; and community in Welty's fiction, 180, 180n3; and *Ponder Heart,* 195

Russia/Soviet Union, 44–5, 170–1, 173, 183, 199

Salter, John, 79, 80

Schlissel, Lillian, 119

Schmidt, Peter, 5, 34

School bus image, 124, 139, 141–2, 144, 153–4

School busing, 11, 124, 142, 144

Schwerner, Michael, 93, 124

Scott, Anne Firor, 31

Segregation. *See* Integration of education; Integration of theaters; Race and racism

Self-portraits, 15, 205, 207–21

Sexism. *See* Feminism; Gendering and gender relations

Shakespeare, William, 75, 95, 131

*Shoe Bird* (Welty), 111n4

Short stories. *See* specific titles of Welty's short stories

Siegal, Estelle, 193

Smith, Gerald L. K., 70, 71

Smith, Gypsy, 29

Smith, Lillian, 22, 144

*Social Gospel in the South* (McDowell), 30–1

Somerville, Nellie Nugent, 31–2

*Song of the South,* 51

Sophocles, 53

Sosna, Morton, 29

*Sound and the Fury* (Faulkner), 62

Southern identities, 2
Southern Literary Festival, 8, 77, 84–6
Southern Renaissance, 22
Sovereignty Commission, 125, 144
Soviet Union. *See* Russia/Soviet Union
Spanish Civil War, 171, 172
Srinivasan, Seetha, 248
Stalin, Joseph, 12, 171
Steinbeck, John, 42
Stevenson, Adlai: Welty's support for, in 1952 presidential election, 7–8, 37, 42, 71–4, 86, 87, 124, 157, 206; on Korean War, 73–4; on McCarthyism in American Legion speech, 73, 173; written text of speeches of, 74; on poverty and tyranny, 165*n*18; on patriotism, 173; Welty's essay on, 72, 179, 179–80*n*2, 198
"Still Moment" (Welty), 3
Strauss, Richard, 56
Suffrage movement. *See* Women's suffrage movement
Sunday, Billy, 29
Swain, Martha, 31
Swann ruling, 124
Symons, Julian, 165*n*18

Tenant farming, 70
Textuality and intertextuality, 91–2, 94–107
*Their Eyes Were Watching God* (Hurston), 13, 244
Thompson, Maude, 13, 167–70, 242
Till, Emmett, 11, 17, 124, 129, 130–6
*Time to Kill*, 7, 49–50, 50–1*n*2
Todorov, Tzvetan, 33–4, 40, 45–6
"Tomato-Packer's Recess" (Welty photograph), 244–5
Totalitarianism, 12–4, 56, 155–77, 165*n*18

Tougaloo Southern Christian College, 8, 75–6, 78, 80, 85
Trilling, Diana, 3–4, 90
Trouard, Dawn, 26, 26*n*10
Truman, Harry S., 69, 70, 197, 197*n*26
Turgenev, Ivan, 45
Turner, Victor, 119*n*13
Twain, Mark, 66
"Two Writers' Beginnings" (Brodhead), 205
Tyranny. *See* Totalitarianism

"Unemployed in Union Square" (Welty photograph), 246–7
"Union Square" (Welty photograph), 248–9
United Daughters of the Confederacy, 228–9
University of Mississippi, 11, 76, 124
University of Wisconsin, 188*n*11, 223

Vande Kieft, Ruth, 89, 103, 104
Vanderbilt University, 128
Vardaman, James K., 20
Violent resistance to civil rights, 2, 10, 38, 47, 80–2, 84–5*n*21, 85, 92–3, 110, 112, 124, 129, 130–1, 152. *See also* Lynchings
Virgil, 95

Waller, Fats, 78–9
"Wanderers" (Welty), 74
Warren, Robert Penn, 52, 85
"Washwoman" (Welty photograph), 223–4, 240
"Washwomen Carrying the Clothes" (Welty photograph), 241
*Waste Land* (Eliot), 10, 102–5
Welch, Lois, 99
Welles, Orson, 75
Wells, H. G., 159

Wells, Ida B., 144

*Welty* (Black), 224

Welty, Eudora: misread as apolitical, 1–4, 17–8, 22–3, 89–91, 107–8, 123–6; on the politicizing of fiction, 1, 2, 4, 6, 8, 9, 12, 21–3, 37, 42–5, 57–8, 62, 82, 89–91, 125–6; and civil rights, 2, 8, 38, 74–86, 110, 124, 157, 179, 206–7, 230; misread as "regionalist," 3–4, 15, 204, 207, 207n6; on story patterns, 4–5; and private versus public spheres, 6, 23–5, 32, 35–8, 40, 41–2, 157–8; political support for Stevenson by, 7–8, 37, 42, 71–4, 86, 87, 124, 157, 179, 198, 206; politics of, 7–9, 37, 42, 69–87, 109–10, 124, 157, 198–9, 206–7; as Millsaps Writer-in-Residence, 8, 82; Southern Literary Festival speeches by, 8, 77, 84–6; speeches of, at Millsaps College, 8, 74–80, 82–3, 84, 86–7; and close ties to Mississippi, 10, 81–2, 112, 125, 162; filial piety and, 10, 80–2, 110–2, 120–1, 213n12; and illness and deaths of mother and brothers, 10, 80–2, 84n21, 110–1, 120–1, 125; photographs by, 12, 13, 16–7, 36, 122, 161, 163–4, 209, 220, 223–51; Americanness of, 15, 207–21; Harvard speech by, 15, 204, 207; family background of, 16, 211–2, 216–9; and feminism, 19, 23, 58, 91–2, 109, 157; on politics, 20–1, 41–6, 62; birth date of, 27, 207; WPA travels of, 27–8, 161–2, 250; and Methodist church, 30; and World War II, 32–5, 38; parents of, 58, 120n16, 216, 217–8; and anger, 59, 90, 208, 208n7; and Democratic Party, 69–70, 109, 124; African American friends of, 75, 81; at Columbia University, 75, 223; Harlem visits by, 75; and aborted Ellison interview, 80–1, 84; and fears of violence, 80–2; use of obstruction in writings of, 98–100, 105; teaching of Millsaps College writing workshop by, 110–1n3; on loss, 122; and AE, 160–1; British publisher for, 171; literary criticism by, 172–7; translations of works by, 173; comic style of, 181; and guilt, 212–5, 213n12, 220; meaning of traveling for, 218; and movement toward abstraction, 219–20; photographic shows for, 223–4. *See also* specific writings

Weston, Jessie, 104

Weston, Ruth, 5, 40

Wheatley, Patricia, 30

"Where Is the Voice Coming From?" (Welty): as response to murder of Medgar Evers, 10–1, 110, 112, 207, 208n7; alternate title for, 11, 110; and race and racism, 17, 21–2n4, 80, 128–9, 131, 132; filial piety in, 111–5, 114n9, 118–20; Welty on, 120n15

"Whistle" (Welty), 26, 70, 166

White Citizens' Councils. *See* Citizens' Councils

White supremacy. *See* Citizens' Councils; Race and racism

Whitfield, Stephen J., 130, 135–6

"Why I Live at the P.O." (Welty), 26

*Wide Net* (Welty), 22, 171

Winter, William, 37, 87

Wolff, Sally, 194–5n21

Women's home mission movement, 30–2

Women's suffrage movement, 31

Woodburn, John, 75

Woodward, Ellen, 31–2

"Words into Fiction" (Welty), 8, 127

World War I, 171, 172, 172n27
World War II, 32–5, 38, 70, 158, 170–2,
     172n27, 174–5
"Worn Path" (Welty), 211
WPA, 27–8, 159, 161–2, 250
Wright, Richard, 53, 60, 205, 215
"Writing and Analyzing a Story"
     (Welty), 180n3

*Writing between the Lines: Race and
     Intertextuality* (Nielsen), 94

Yaeger, Patricia, 26, 96
Yardley, Jonathan, 23, 27, 58